The Medieval Dragon

The Nature of the Beast
in Germanic Literature

The Medieval Dragon

The Nature of the Beast
in Germanic Literature

Joyce Tally Lionarons

Hisarlik Press
1998

Published by Hisarlik Press, 4 Catisfield Road, Enfield Lock, Middlesex EN3 6BD, UK. Georgina Clark-Mazo and Dr Jeffrey Alan Mazo, publishers.

British Library Cataloguing-in-Publication data available.

ISBN 1 874312 33 8

5 4 3 2 1

Printed in Great Britain by Redwood Books, Trowbridge, Wiltshire

Contents

Preface

A man is a man, and a beast is a beast, but a dragon is a dragon is a dragon.
(Gwynn Jones, *Kings, Beasts and Heroes*)

This book arose out of two simultaneous projects. The first was an experiment inspired by the Ursinus College Faculty Discussion Group's examination of contemporary narrative theory: I wanted to prove both to the group and to myself that it was possible to apply twentieth century theoretical perspectives successfully to medieval heroic literature. I also wanted to try to answer a simple question that had been put to me years ago at my dissertation defense: "What is a dragon anyway? Why is one different from, say, Godzilla?" Although I apparently answered the question well enough then to satisfy my examiner, I did not satisfy myself. Therefore, my second objective in this book has been to investigate the concept of *draconitas* or 'dragonness.' When I began, I intended merely to write a conference paper or two, but, like the tiny serpent in *Ragnars saga loðbrókar*, the work grew in the writing to dragon's size, and needed larger living room. The book thus concerns itself with the nature and characteristics of Germanic literary dragons and dragon slayings as they relate to contemporary ideas about myth and narratological theory, especially those theories put forward by René Girard, Mikhail M. Bakhtin, and Hans Robert Jauss. In particular, my work explores the relationship between the dragons of medieval Germanic literature and the chaos monsters of Indo-European myth on one hand, while on the other it looks for the reasons behind the often uncanny similarity between dragons and the dragon-slayers who are their antagonists.

Along the way I have incurred many debts, as writers always do. I owe Ursinus College a great deal of gratitude for giving me a sabbatical leave which enabled me to write a first draft of most of the manuscript. I want to thank Raymond P. Tripp, Jr and Alexandra Hennessey Olsen for teaching me Old English and Old Norse to begin with, and for first interesting me in the question of dragons. Patricia Schroeder, Cindy Vitto, Margot Kelley, and Celia Millward all read and commented on various parts of the text at different stages in its development. Lynn Thelen was invaluable for her help on *Das Nibelungenlied*; Ann Matter provided inspiration at a difficult juncture. Special thanks and love go to Edward R. Haymes for reading the entire manuscript and offering detailed commentary and wisdom—with the usual assurances that the mistakes that remain are my own. I also want to thank Sheroo Meyer, Mary Tiryak, Loren Gruber, Gina and Leon Oboler, Peter Perreten, Bill Schipper, Derk Visser, Colette Hall, and Sherry Linkon for their encouragement and advice. Finally, of course, I need to thank John Lionarons for his love, his music, his patience, and his repeated and tireless proofreading. This book is for him.

Portions of Chapter V were published as "The Sign of a Hero: Dragon-Slaying in *Þiðreks saga af Bern*"in the *Proceedings of the Medieval Association of the Midwest* 2 (1993), 47–57; an article based on Chapter 2 appeared as *"Beowulf:* Myth and Monsters"in *English Studies* 77 (1995), 1–14.

1

Dragons and Dragon-Slayers

Wer mit Ungeheuern kämpft, mag zusehn, daß er nicht dabei zum Ungeheuer wird. Und wenn du lange in einen Abgrund blickst, blickt der Abgrund auch in dich hinein. (Friedrich Nietzsche, *Jenseits von Gut und Böse*)

THE FAMILIAR IMAGE of a knight in shining armor who fights a solitary battle against a winged, fire-breathing dragon in order to win the hand of a fair lady is an image more common in contemporary popular culture than it is in medieval literary fiction. In fact, the popular conception of the dragon fight as a mainstay of medieval literature as well as of twentieth-century fantasy novels can make dragons a difficult subject for a literary critic to write about. In 1936, when J.R.R. Tolkien published his influential study "*Beowulf*: The Monsters and the Critics,"[1] he found it necessary to defend his topic against accusations of triviality: dragons in literature were not considered a serious subject for critical inquiry. Today the problem is somewhat different. After the plethora of scholarly articles published in the 1960s and 1970s about *Beowulf*'s dragon, which Tolkien's essay encouraged if it did not engender, and after the popular dragon fad of the 1970s and early 1980s (generated in part by Tolkien's Middle Earth and its inhabitants), the publication of yet another book having to do with dragons may strike some readers as superfluous at best. Certainly we all know what a dragon is by now.

But do we? Perhaps the recent cultural omnipresence of the dragon is itself ample justification for the present work. The assumption that we all do know what a dragon is, that the dragon as a standard feature of certain types of modern and medieval literature is self-explanatory and transhistorical because "a dragon is a dragon is a dragon,"[2] has been so deeply rooted in our cultural imagination that even scholars have been wont to speak casually of 'dragons' as if the word required no interpretation—as if its meaning were single, transparent, or even, at the risk of seeming fanciful, dependent upon a physical referent in the natural world.

Recently, however, contemporary linguistic and literary theory has taught us that it is dangerous to treat any word—even one which has a physical referent in the natural world—as if it were a transparent medium for the communication of a single, monologically determined meaning. This danger is compounded when we try to discover the meaning of a word like 'dragon' in its literary-historical context, for the dragon—in myth, in literature, and in history—has always been a purely imaginary, and thus primarily a linguistic, phenomenon. It exists as a word within discourse, as part of a dialogue (in the broad Bakhtinian sense) rooted in a specific time and a specific place. The meaning of a particular usage of the word 'dragon' in a particular work of literature can therefore be determined only within that work's specific discursive context. We do not always already know what a dragon is.

However, we do not *not* know what a dragon is either. When the word enters actual usage it is not semantically empty; that is, it is not open for easy appropriation by a speaker or writer wishing to invest it with privately determined meaning. M.M. Bakhtin's description of the polysemous and heteroglot nature of language in general provides a useful reminder that, when a speaker appropriates a word,

> it is not as a neutral word of language, not as a word free from the aspirations and evaluations of others, uninhabited by others' voices. No, he receives the word from another's voice and filled with that other voice. The word enters his context from another context, permeated with the interpretations of others. His own thought finds the word already inhabited.[3]

Thus, the word interacts externally with a shifting array of intertextual voices, deriving its meaning in part from varying interpretations of any number of separate and even contradictory linguistic usages—in this case, from many other 'dragons.' Moreover, within any particular utterance or text a word is always internally dialogic as well:

> The word is born in a dialogue as a living rejoinder within it; the word is shaped in dialogic interaction with an alien word ... [and] is directed toward an *answer*.[4]

The attentive reader's task is to discover and articulate the dialogue within which the word participates. In order to understand the meaning of the word-image 'dragon' in medieval literature it is therefore necessary to reconstruct from each individual text both the internal and external questions to which the dragon is an answer, as well as the answers to which it serves as question.[5]

This task is complicated in the case of medieval texts by the historicity of the questions and answers involved. The positivistic view of a work of art as an object that timelessly and transparently presents its meaning to any sufficiently attentive and perceptive reader has for the most part been rejected by students of past literatures;[6] we recognize the need to remain conscious of what Hans Robert Jauss has called the essential otherness, the 'alterity' of the medieval past.[7] Additionally, we have become increasingly aware that it is impossible for a modern reader wholly to shed twentieth-century assumptions in order to recreate the lived medieval experience of a text; as Thomas Hahn puts it, "no modern scholar is in dialogue with 'the medievals'; she can only draw from or address the interests of contemporary [modern] discourses."[8] Moreover, one can question whether recreating the medieval experience is, or should be, our final goal. Certainly if a text has literary, rather than purely antiquarian value, it will have something to say to us in our historical condition, albeit something that is perhaps different from what it said to its original audience.

Hans Robert Jauss has proposed a hermeneutics of reception as one way of dealing with the alterity of medieval texts without denying either the otherness of the authorial voice or the modernity of the scholar's discourse. In his 1979 essay, "The Alterity and Modernity of Medieval Literature," Jauss outlines a basic three-part "methodology of literary hermeneutics":

> The immediate or prereflective reader experience...constitutes the necessary first hermeneutic bridge.... [O]ne becomes aware of the astounding or surprising otherness of the world opened up by the text.... [A] reflective consideration of its surprising aspects is called for, an activity which methodologically entails the reconstruction of the horizon of expectation of the addressees for whom the text was originally composed. This second hermeneutic step meanwhile cannot in itself be the absolute goal of understanding if the knowledge of the otherness of a distant text-world so gained is to be more than simply a sharpened variation of historical reification, objectified through the contrast of horizons. [Third,] ... the question of a significance which reaches further historically, which surpasses the original communicative situation, must be posed.[9]

The original horizon of expectations of a work of literature can be reconstructed by an exploration of the work's conscious and unconscious intertextuality. Jauss recommends "foreground[ing] it against those works that the author explicitly or implicitly presupposed his contemporary audience to know."[10] However, in those cases where explicit indications of an author's presuppositions are lacking, one can determine at least part of the horizon of expectations through an examination of, first,

> familiar norms or the immanent poetics of the genre; second, through the implicit relationships to familiar works of the literary-historical surroundings; and third, through the opposition between fiction and reality, between the poetic and the practical function of language.[11]

Once the specific alterity of the work's original horizon of expectations has been established, a dialogue between text and reader begins, in which "the content of the horizon of one's own experience [is] brought into play, and mediated through the alien horizon in order to arrive at the new horizon of another interpretation."[12] The alterity of the earlier text is thus used rather than transcended, allowing multiple textual meanings to emerge that could not have been anticipated by the contemporary medieval audience.

Paradoxically, the greatest danger in attempting to reconstruct a medieval horizon of expectations for the dragon is not the creation of too many meanings, but rather reductionism: it is all too easy to limit the dragon's significance dogmatically or arbitrarily to a single, 'medieval' interpretation. To avoid such reduction, we must recognize that medieval dragons and dragon-texts, like modern novels, are often polyglot, heteroglot baggy monsters. But as Bakhtin has pointed out, it is sometimes difficult for modern readers to recognize heteroglossia in

> works from distant times and alien languages, where our artistic perception cannot rely for support on a living feel for a language. In such a case (figuratively speaking) the entire language—as a consequence of our distance from it—seems to lie on one and the same plane; we cannot sense in it any three-dimensionality or any distinction between levels and distances.[13]

Detailed historical-linguistic analysis can provide some help here; in addition, reception history can aid us in determining the 'levels and distances' of a medieval text by enabling us to see what Jauss calls the "dialogic and at once processlike relationship between work, audience, and new work that can be conceived in the relations between message and receiver as well as between question and answer, problem and solution."[14] It is important to remember that this "processlike relationship" is in fact dialogic, not dialectic: that is, it assumes neither an eventual interpretive synthesis nor a teleological evolution of significance towards an ultimate totality of meaning. Instead, the progression from work to audience to new work comprises "an ever-different variation on a basic pattern.[15]

Accordingly, medieval texts dealing with dragons do not present a monologic repetition of a single dragon motif so much as they depict a progression of individual, intertextually related dragons, a series of particular historical expressions of a varying notion of *draconitas*, or 'dragonness.' Like any other traditional element within the corpus of medieval literature, the dragon is predicated upon an assumption of "continuation within imitation."[16] Thus, in order to understand those dragons which play important roles in medieval texts, we must first determine the horizon of expectations out of and against which those dragons emerged, i.e., the tradition of dragon lore and its significance as it existed both before and during the Middle Ages, and then distinguish the variations played upon that tradition within specific works of literature.

To do this requires an examination of those intertexts, both oral and written, which participated in the medieval audience's horizon of expectations. These may be roughly categorized into four groups: (i) *mythological* texts, stories and poems which endow the dragon with forms and associations spanning the entire Indo-European linguistic and literary tradition; (ii) *natural-historical* texts, including bestiary accounts, historically recorded 'sightings' of dragons, and discussions of such natural analogues to the dragon as serpents, meteors, and the like; (iii) *historical-political* texts, documenting the uses to which the idea of the dragon has been put by the Indo-European cultures of which it is a part; and (iv) *Biblical and hagiographical* texts, which record the specifically Christian manifestations of the dragon as it has entered into the religious/political culture of the Western world.

MYTHOLOGICAL DRAGONS

In 1919, in a remarkable book entitled *The Evolution of the Dragon*, the mythographer G. Elliott Smith asserted that "the dragon has been identified with all of the gods and all of the demons of every religion."[17] This is, of course, an exaggeration of the facts, but certainly the earliest texts concerning dragons are mythological accounts of the destruction of a monster, often in the form of a gigantic serpent, by a god or semi-divine hero. In fact, although the dragon slaying is a recurrent pattern in a large number of mythologies, it occurs so frequently in Indo-European myth that comparative linguist Calvert Watkins has asserted that "it may be a quasi-universal."[18]

By definition, myth is the site of what contemporary students of narrative would call 'monologic' discourse; that is, a myth speaks in a single, seemingly uncontested voice from a single, authoritative point of view. Its events transpire *in illo tempore*, "in *that* time," a time which privileges origins and assumes the perfection—in both the colloquial and grammatical senses of the term—of first things. Bakhtin, who associates mythic time with the epic, calls it the "absolute past":

> It is both monochronic and valorized (hierarchical); it lacks any relativity, that is, any gradual, purely temporal progressions that might connect it with the present. It is walled off absolutely from all subsequent times.[19]

Myth relies for its status as myth on the fiction that its existence precedes and is thus independent of any particular textual embodiment, which must of necessity occur in *this*, historical, time; by so doing, it both denies the possibility of intertextual exchange and suppresses intratextual dialogue. As Jauss puts it, "the mythic process . . . renders things unavailable for questioning."[20] Nevertheless, any particular mythic *text* becomes open to both inter- and intratextual dialogic exchange—that is, to the emergence of other, even contradictory, textual voices—when it gains literary form through the appropriation of the myth by a particular, historically situated author, whose narrative voice is necessarily embedded in an intertextual matrix comprised of all previous versions of the narrative, and whose language necessarily permits multiple interpretations. More than a dialogue, the mythic text becomes the site of what Jauss calls a "polylogue between later writers, their norm-giving predecessors, and that absent third party, the myth itself."[21]

When, as is the case in the four medieval dragon-slaying texts to be considered in this study, a traditional heroic narrative appropriates monster killing into its legendary/historical discourse, its intertextual matrix tends to partake in large part of the myriad retellings of dragon myths which occur in each of the Indo-European languages. Calvert Watkins' comparative analysis of these myths indicates that while the circumstances, motives, and cultural prerequisites of the dragon slaying differ from language to language and narrative to narrative, the discursive kernel of the myth remains the same: an Indo-European dragon slaying is a polyglossic event characterized in each language by a simple verb-object formula[22] 'kill serpent,' which is in turn particularized first by the presence of a semantically marked 'dragon slaying' verb, a cognate of the reconstructed I.E. form *$g^w hen$-, which may be used bidirectionally whenever a hero kills or is killed by a dragon, and second by the usual absence of an overt subject in the clause containing the verbal formula (*HK*, 276–77). Examples of this formula may be found in Indic, Old Iranian, Old Hittite, Middle Iranian, Greek, and Germanic texts, to cite only those instances attested to by Watkins (*HK, passim*). The Germanic languages, however, have recourse to the periphrasis 'become slayer to' (O.E. *to bonan weorðan*, O.N. *at bana verða*, O.H.G. *ti banin werdan*), which is

> regularly used of more than ordinary killings: it is semantically marked. It is found characteristically in narration of killing of or by a dragon or other monster (bidirectionality), of fratricide or other kin-slaying, and of awesome exploits of the hero, or of awesome victims. (*HK*, 290)

This periphrasis is equivalent to *$g^w hen$- "as not merely a typological semantic parallel, but a genetic equation" (*HK*, 292).

The existence of a semantically marked 'dragon slaying' verb is significant for the interpretation of mythic texts because it sets the destruction of the monster (or the destruction of the hero *by* the monster) off from other, lesser sorts of killings narrated within the myth, thereby particularizing the event as a special, unusual action which must be performed by a special, unusual actor. That this actor is not overtly named within the formula has a subtler implication in that it tends to turn the formulaic phrase into "a sort of predicate which *defines* the Indo-European hero" (*HK*, 276), an implication strengthened in the Germanic versions of the dragon slaying myth, where the periphrasis can be nominalized into an epithet, as when Þórr is referred to as *orms einbani*, "serpent's single bane" (*HK*, 290). Moreover, such an epithet is itself bidirectional in that it makes simultaneous interpretive assertions about both the monster and the hero it describes: if the killing of a dragon constitutes the definition of a hero *par excellence*, then the dragon is also defined, by implication, as the ultimate adversary. Even more interesting, however, is the bidirectionality of the verb, for its reversibility suggests a covert similarity between subject and object, hero and dragon, that the myth's overt language denies.

The Indo-European dragon slaying myth is most often embedded in narrative accounts of the creation of the world or of cosmic order in which a serpentine monster is destroyed or subdued by a hero in order to establish the prevailing cosmic regime: the myth explains and legitimates the religious and political status quo. It occurs in the 'absolute past' in order to give the legitimating function of the myth its full potency: "The *fascinosum* of this basic etiological

model stems from the belief in the perfection and higher worth of first things."[23]
The political elements of the myth stand out most clearly when the dragon fight
is combined with what C. Scott Littleton calls the "kingship in heaven" theme,
in which a dragon arises to challenge a hero/god who has established himself as
king over the world.[24] Although in some cases the monster seems simply to
embody the chaos of an untamed, uncivilized cosmos, in others it is a clear
manifestation of or agent for a deposed god/king. In either situation, the myth
contends that the dragon must be destroyed in order for the world—and its
living gods and peoples—to exist. The life-threatening aspect of the monster
may be emblemized by the dragon's guarding or hoarding water in the form of
a stream or well, or by its propensity for devouring human beings. But by setting itself up as an adversary to and potential usurper of the godhead, the dragon
becomes *de facto* 'monstrous,' and this fact justifies its slaughter by the god/
king.

An early example of this motif occurs in the story of Indra and Vṛtra as it is
set forth in the Indian *Rig-Veda*. Vṛtra is a dragon which has imprisoned all the
waters of the cosmos in a mountain. When the monster is slain by the god Indra,
the waters are set free. The story is told in miniature in the first strophe of the
Rig-Vedic hymn 1.32:

> índrasya nú viryàni prá vocam
> yáni cakára prathamáni vajrí
> *áhann áhim* ánv apás tatarda
> prá vaksána abhinat párvatanam
>
> [I tell now the manly deeds of Indra,
> the foremost which he did armed with the cudgel.
> He slew the serpent, drilled through to the waters
> He split the belly of the mountains.]
> (cited in *HK*, 273; emphasis in Watson's text)

The words *áhann áhim*, "slew the serpent," contain the Indo-European dragon
slaying formula, here characteristically lacking an overtly stated subject and
combined with the explicit mention of the imprisonment and liberation of the
life-giving waters of the world. Other examples of mythological dragon slayings include, but are not limited to, the Iranian story of the combat between
Thraetaona, son of Athwya, and the serpent-monster Aži Dahaka; the Babylonian
myth of Marduk, who fights and kills the dragon Tiamat in order to create the
sky and the earth from the two severed halves of her body; Egyptian tales of the
battle between the serpent Apep or Apophis, who represents darkness, and the
sun god Ra or Seth; Canaanite stories of the destruction of a seven-headed
serpent, Lotan, by Baal, a myth which enters the European tradition in the
Biblical accounts of Leviathan; and Old Norse accounts of the conquest, albeit
not the destruction, of Miðgarðsormr by the god Þórr.

Perhaps most familiar to Western readers are the battles between gods and monsters in Greek and Roman mythology. Littleton cites the example of Zeus and Typhon as part of the 'kingship in heaven' pattern, noting that Typhon, while certainly not a dragon *per se*, is represented as having snakes growing from his body.[25] Watkins mentions Bellerophon's slaying of the Chimaira (a fire-breathing monster with a serpent's tail, although a lion's head and a goat's middle), as well as the destruction of the snake-haired Gorgon by Perseus, as Greek instances of the dragon slaying formula (*HK*, 280–83). Roman literary versions of the dragon myth include Ovid's accounts of the fight between Apollo and Python and of the destruction of the Mars Serpent by Cadmus, related in *Metamorphoses* I and III.

What is perhaps most significant in all of these narratives is that in virtually every case the destruction of the monster and the creation of cosmic order comprise a single narrative act: order in the myth is established only through an act of violence. And because violence functions as what David Danow has termed "the negative correlative of dialogue,"[26] that is, because it first silences and then replaces dialogic interaction, it occurs when an engagement between one potentially speaking subject and another becomes instead a confrontation between a monologic subject and a silenced object. This violent muting of an objectified other—the dragon slaying—simultaneously creates and legitimizes the status quo by ensuring that only one voice remains after the violence is done, thereby creating the single, authoritative, monologic discourse of myth.

The phenomenon of cosmic and/or cultural order resulting from an original act of violence has been explored most thoroughly by René Girard in his *Violence and the Sacred*,[27] where he argues that the only essential feature of order-creating violence is the impossibility of violent reprisal (as well as, I would add, of dialogic rejoinder) on the part of the victim or the victim's advocates: the sole qualification for the role of victim—and thus of mythical monster—is the condition that no voice be raised on one's behalf, no vengeance taken for one's murder. The monster/victim is a scapegoat who dies to put an end to what the myth depicts as an ever-escalating cycle of reciprocal violence threatening existence itself. The victim's death assures both that a life-sustaining cosmic order can be (re)established without further challenge and that the mythic version of events can assert itself as truth without question or dissent. Consequently, even though the victim is generally accused within the myth of having committed crimes against nature and the community—i.e., of 'monstrous' behavior—specific guilt or innocence is never an issue; myth as myth disallows dialogic inquiry. The victim attains his or her 'monstrous' status retrospectively and only within the discourse of the myth which documents the violence: victims of violence are designated monsters because they have fulfilled the role of victims; they are not victimized because they are monsters. The scapegoat myth thus represents the ultimate in monologic ideological discourse, for it is "nothing more than the camouflaged victory of one version of the story over the other . . . thereafter held to be the true and universal version, the verity behind the myth itself" (*VS*, 73).

In fact, the monster/victim is frequently represented as the twin or double of the monster-killing hero, for the two signify, respectively, the maleficent and beneficent aspects of the same mythic violence.[28] Because human, reciprocal violence tends to efface any differences between those culturally situated individuals participating in it, such violence destroys the semiotic basis for meaningful cosmic order or societal structure (*VS*, 164); in addition, the silencing of human discourse that results whenever verbal dialogue is replaced by the pseudo-dialogue of violence effaces linguistic difference, and therefore meaning itself.[29] A more authoritative language, the monologic discourse of myth, must intervene to reestablish linguistic and ideological difference and with it linguistic and political meaning: 'good' violence is split from 'bad,' the victorious hero is differentiated from the defeated monster, and the objectified and silenced victim meets "his death in the guise of the monstrous double" (*VS*, 251).

Creation of order is therefore dependent within the myth on the suppression of both reciprocal, merely human dialogue and reciprocal, merely human violence. Unilateral, monster-slaying violence is by contrast deemed 'sacred' violence and portrayed as enacted between supernatural beings for the benefit of humanity; likewise, the monologic discourse of myth is deemed 'sacred' narrative, discourse originated by the gods themselves. As a "radically new type of violence" (*VS*, 27), sacred violence needs a distinct verbal formula to differentiate it from ordinary human, reciprocal violence. And, as noted above, sacred violence in the dragon myth is designated in the Indo-European languages by just such a special, semantically marked verb, bidirectional as a reflection of the 'doubling' of hero and victim, and quite logically needing no overtly expressed subject. The enshrinement of sacred violence in myth, according to Girard, is "part of the process by which man conceals from himself the human origin of his own violence, by attributing it to the gods" (*VS*, 161).

One need not posit, with Girard, an originary act of physical community violence against an historical victim to accept the significance of his hypothesis with regard to the dragon myth. As we have seen, the distinction between good and evil violence, signified by the appearance of the hero and the monstrous double, takes place within the myth precisely in order to differentiate what the violent suppression of dialogic discourse has caused to become undifferentiated, which is to say, in order to create the ideological conditions which allow the monologic discourse of the myth to exist in the first place. The ordering of the cosmos comes about through this differentiation, or, rather, is itself the same process of differentiation, for cosmic order consists of the articulation of reality and the ordering of events into the ideologically coded, monologic discourse which constitutes myth. Without differentiation, of course, meaning—and with it the human community as an ordered society conscious of itself—could not exist. The myth thereby equates the establishment of the prevailing cosmic order with the establishment—the coming into consciousness—of Being itself.

On this ontological level of the myth, the image of the dragon gains additional significance. If the system of differences which constitutes language permits consciousness of Being, it also, as Kenneth Burke has pointed out, brings negativity, consciousness of the possibility of non-Being, into the world for the first time.[30] Language creates absence—non-Being—as a condition of meaning when it asserts presence; at the same time, it attempts to conceal that absence through the addition of even more language, i.e., through the creation of mythic discourse. Originary myths thus become, as Eric Gould has argued, the "symbolic order of our fear of nothing at all."[31] The need for an originary myth arises at least in part out of human awareness and terror of non-Being:

> No metaphorical language confronts non-being quite so squarely and definitively as myth. Mythicity . . . is the condition of filling the gap with signs in such a way that Being continues to conceal Nothing as a predication for further knowledge.[32]

Moreover, Gould points out, "language even has the capacity to nihilate Nothing. . . . [I]t alone retains the ability to comment on its own incompleteness. It can assert the necessary presence of absence."[33]

On this level, the dragon myth would seem to be an early expression of the creation of meaning through language: the dragon arises as a signifier through the differentiation of Something from Nothing; its significed is the absence created and concealed by language. And although it signifies "the necessary presence of absence," as an image the dragon is itself present within the myth, since any image must be an image *of* something.[34] In its character as a present absence, the dragon again becomes a sort of obverse image, a 'monstrous double' of the victorious hero/god who asserts his own ontological presence by triumphing over absence in the form of a monster. The dragon myth may thus be interpreted as an assertion of human desire for Being, for a presence which can conquer absence. "Desire," Girard states, "clings to violence and stalks it like a shadow because violence is the signifier of the cherished being, the signifier of divinity" (*VS*, 151).

Unchecked, such desire could easily break out of the constraints of dialogic interchange and engender the Girardian scenario of unending reciprocal violence: hence "the real reason for surrogate victims and controlled forms of violence in society [is] . . . our need to systematize human desire."[35] The dragon exists to simultaneously conceal and reveal the ontological knowledge that the myth contains: behind presence lies absence, behind existence lies the void. For this reason the dragon is associated within the myth with death and the grave, with primordial chaos (and therefore with water), but also with hidden treasure and esoteric knowledge.

The significance of the dragon myth on both the ideological and ontological planes is probably clearest in Norse versions of the story, which in fact feature two dragons: one, Miðgarðsormr or the World Serpent, is subdued by Þórr in one variant of the Indo-European dragon slaying myth; as the signifier of absence, however, Miðgarðsormr continues its existence in the depths of the sea, encircling and underlying the created world. It will rise again at the Ragnarǫk, the last battle between gods, men, and monsters which will result in the inevitable destruction of the world, but which may also give rise to a new, regenerated cosmos. A second dragon, described in the Eddic poem *Vǫluspá*, is Níðhǫggr, a flying serpent which lives in the well Hvergelmir and gnaws perpetually at the root of Yggdrasill, the World Tree. Each dragon is concealed from the everyday sight of humanity; each exists as a perpetual signifier of absence, of the Nothing which underlies Being; each threatens an end to created order and thus to signification. Even after the Ragnarǫk, when a new cosmos is prophesied to arise, Níðhǫggr will fly into the new world (*Vǫluspá*, 66);[36] there can be no creation without monsters, no presence without absence. The dragon's name, 'Striker-that-destroys,'[37] indicates a related function in the myth: Níðhǫggr is represented as carrying corpses on his wings and is thereby associated with the inevitable loss of physical being by individuals. As Ellis Davidson puts it, the dragon is "a natural image for devouring death."[38]

When the dragon descends from the myths of cosmic origins into folktale and legend, it retains and even strengthens its associations with death, for here it tends to signify absence—and violence—on a social and individual rather than a cosmic level. The Germanic dragon in particular is said to inhabit a grave-mound or barrow, where it guards a treasure. An Old English gnomic verse states:

> Draca sceal on hlæwe
> frod, frætwum wlanc.[39]

[The dragon must be on the grave mound, old and wise, proud of the treasure.]

The wisdom of the dragon is here associated not only with its age but also with its gold: the treasure, as David Williams points out in regard to the *Beowulf* dragon's hoard, "is the symbol of wisdom as yet unattained and a challenge as yet unmet."[40] More specifically, the treasure signifies the hidden knowledge of the dragon, the secret that behind presence lies absence, behind Being lies Nothingness. The hero's desire to wrest the treasure from the dragon signifies his desire for Being, which can be gained only through a confrontation with non-Being in the form of the hero's obverse, negative image, the monstrous double. To lose that contest is to die; to win is to legitimate oneself and gain the name of a hero, but it is not finally to annihilate the dragon. Instead, the dragon conceals its existence in a new form that simultaneously reveals itself in the 'dragonish' characteristics acquired by the dragon slayer: Siegfried's horn-hard skin or his knowledge of the language of birds.[41]

Moreover, the dragon's ideological function as a scapegoat retrospectively defined as monstrous by the victorious official discourse, primary in the Indo-European creation myths surveyed above, survives into legend on another level

as well, a level on which the dragon appears to threaten social rather than cosmic order. Linguistically, this is indicated by extensions of the Indo-European
dragon slaying formula to refer (again bidirectionally) to killings of or by a
person who has been defined as monstrous (or 'dragonish') within the authoritative discourse of the text because of his or her violations of the fundamental
rules of civilized social behavior, and more precisely of violations of the codes
regulating hospitality between host and guest. Watkins cites examples of the
'monstrous guest/host' motif from Indic, Iranian, Hittite, Germanic, and Greek
sources. He concludes with two "final comparative details" which, he says,

> demonstrate both the well-foundedness of our identification HERO =
> GUEST, SERPENT = ANTI-GUEST, and . . . its legitimate status as an
> Indo-European theme. The first is the fact that the Hittite Illuyanka-ser-
> pent is an invited guest at a feast, where he is made drunk and thereby
> overpowered . . .
>   The second is a 'singular detail' in a dragon-slaying [*sic*] episode of
> Grettir's Saga. When Grettir came to the young wife Steinvǫr's house, with
> the purpose of ridding it of the unknown monster who had carried off her
> husband, "he concealed his identity and called himself *Gestr.*" (*HK*, 297)

These extensions of the dragon slaying formula to include human beings reflect
and tend to reinforce the idea of the 'monstrous double' that is inherent in the
dragon myth as a whole, for, as the common etymology of the two words suggests, the host/guest relationship is also bidirectional and interdependent. Only
the presence of a guest articulates the host as host; in the absence of a guest, the
host cannot be differentiated as such; the guest, on the other hand, requires a
host in order to exist as a guest. Just such a relationship obtains between the
hero and the dragon: the hero is articulated as hero in the dragon slaying, while
his victim is defined as monstrous by virtue of his or her defeat. If a dragonish
guest (or host) must be destroyed, it is because his or her presence within the
legend has become ideologically threatening to the social order, which main-
tains its hegemony in part through the monologic discourse of dominant cultural and social myths.

NATURAL-HISTORICAL DRAGONS

The medieval horizon of expectations for a story featuring a dragon is not,
however, limited to associations drawn from the Indo-European dragon myth.
Because the most consistent characteristics of the dragon are not in any way
supernatural, but can be found in nature (e.g., its reptilian form, its ability to
fly, its poisonous bite, even the light and heat from the fire said to burn in its
belly) the dragon easily moves out of myth and into such quasi-literary texts as
histories, chronicles, bestiaries, and travellers' tales. These works form the second intertextual layer of the dragon's horizon of expectations.

The serpentine qualities of the dragon are emphasized in medieval bestiaries, which generally follow a standard form first found in Isidore of Seville's *Etymologica* in the entry beginning "Draco maior . . .":

> Draco maior cunctorum serpentium, sive omnium animantium super terram. Hunc Graeci δράκων vocant; unde et derivatum est in Latinum ut draco diceretur. Qui saepe ab speluncis abstractus fertur in aerum, concitaturque propter eum aer. Est autum cristatus, ore parvo, et artis fistulis, per quas trahit spiritum et linguam exerat. Vim autem non in dentibus, sed in cauda habet, et verbere potius quam rictu nocet. Innoxius autem est a venenis, sed ideo huic ad mortem faciendam venena non esse necessaria, quia si quem ligarit occidit. A quo nec elephans tutus est sui corporis magnitudine, nam circa semitas delitescens, per quas elephanti soliti gradiuntur, crura eorum nodis inligat, ac suffocatos perimit. Gignitur autem in Aethiopia et India in ipso incendio iugis aestus.[42]

> [The dragon is the largest of all serpents and of all living creatures on earth. The Greeks call it *drakón*; and this was taken into Latin so that it was called *draco*. And frequently the dragon rushes from caves into the air, and the air is agitated on account of it. It is crested, has a small mouth with a narrow opening through which it draws its breath and thrusts out its tongue. Its strength is not in its teeth but in its tail, and it can harm through its stroke, rather than its jaws. It is harmless in terms of venom, but venom is not necessary for it to cause death, because it kills whatever it has entangled in its coils. And the elephant is not safe from it because of its size, for it lies hidden near the paths on which elephants usually walk, and entangles the elephant's legs in its coils, and kills through suffocation. It grows in Ethiopia and in India, in the burning of perpetual heat.]

This passage, with its emphasis on the extraordinary size and snake-like habits of the dragon, clearly has little in common with either the popular conception of a flying, fire-breathing monster or with the semi-divine, cosmos-threatening creatures of Indo-European myth. Isidore's dragon is a mere snake, however large or exotic, closer to the boa constrictors of classical natural history than to the dragons of later literature. In fact, Pliny the Elder's account of African constrictors in Book VIII of his *Historia Naturalis*, where he describes one serpent killed in the Punic Wars as being 120 feet long and tells stories of dragons in India killing elephants, is likely to have been among Isidore's sources.

Nevertheless, the fact that Isidore's dragon lives *in ipso incendio iugis aestus*, "in the burning of perpetual heat," could provide ample inspiration for the conscious or unconscious transferral of perpetual burning from the environment to the dragon's body and breath. And not only does the dragon rush *in aerum*, "into the air," in so doing it also causes distinct aerial disturbances, events which provide a hint of flight that is made explicit in Isidore's further distinction between *angues*, *serpentes*, and *dracones* when he states that the "*anguis* lives in the sea, the serpent on earth, the dragon in the air."[43] This might have been enough to supply the dragon with wings in medieval texts, even if more graphic descriptions of winged serpents had not been available. Such descriptions did exist, although medieval bestiary accounts did not as a rule make use of them. The most notable authority for winged snakes is Herodotus, who mentions Arabian serpents characterized by bat-like wings twice in his *Historia*, once in a simple description (II, 75), and once in terms of an annual battle between these serpents and the Egyptian ibis (III, 109). One final characteristic of the medieval literary dragon, its function as the guardian of a hoard of gold, finds a possible intertext in Herodotus' statement that "gold-guarding griffins" inhabit northern Europe (*Historia* III, 116; IV 13, 27).[44]

Medieval texts concerning the marvels of the classical and especially of the Asiatic world tend to echo these natural historical descriptions of dragons. The Old English *Wonders of the East*, for example, found in the same manuscript as *Beowulf*, describes dragons:

> Þa beoð on lenge hundteontiges fotmæla lange . & fiftiges hy beoð greate swa stænene sweras micle . for þara dracena micelnesse ne mæg nan man na yþlice on þ land gefaren.[45]

> [that are one hundred and fifty feet long in length; they are as great as large stone columns. Because of the size of the dragons no one may travel easily in that land.]

Neither the medieval nor the classical accounts of such 'natural' dragons move the monster out of exotic natural history into symbol or metaphor; neither seem particularly influenced by the Indo-European myths concerning dragons. Nonetheless, the metaphoric association of Indo-European mythic dragons with death could be reinforced by the easily drawn analogy between dragons and the snakes and worms found in grave-mounds; in fact, the most common term for the dragon in medieval Germanic literature is not the Latin-derived OE *draca* or ON *dreki*, but the native OE *wyrm* and ON *ormr*, either of which can signify 'worm' or 'snake' as well as 'dragon'.[46] Nora K. Chadwick interprets ON *ormgarðr*, 'snake's dwelling,' as a possible kenning for "the place of the dead, even Hell";[47] it is likewise possible that the cognate OE words *wyrmgeard* and *wyrmsele* would come to represent not only the literal 'grave,' but the metaphorical 'dragon's lair' as well.

Moreover, when we turn away from dragon-texts concerning serpents and constrictors to those representing naturally occurring celestial phenomena (i.e., comets, meteors, lightning, the *aurora borealis*) as dragons, the dragon immediately leaves the sphere of natural history and becomes a vehicle for metaphor. The basis for the metaphor, the attribution of fiery breath to the dragon, is a comparatively late addition to dragon lore and was probably influenced by specifically Christian ideas.[48] Nevertheless, by 793 some types of celestial lights could be called dragons, as this often-cited entry in the *Anglo-Saxon Chronicle* makes clear:

Her wæron reðe forebecna cumene ofer Norþanhymbra land, and þæt folc earmlice bregdon: þæt wæron ormete ligræscas, and wæron geseowene fyrene dracan on þam lyfte fleogende.[49]

[In this year dire portents came over Northumbria, and badly frightened that people. There were huge lightning flashes, and fiery dragons were seen flying in the air.]

Precisely what sort of "fiery dragons" the chronicler refers to in this passage may be debated. The most fanciful solution—that the Northumbrians observed what they believed to be genuine flying serpents in their skies—may be attractive, but it is more likely that here the term *dracan* refers metaphorically to some sort of unusual, but not supernatural, celestial lights, interpreted locally as an ominous portent of the Viking raids which occurred later that year. Late medieval usage of the term 'firedrake' to refer to a meteor suggests one possible solution; the *aurora borealis* has also been proposed.[50] In addition, the assumption that the sight of such 'dragons' portends evil, even if the dragons are not assumed to be actual monsters, could have been underscored by specifically Christian associations of the dragon's fiery breath with the fires of hell. The metaphor may also carry with it some hint of the 'monstrous guest' motif which we have found in conjunction with the Indo-European dragon slaying myths, for the Vikings (who, it should be remembered, often sailed in dragon-prowed ships) would certainly fit the description of 'dragonish' guests who arrive to disrupt the established social order.

In sum, the medieval horizon of expectations concerning dragons can be seen so far to encompass mythic narrative, metaphor, and representations of analogues to the dragon in the natural world. The 'natural-historical' representations of the dragon, however, are not always neatly differentiated from the mythic layer of the horizon of expectations; instead, they can slide into metaphor as myth and natural history conduct their own intertextual dialogue about dragons.

HISTORICAL-POLITICAL DRAGONS

That the dragon was often used as an image for the deadly ferocity of an army—by the army itself—is a matter of historical fact. The dragon ships of the Vikings have already been noted; other examples include the use of dragon banners and insignia by peoples as diverse as the Romans, Indians, Persians, Parthians, Scythians, and Saxons.[51] This proliferation of dragon standards and insignia suggests that if the dragons of Indo-European myth were considered the ultimate adversaries of legendary heroes, then there were apparently many warriors who wished to see themselves, and to be seen, as equal to dragons in their fighting prowess.

Isidore of Seville, in a text which associates the historical-political dragon with the dragons of myth, claims that such dragon banners were originally devised to commemorate Apollo's victory over Python (*Etymologica* XVIII, iii, 3). Semantically speaking, the use of dragon insignia by an army or military host provides an example of yet another dialogic interaction between the word/image 'dragon' and various cognates of Latin *hostis*, 'stranger, enemy,' the word which underlies both 'host' and 'guest' in English and other Germanic languages (cp. German *Gast*, 'guest,' and *Gastwirt, Gastgeber*, 'host'). An army, of course, is a host whose significance and behavior differ from that of a (social) host welcoming a guest, while as visitors an army cannot help resembling the 'monstrous' guests of Indo-European dragon legends. 'Hostile' behavior is the norm for a military host, but that behavior is no less monstrous—that is, dragonish—for being expected. Although we have seen that the dragon already inhabits the semantic field of 'guest/host' when that field includes a violent breach of hospitality, its use as military insignia further illustrates its relationship to such terms as '(military) host,' 'hostile,' and 'hostage'—all words signifying in one way or another the breakdown of reciprocal hospitality (and thus dialogue) into violence and coercion.

At the same time, the dragon's role as a military emblem could be generalized into a symbol for the people whom the dragon army protected; in Jacques LeGoff's words,

> the standard-dragon developed a symbolism of its own, the upshot of which was to make the dragon the emblem first of a military community, then of a nation. The *draco normannicus*, or Norman dragon, was merely a metaphor for the people of Normandy.[52]

Dragons used as emblems for entire populations act as intertexts for stories of mythical dragon fights to produce originary narratives which serve to document, not the divine establishment of cosmic order, but the human formation of social order: victory over the dragon thus becomes a "symbolic victory of the civilizing hero, the cathedral builder or land clearer, organizer of the feudal order."[53]

The widespread military use of dragon insignia has also inspired Mircea Eliade's hypothesis that legendary or literary dragon battles arise when a

> historical personage is assimilated to his mythical model (hero, etc.) while the event is identified with the category of mythical actions (fight with a monster, enemy brothers, etc.).[54]

Otto Höfler calls such dragon legends 'historical' dragon fights: that is, he asserts that the dragon stories refer to actual battles fought by men which are symbolically represented as dragon fights in a kind of secular euhemerization.[55] Such a hypothesis leads naturally to the question of which historical battles are the basis for specific dragon tales, and for the Siegfried/Sigurðr legend Höfler provides an answer: he believes that Siegfried is the legendary/literary representation of the Cheruscan Arminius, whom Tacitus says was celebrated in the songs of the Germans (*Annals* II, 88) and who ambushed and annihilated the

Roman host of Varus in the first century CE. In a similar vein, Annelise Talbot has suggested that the dragon fight attributed to Siegfried's father Sigemund in *Beowulf* is "a symbolic description of the conquest and burning of Vetera, with its hoard of Roman loot from German tribes" by the Batavian leader Civilis in or around 69 CE[56]

As problems of literary history, these theories are difficult to prove or disprove. For our purposes, however, they serve as ready examples of the vital difference between source and intertext. While it is possible that a battle against an army bearing a dragon standard could be transformed in the telling into a fight against a dragon, once the metaphorical transformation has been made, the forgotten historical *source*—i.e., the specific battle underlying any one particular dragon fight—is irrelevant to further legendary/literary representations of the dragon; it does not become an intertextual component of the medieval horizon of expectations concerning dragons in the way that the more generalized use of dragon standards by historical armies does. The primary danger of confusing source-study with the reconstruction of an intertextual horizon of expectations contemporary with the work of literature under consideration lies again in the possibility of interpretive reduction: it is all too easy to assume that the discovery of a specific source 'explains' the figure of the dragon as it appears in a work of literature. In Paul Zumthor's words, the "'search for sources' . . . articulates a possibility, nothing more. . . . [I]t reifie[s] a referential illusion."[57] Just as the medieval literary dragon is not a univocal repetition of the dragons of Indo-European myth, it is also not 'really' a meteor or an army with a dragon banner: it is a textual image which may or may not retain specific associations with its historical source materials. I do not, of course, mean to suggest that literary historians like Höfler and Talbot are themselves trying to 'explain away' the dragons in their analyses of political analogues; nonetheless, it is easy to make the mistake of assuming that a difficult or enigmatic work may be fully illuminated by discovering its source.

BIBLICAL/HAGIOGRAPHICAL DRAGONS

Traditionally considered the most pervasive of intertexts for the medieval literary dragon are the descriptions of dragons and other monsters found in the Bible, where the dragon appears as a direct manifestation of Satan and therefore takes on connotations of absolute evil—something not found in the use of dragons as military standards, in classical natural history or in the earliest bestiary accounts, or even in the monstrous doubles of Indo-European myth. The bestiary analogy between the dragon and the serpent does, however, recall the serpent of Genesis 3:1, referred to in the Vulgate as *callidior cunctis animantibus terrae*, "more subtle than any of the beasts of the earth," who precipitates the Fall by tempting Eve, and who is cursed by God:

> Quia fecisti hoc maledictus es inter omnia animantia et bestias terrae; super pectus tuum gradieris, et terram comedes cunctis diebus vitae tuae. (Gen. 3:14)
>
> [Because you have done this thing, you are cursed among all animals and beasts of the earth; you shall go upon your breast, and you shall eat earth all the days of your life.]

Fire-breathing serpents are also described in the Bible and provide yet another important intertext for the medieval literary dragon. The fiery breath of the dragon may be attributed first to the Biblical accounts of the *ignitos serpentes*, "fiery serpents," which plagued the Israelites in the desert (Numbers 21:6) and which are also referred to in Deuteronomy 8:15 (*serpens flatu adurens* "the serpent burning with his breath"), and second to the description of Leviathan in Job 41:9–12:

> Sternutatio eius splendor ignis, et oculi eius, ut palpebrae diluculi. De ore eius lampades procedunt, sicut taedae ignis accensae. De naribus eius procedit fumus, sicut ollae succensae atque ferventis. Halitus eius prunas ardere facit, et flamma de ore eius egreditur.
>
> [His sneezing is like the shining of fire, and his eyes like the eyelids of the morning. From his mouth lamps go forth, like torches of lighted fire. From his nostrils comes smoke, like that of a pot heated and boiling. His breath kindles coals, and a flame comes forth out of his mouth.]

This monster would also be likely to have been associated with the gold-guarding Germanic dragon because *sub ipso erunt radii solis sternet sibi aurum quasi lutum*, "under him are rays of light; he strews gold from himself like mire" (Job 41:21).

Some human enemies of the Israelites—who may be defined by their behavior, in keeping with the Indo-European dragon slaying myth, as monstrous or 'dragonish' hosts—are also referred to in the Old Testament as resembling dragons, most notably Nabuchodonosor (Jeremiah 51:34) and Pharoah, who is called *draco magne* "the great dragon" (Ezechiel 29:3). But the most important dragon appears in the New Testament, in the Apocalypse of Saint John, where we find *draco magnus rufus, habens capita septum, et cornua decem, et in capitibus eius septum diademata*, "a great red dragon, having seven heads, and ten horns, and seven diadems on his heads" (12:3). This is *draco ille magnus, serpens antiquus, qui vocatur diabolus et Satanas*, "the great dragon, the ancient serpent, who is called the devil and Satan" (12:9). Here the dragon is explicitly identified as Satan, an identification which led the Church Fathers and their medieval descendants to the subsequent glossing of virtually all the Biblical monsters as types of the devil.

This seemingly monologic discourse of the Bible concerning dragons does, however, at times interact dialogically with other classical and medieval voices on the subject, as we have seen in the case of the 'monstrous hosts' noted above.

To cite another example, the natural-historical dragon is invoked in Psalm 148 when the dragons (*dracones*) of the earth and the sea are called upon to praise God (148:7)—an activity that cannot be reconciled with the patristic notion that all dragons are types of Satan. Augustine glosses this problematic text as "referring to dragons only as the largest living creatures on Earth"[58] in an obvious reference to classical sources on the subject. In addition, the Biblical dragon is intertextually bound to the monsters of Indo-European dragon myths through the Canaanite figure of Leviathan, and is therefore subject to the same sort of interpretation as the dragon of myth. Yet in medieval practice the Bible functions effectively as a separate intertext for the dragon legend. If the dragon's horizon of expectations contains elements of the mythic or natural-historical dragon on the one hand and of the demonic or Satanic dragon on the other, for the Middle Ages the two serve as discrete conceptions of *draconitas* which meet one another anew in the literary text.

The Biblical influence on medieval dragons can be clearly seen in the later bestiary accounts. As noted earlier, the classical sources for the bestiaries presented the dragon as an animal like any other, larger than most and exotic in that it inhabited remote places like Ethiopia or India, but still of primarily zoological interest. However, the medieval practice of Christianizing and allegorizing the texts of the classical world led to the addition of moralizing passages to the bestiaries to explain the allegorical significance of each animal. T.H. White's translation of a twelfth-century bestiary concludes its section on the dragon with an exemplary comparison between the dragon and the devil:

> The Devil, who is the most enormous of all reptiles, is like this dragon. He is often borne into the air from his den, and the air round him blazes, for the Devil in raising himself from the lower regions translates himself into an angel of light and misleads the foolish with false hopes of glory and worldly bliss. He is said to have a crest or crown because he is the King of Pride, and his strength is not in his teeth but in his tail because he beguiles those whom he draws to him by deceit, their strength being destroyed. He lies hidden round the paths on which they saunter, because their way to heaven is encumbered by the knots of their sins, and he strangles them to death. For if anybody is ensnared by the toils of crime he dies, and no doubt he goes to Hell.[59]

The same sort of allegorized dragon appears in the Old English poem "Panther," itself part of a fragmentary Anglo-Saxon *Physiologus* preserved in the Exeter Book.[60] The panther functions in the poem explicitly as a figure for Christ, who is called *æghwam freond . . . butan dracan anum*, "a friend to each one . . . except the dragon alone" (15b–16b). The dragon, which is called *se ealda feond*, "the ancient enemy" (59b), in a deliberate evocation of the Biblical *hostis antiquus*, is also termed *attorsceapan*, "poisonous enemy" (33b) and *fyrngeflitan*, "ancient enemy" (34a) and functions within the allegory as a figure for Satan. This dragon is:

Se ealda feond,
þone he gesælde   in susla grund
ond gefetrade   fyrnum teagum,
biþeahte þreanydum... (59b–61a).

[the ancient enemy, whom he [the panther/Christ] put into the tormented ground and fettered with fiery fetters, covered with misery....]

In the same way classical accounts of dragon slayings, such as the slaying of the Mars serpent in Ovid, could be given allegorical interpretations and thus 'moralized.'

The Biblical conception of the Satanic dragon may also be found in numerous saints lives written during the Middle Ages. Although a complete survey of hagiographical dragon lore would be out of place here and in any case would require a book of its own, it may suffice to mention that a list of dragon-slaying saints in the Western Church alone would include over forty names.[61] The tale of St George and the dragon is probably the most familiar to English-speaking readers, but in this story the dragon is a late and somewhat atypical addition. Some versions of the legend even feature the saint mounted like a knight on his charger attacking the monster with drawn sword, a variant which makes the legend more similar to secular romances than to other hagiographic dragon fights. More typical of the saints legends is the story of St Margaret of Antioch:

> While in prison, Margaret besought the Lord to make manifest in visible form the enemy who was striving against her. Then there appeared to her a hideous dragon, who sought to throw himself upon her and devour her. But she made the sign of the cross, and the dragon vanished.[62]

Other dragon-slaying saints are St Michael, St Philip the Apostle, St Martha, St Florent, St Clement, St Ammon, St Simeon Stylites, St Julian, St Hilary, St Donatus, St Sylvester, St Germanus, St Victor and St Victoria. Taken together, these saints' legends serve to underscore the idea of the dragon as a demonic rather than a natural-historical or mythical creature, and they must have added an element of sanctity to the horizon of expectations regarding the heroes of even the most secular dragon fights in literature.

Conversely, the presence of a dragon in a particular tomb or grave could be interpreted as a sign of damnation in a metonymic conflation of the Satanic dragon of the Bible with the grave-dwelling Germanic dragon. The dragon St. Marcellus fought outside Paris in the fifth century was said to have emerged from the grave—perhaps even from the corpse—of an adulterous woman.[63] Another example of this type has been cited by H.M. Chadwick, who tells the ninth century story of the opening of Charles Martel's grave:

> St Eucherius, bishop of Orleans, in a vision saw Charles in hell, and on coming to himself begged St Boniface and others to go and inspect the prince's burial place. On opening the tomb they saw a dragon dart out suddenly and found the grave all blackened as though it had been burnt up.[64]

Whatever the source of the fire in the tomb, the saints immediately interpret it as a 'dragon,' and the dragon as a sign that Charles is indeed in hell. Perhaps they saw the dragon as representing Charles himself, thereby literalizing a common homiletic metaphor found, among other places, in this admonition from the early eleventh century Old English *Byrhtferth's Manual*:

> & ure stafas syn on urum handum to sleanne þa wyrmas, & eac þa næddran, gif hig wyð us wyllað winnan oððe us derian. Hwæt synt þa wyrmas buton lyðre men & geflitgeorne & Godes fynd & heora agenra sawla forwyrd?

> [and let our staves be in our hands to strike the dragons, and serpents also, if they desire to fight against us or to injure us. What are the dragons but people who are evil and contentious and enemies of God, and the ruin of their own souls?][65]

Obviously dragons in literary texts can be many things besides evil and contentious people, something the critical reader needs to remember, even if homilists and early scientists like Byrhtferth of Ramsey can forget.

DRAGONS IN EPIC AND SAGA

The question of how to interpret the dragons and dragon fights in specific works of medieval literature remains. The precise horizon of expectations held by individual historical audiences is hard to pinpoint, yet the extension of that horizon by a particular literary text and with it the significance of any one dragon story may be gauged only by measuring the distance between that dragon fight and the expectations of its audience. "Significance," Jauss asserts, ". . . is no atemporal, basic element which is always already given; rather it is the never completed result of a process of progressive and enriching interpretation."[66] The intertextual possibilities articulated here interact in each individual text, and each individual dialogic interaction will point toward a different interpretation of any one dragon.[67] The significance of a medieval dragon can be ascertained only by carefully listening to the voices of the text which it inhabits, in order once again to ask questions to which the textual voices can provide answers.

One reason this has so rarely been done, of course, is that there are a large number of generic dragons about. Most dragons in literature are not given important roles to play; their presence in a text often does not expand or change the horizon of expectations in any important or interesting fashion. As J.R.R. Tolkien has remarked,

> dragons, real dragons, essential to both the machinery and the ideas of a poem or tale, are actually rare. In northern literature there are only two that are significant. If we omit from consideration the vast and vague Encircler of the World, Miðgarðsormr, the doom of the great gods and no matter for heroes, we have but the dragon of the Völsungs, Fáfnir, and Beowulf's bane.[68]

Following Tolkien's lead, I have limited my consideration of medieval dragons to the two he singles out as significant, and thus explicitly to the study of the dragon as it occurs in the heroic literature of the Germanic Middle Ages. The story of the *Beowulf* dragon has been told once, that of Siegfried and Fáfnir repeatedly. I have chosen to include three of those tellings in my study: *Vǫlsunga saga*, *Das Nibelungenlied*, and *Þiðreks saga af Bern*. Each narrative constitutes an historically situated variation on and expansion of a similar intertextual event; each dragon reveals its own 'continuation within variation' of the medieval polylogue about dragons. Because these dragons arise in specifically heroic, as opposed to romantic or hagiographic, literature, their primary intertexts are those of Indo-European myth; however, they are not themselves mythic texts, and cannot be explained merely by reference to that myth. Dragons in literature are answers to historically posed questions, and question in their turn historically assumed answers. If we are to understand them at all from this historical distance, we must listen carefully to them, question their answers, and answer their questions.

2

Beowulf and the *Beowulf* Dragon

It might be dangerous not to decide who is the host and who is the guest, who gives and who receives, who is the parasite and who is the *table d'hôte*, who has the gift and who has the loss, and where hostility begins within hospitality.(Michel Serres, *The Parasite*)

Perhaps no dragon in literature has provoked more critical discussion than the *Beowulf* dragon.[1] The question of how this particular dragon could have become the object of an interpretive controversy may be answered in part by reference to the various possibilities for interpretation suggested by the different intertexts for medieval dragons surveyed briefly in Chapter I, and in part by the desire of many literary critics for interpretive closure. On the whole, scholars have argued that the *Beowulf* dragon must be understood in the light of only one particular intertext or, as the conflict has generally been framed, as having been drawn from only one particular source: patristic *or* natural-historical *or* political *or* mythic. As we have seen, however, the Jaussean idea of a horizon of expectations for the medieval dragon which is historically consti-tuted by any number of different and possibly conflicting intertexts, and which can be influenced and modified even by the text under discussion, relieves us of the difficulty of providing, arguing for, and thus 'proving' the existence of a single textual origin for this particular dragon. Instead, we will seek to deter-mine the specific, distinctively Anglo-Saxon horizon of expectations for the *Beowulf* dragon by looking first at the external textual contexts—Anglo-Saxon, Latin, and Scandinavian—within which the *Beowulf* dragon is inscribed, and then at the dragon itself as it appears in the internal context of the poem as a whole.

THE *BEOWULF* DRAGON IN ITS CONTEXTS

The most immediate external context for the *Beowulf* dragon is of course the *Beowulf* manuscript, Cotton Vitellius A. xv., and more precisely that portion of the manuscript dating from the late tenth or early eleventh century which is referred to as the Nowell codex.[2] Two scribes created the codex; in the first hand are three Old English prose translations of Latin works: (i) a fragmentary *Life of Saint Christopher*, (ii) an illustrated copy of *The Wonders of the East*, and (iii) *Alexander's Letter to Aristotle*.[3] These texts are followed by *Beowulf*, which was copied by the first scribe up to line 1939, then finished by a second scribe. After *Beowulf,* and possibly a later addition to the codex although still in the hand of the second scribe, is the Old English poem *Judith.* Because the three prose texts and *Beowulf* all have to do with monsters and prodigies of nature in one way or another, it has been conjectured, most notably by Kenneth Sisam, that the codex was compiled as a sort of *"Liber de diversis monstris, anglice."*[4] This designation has not been widely accepted,[5] but the monsters of the prose texts do provide a meaningful Old English literary context for the *Beowulf* dragon, perhaps all the more meaningful in light of recent arguments for a tenth or eleventh century date of composition for *Beowulf.*[6]

The dragons of *The Wonders of the East,* already cited in Chapter I, are described as 150 feet long (fully three times the size of the *Beowulf* dragon), but no specific dragon battles are narrated in the text; the serpents are merely said to inhibit easy travel.[7] *Alexander's Letter to Aristotle,* on the other hand, describes a night of continuously escalating battles against progressively larger and more frightening specimens of *wyrmcyn,* "the race of serpents/dragons." After two violent encounters with *wyrma micel mænegeo,* "a great multitude of dragons,"[8] Alexander and his companions are attacked by a third group of monstrous serpents:

> . . . þa cwoman þær nædran eft wundorlicran þonne ða oþre wæron & eges licran. þa hæfdon tu heafda & eac sume hæfdon þreo. wæron hie wundorlicre micelnisse, wæron hie swa greate swa columnan ge eac sume uphyrran & gryttran cwoman þa wyrmas of þam neahdunum. . . . þonne hie eðedon þonne eode him of þy muðe mid þy oroþe swylce byrnende þecelle, wæs þæra wyrma oroð & eþung swiðe deadberende & æterne & for hiora þæm wolbeorendan oroðe monige men swulton.[9]

> [. . . there came again serpents more wonderful than the others were and more frightening. They had two and sometimes three heads. They were of wondrous size; they were as large as stone columns, and some even taller and larger came from the neighboring hill. . . . [W]hen they breathed, out of their mouths came breath like a burning torch. The breath and breathing of the dragons was deadly and poisonous and because of their pestilential breath many men died.]

These serpents are called *wyrmas,* which can mean either 'snakes' or 'dragons,' and *nædran,* which usually simply means 'serpents.' And 'serpents' are exactly what these *wyrmas,* like the 150-foot *dracan* of *The Wonders of the East,* are: they are the same sort of natural-historical 'dragons'—having neither supernatural traits nor symbolic/allegorical significance—as those described by Pliny and Herodotus. In the same natural-historical tradition are the exotic serpents described in the *Liber Monstrorum,* a Latin work likely to have been compiled in Anglo-Saxon England which is already intertextually related to *Beowulf* in that it describes among its human 'monsters' a certain *Higlacus Getorum rege,* obviously the *Beowulf* poet's Hygelac, king of the Geats.[10] In fact, the *Liber Monstrorum* seems to make a distinction between dragons and other serpents, in that while it does not include an entry for *draco* among its twenty-four types of monstrous snakes, it does include one serpent which has *draconis dentes*, "dragon's teeth."[11]

Another medieval Latin intertext for *Beowulf* and the *Beowulf* dragon is the *Gesta Danorum* of Saxo Grammaticus, which describes the slaying of a gold-guarding dragon by one Frotho, king of the Danes. Dorothy Whitelock points out that this king, although not appearing by name in *Beowulf*, nevertheless "occupies in the genealogies precisely the place of Beowulf [Beaw] the Dane, son of Scyld,"[12] an association which strengthens the intertextual relationship between the Latin and the Old English work. This in turn raises the question of whether the name 'Beowulf,' or more precisely 'Beaw,' could have been traditionally associated with a dragon slaying, or even if Beowulf the Geat could have acquired his dragon through association or confusion in the mind of the poet or his source with Beowulf the Dane—a suggestion impossible to prove, but one which Whitelock calls "no more far-fetched than many theories that have won general recognition."[13]

Specific plot correspondences between Frotho's dragon battle as described by Saxo and Beowulf's dragon fight are so commonplace as to be virtually meaningless, but this is not entirely true of the dragon battles described in a British-Latin intertext for the poem, the *Life of Saint Sampson*, which shares with *Beowulf* such plot elements as

> the close relation or personally devoted follower who seeks to join the hero; the less close companions and warbands left standing in the middle distance, with—in the second episode—the message of the outcome transmitted to the military leadership by the follower; the method of disposing of monsters over cliffs; and mutatis mutandis the cleansing of the den and the memorial bearing the victor's name (St. Sampson's Monastery or Biowulfes Biorh).[14]

Whether the *Beowulf* poet knew a version of the *Life of Saint Sampson*, as James Carney has suggested,[15] or whether the common elements merely indicate conventional details and story-types, is less important than the fact that the hagiographic text, unlike the prose texts of the *Beowulf* manuscript or Saxo's Latin *Gesta*, provides the heroic poem with a correspondingly heroic intertext that clearly attributes Christian allegorical significance to the serpents slain by the saint. In Alan K. Brown's words, "Allegory is unavoidable in the first episode's picture of a monk prevented by a dragon from returning to his cloister."[16] How much of that allegory adheres to the *Beowulf* dragon remains to be determined.

Certainly within a Scandinavian context the *Beowulf* dragon would for the most part have eluded Christian allegorization. In her 1959 essay "The Monsters and *Beowulf*," Nora K. Chadwick discusses a series of Old Norse saga analogues to the three monster killings in the Old English poem, including *Hrólfs saga kraka*, *Herrauðs saga*, *Hálfdanar saga Eysteinssonar*, *Valspáttr*, *Gullþóris saga*, and the *Þáttr of Ormr Stórólfsson*, showing that, in each of the sagas, the hero overcomes a triple group of monsters having some apparent connexion with one another, and these monsters individually have features which appear to reflect those of the monsters in *Beowulf*.[17]

In fact, the heroes of these sagas all seem to be members of a family of the Gautar—who have been equated with the Geats of *Beowulf*—or of "the Hálogaland family of Ketill Hǽngr,"[18] making the three interconnected monster-fights a sort of "inheritance to which various members of a noble family . . . succeed."[19] In Chadwick's words,

> all are engaged in waging a feud to the death against an allied or related group of 'monsters'—the *draugr* Agnarr and his variants; the dragon Hárekr; and an evil supernatural woman. The feud and the rôle of the personnel remain constant, no matter what generation we happen to be studying.[20]

Aside from the fact that such a traditional story-line would suggest that the medieval Scandinavian audience, at any rate, would be expecting a dragon to appear in a narrative containing the other monsters, the importance of these intertexts for the Anglo-Saxon dragon's horizon of expectations lies in the textually described origins of the monsters fought by these heroes: they are conceived of as men who magically transform themselves at will into dragons, often the better to guard their ill-gotten gold, at times merely to improve their fighting skills. In *Hálfdanar saga Eysteinssonar*, for example, King Hárekr of Bjarmaland *varð . . . at flugdreka*, "became a flying dragon" during a pitched battle against the Gautar Hálfdan and Skúli, but was nevertheless unable to save his own life:

> Skúli hjó í móti ok af konungi eyrat ok vangafilluna, svá at berir skinu við jaxlarnir. Þá varð Hárekr at flugdreka ok sló Skúla með sporðinum, svá hann lá í óviti. Þá kom at sá kappi, er Grubs hét, ok hjó fót undan drekanum, en drekinn krækir annarri klónni til Grubs ok reif hann á hol á náranum. Þá kom at Hálfdan ok hjó til drekans á hálsinn, ok var þat hans bani.[21]

> [Skuli hit back, slicing off one of the king's ears and all the flesh on one cheek, leaving his back teeth bare. Then Harek turned into a winged dragon and swung his tail at Skuli, laying him out completely. Up came a fighting man called Grubs and hacked off one of the dragon's legs, but the dragon hooked his remaining talons into Grubs's belly and ripped him open just above the loins. By then, Halfdan was back in action, and he struck at the dragon's neck, and so the creature died.][22]

King Hárekr's nephew Valr and his sons also have the ability to become dragons, transforming themselves into large gold-guarding serpents when they are pursued by the Gautar prince Oddr Skrauti and his companions to a cave hidden behind a waterfall:

> Hellir stórr var undir fossinum, ok kǫfuðu þeir feðgar þangat ok lǫgðust á gullit ok urðu at flugdrekum ok hǫfðu hjálma á hǫfðum, en sverð undir bægslum, ok lágu þeir þar, til þess at Gull-Þórir vann fossinn.[23]

[A large cave was under the waterfall, and the father and sons dove into it and lay on the gold and became flying dragons, and they had helms on their heads and swords under their shoulders, and they lay there until Gull-Þórir gained control of the waterfall.]

Gullþórir himself, as is told in *Þorskfirðinga saga* (*Gullþóris saga*), having slain the dragons in the cave and obtained their gold, eventually takes the chests full of treasure and:

plunges with them into the ravine and is seen no more; but the general belief is that he has changed himself into the likeness of a snake, for long afterwards a dragon is seen flying down into Gullfoss and above the ravine into which Gullþórir has been seen to disappear.[24]

And of course the most famous transformation of a man into a dragon occurs in the Eddic poems and *Vǫlsunga saga*, when Fáfnir becomes a dragon to guard a hoard of gold.

Differing interpretations of *Beowulf* tend to privilege one external context or set of intertextual relations for the dragon over the others. While it is danger-ous, if not impossible, to try to divide *Beowulf* critics and criticism into neat categories, the choice of a privileged context or set of intertexts is often de-pendent at least in part on whether the poem is regarded as fundamentally oral in its composition (an assumption which tends to privilege traditional vernacu-lar, usually secular intertexts)[25] or as purely literary (an assumption which often privileges Latin, specifically Christian intertexts).[26] Many recent commenta-tors on the poem have opted to place the *Beowulf* dragon into a natural-histori-cal context, believing that whatever metaphoric significance the monster may have within the thematic structure of the poem, as a dragon it is neither de-monic nor human, but is instead purely bestial in nature.[27] Others privilege the Biblical and hagiographic intertexts, interpreting the dragon as an allegorized figure of Satan or of a particular sin, such as avarice or pride.[28] And the human dragons of the sagas have in their turn given rise to speculations about the possible human origins of the *Beowulf* dragon, either in a lost earlier version of the poem or in a restored text of the extant version.[29]

But as the various Anglo-Saxon, Anglo-Latin, and Norse texts cited above would indicate and as the interpretive controversy would appear to confirm, the text of *Beowulf* does not itself privilege any one external context for the dragon. Furthermore, owing to the multiplicity and diversity of possible intertextual associations for the dragon, it is unlikely that the Anglo-Saxon audience of the poem would have automatically or *a priori* privileged any one of the interpre-tive contexts embedded in the intertexts cited; i.e., it would not have had a single preconceived idea about the nature of dragons. Instead, the Anglo-Saxon audience of *Beowulf*, like any audience of an unfamiliar text, would most likely have anticipated that some of their expectations would be confirmed and others challenged within the internal context of the poem.

At first glance, however, there would seem to be nothing new or challenging about the *Beowulf* dragon at all, for either a medieval or a modern audience. In fact, its challenge lies in the peculiar *lack* of interpretive indicators within the text to guide an audience to a conclusive interpretation by confirming or disputing contradictory elements within the audience's horizon of expectations. The *Beowulf* dragon confusingly offers evidence to confirm all the commonplace yet conflicting views on the general character of dragons while denying none. This indeterminacy makes *Beowulf* the site of a kind of multicultural dialogism, a polylinguistic conversation about the nature and significance of monsters that is never resolved in favor of any one interpretation.

Although W. P. Ker's comments on the monsters of the poem—that the *Beowulf* poet put the "irrelevancies in the centre and the serious things at the outer edges"—became somewhat notorious after Tolkien's eloquent rebuttal of this view,[30] I would argue that his assessment of the nature of the dragon episode is on the whole still accurate:

> The latter part of *Beowulf* is a tissue of commonplaces of every kind: the dragon and its treasure; the devastation of the land; the hero against the dragon; the defection of his companions; the loyalty of one of them; the fight with the dragon; the dragon killed, and the hero dying from the flame and venom of it; these are commonplaces of the story. . . . Everything is commonplace, while everything is also magnificent in its way. . . . [31]

Ker is certainly right about the commonplaces of the story; no real challenge to the audience's horizon of expectations appears in the plot. The characterization of the *Beowulf* dragon seems equally conventional. Nonetheless, it will prove useful to look for a moment at how the monster appears in its own narrative context.

The *Beowulf* dragon is never described outright or in detail; one must infer its nature and appearance from the discourse within which it is embedded, that is, from the language chosen by the poet to designate the dragon and its characteristics. That language is, to use Bakhtin's terminology, "polyglot,"[32] i.e., it contains within itself an implicit, largely unconscious yet nonetheless inescapable dialogue between two and sometimes three discrete languages and the cultures they represent, in this case between Latinate (i.e. classical or Biblical) and Germanic (i.e. English or Scandinavian) notions of the dragon. The Latin-derived word *draca*, 'dragon' occurs as a simplex in the poem five times;[33] it appears an additional six times as an element in compounds: *niðdraca*, "hostile dragon" (2273a); *ligdraca*, "fire dragon" (2333a, 3040b); *fyrdraca*, "fire dragon" (2689a); and *eorðdraca*, "earth dragon" (2712a, 2825a). The Old English term *wyrm* (cognate to O.N. *ormr*), by contrast, appears eighteen times in the dragon episode,[34] although only once in a compound, *wyrmhord*, "dragon's hoard" (2221b).[35] In addition, *draca* occurs once in reference to Sigemund's dragon (892b), which is also otherwise designated *wyrm* (886b, 891a, 897b). The usage of both words may set up a miniature linguistic dialogue between the two terms that would serve to emblematize the corresponding dialogue (or, better, polylogue) between the possible intertexts for the dragon, whether classical, Biblical, or Germanic. It is of course impossible to know just how actively the etymological distinction between the two words was made by the poet or his audience, given that the loan word *draca* entered the Old English vocabulary early enough to have been thoroughly assimilated into the language. Nevertheless, there is evidence that quite sophisticated etymological wordplay had a significant role in traditional Germanic literatures.[36] There is nothing sophisticated about the etymologies involved here; however, even on this elementary semantic level the poet's discourse about his Germanic dragons functions against a background of Latin language and Latin concepts. To transpose Bakhtin's discussion of polyglossia in the Roman world into an Anglo-Saxon context, in Old English texts the English "literary word views itself in the light of" the Latin word, "*through the eyes of*" the Latin word; it becomes a word "with a sideways glance."[37] The "sideways glance"is particularly acute in diglossic compounds like *eorðdraca* or *sædraca*, in which the Anglo-Saxon world of earth and fire, sea and strife, is compelled to look at itself, ever so quickly, through the eyes of the learned, ecclesiastical Latin culture.

Other compounds emphasize those aspects of the dragon most important for the audience of the poem to remember: the dragon has wings and can fly; hence, it is called *lyftfloga*, "air flier" (2315a); *widfloga*, "far flier" (2536b, 2830a); *guðfloga*, "battle flier" (2528a); and *uhtflogan*, "dawn or night flier" (2760a). It is hostile to humanity, and is thus designated a -*sceaða*, "one who does harm, an enemy"in several compounds: *uhtsceaða*, "enemy at dawn" (2271a); *ðeodsceaða*, "people's enemy" (2278a, 2688a); *guðsceaða*, "war enemy" (23-18a); *mansceaða*, "evil enemy" (2514b); and *attorsceaða*, "poisonous enemy" (2839a). Guarding treasure in a grave mound or barrow is the usual occupation of a dragon in Germanic tradition, and the poem emphasizes the dragon's guardianship of its hoard; the dragon is a *weard*, "guardian" (2413b, 3060b); *hordweard*, "hoard guardian" (2293b, 2302b, 2554b, 2593b); *beorges hyrde*, "barrow guardian" (2304b); *beorges weard*, "barrow guardian" (2524b, 2580b, 3066b); and *frætwe hyrde*, "treasure guardian" (3133b).

Interestingly enough in the light of the mythic intertexts discussed in Chapter I, the dragon is also referred to as a *gæst*, "stranger, guest" several times; the word may also mean "ghost, spirit, or demon." I will discuss this word in detail later on in this chapter; at this point I would merely suggest that the poet is able to emphasize in one word both the alien status and the supernatural qualities of the dragon: *gæst* (2312a); *gryregieste*, "dreadful stranger" (2560a); *atol inwitgæst*, "terrible malicious stranger/spirit" (2670a); *niðgæst*, "hostile stranger/spirit" (2699a).

The *Beowulf* dragon breathes fire, although it kills *biteran banum*, "with sharp teeth" (2692a), which are poisonous (2711b-15a). Its fire is not only dangerous to its enemies, but also seems to affect the dragon's own body, which is *fyrwylmum fah*, "marked by the surging flames"[38] (2671a) and *grimlic gryrefah gledum beswæled*, "grimly terrible with his many colors, burned by the flames" (3041). We are told that it is *fiftiges fotgemearces lang on legere*, "fifty feet long in the place where it lay" (3042b–43a) after it is dead; living, the dragon fights coiled like a snake: it is a *hringbogan*, "coiled creature" (2561a) and *wyrm wohbogen*, "coiled worm/snake" (2827a). It may or may not have scales like a serpent, being described only as *nacod*, "naked" (2273a), a term which may imply the smoothness of scales,[39] but which may also suggest that the dragon is revealed or manifest, as in the modern English usage "naked hate."[40] It is *eald*, "old" (2771a, 2760a) and *wintrum frod*, "old and wise with winters" (2277a), having guarded its hoard for *þreo hund wintra*, "three hundred winters" (2278b).

Like Grendel, the dragon seems bound to its lair by day, venturing out only after dark:

> Hordweard onbad
> earfoðlice,   oð ðæt æfen cwom;
> wæs ða gebolgen   beorges hyrde,
> wolde se laða   lige forgyldan
> drincfæt dyre. (2302b–2306a)

[The hoard guard waited restless until evening came; then the barrow-keeper was in rage: he would requite that precious drinking cup with vengeful fire.]

Finally, the dragon is an *aglæca* (2520a, 2557a, 2534a, 2905a), a curious epithet that is glossed, according to its context, either as 'monster' (referring to an evil character) or 'hero, warrior' (in reference to a good character), and which has in its duality inspired a minor interpretive controversy of its own.[41]

In fact, linguistic analogues to *aglæca* exhibiting the same kind of duality of meaning occur in many cultures, sometimes even in reference to dragons. According to Emile Benveniste, Greek *krateros*, "divinely strong, supernaturally powerful," is "favorable when it accompanies the word *amumon*, 'without reproach' (*Theog.* 1013), unfavorable when it describes . . . a dragon (*Theog.* 328)."[42] Moreover, René Girard points out in his discussion of the relationship between violence and the sacred that Latin *sacer* can mean either 'sacred' or 'accursed' (*VS*, 257), a duality retained to a certain extent in French *sacré* (*VS*, 263). Non-Indo-European analogues of the same type include Melanesian *mana*, Lakota *wakan*, and Iroquois *orenda* (*VS*, 257). In *Beowulf* the word *aglæca* seems to have little to do with the sacred *per se*; it does, however, have to do with a particular kind of violence—unilateral violence against monsters—which as we have seen in Chapter I is associated with the 'sacred' violence of myth. Textual occurrences of *aglæca* are limited to references to the monsters (Grendel, Grendel's mother, Beowulf's dragon, Sigemund's dragon) and to the monster-slaying heroes. The term is never used to denote Beowulf's men, Hroðgar or his retainers, the warriors of the Finn episode, or those taking part in Hygelac's Frankish expedition. Of the human characters, only Beowulf and Sigemund, men willing to fight the monsters alone, are designated *aglæcan*. Both are 'warriors,' to be sure, but both are warriors set apart from humanity through superhuman abilities for good or evil. Each is alone, exiled or alienated or elevated away from society by his very nature. By the end of the poem, all of the *aglæcan*—monsters and heroes—are dead.

Nonetheless, despite speculations concerning the elusive signification of *aglæca*, there are in fact no surprises in the characterization of the *Beowulf* dragon, nothing which could not be said of many of the dragons in literature, nothing which would force the poem's audience to modify its horizon of expectations. There is likewise nothing which would tend to reinforce any one particular interpretation of the dragon or rule out another one—no specific pointers toward allegory, no distinctions between human and bestial nature, no explicitly mythic or supernatural dimensions.

What does exist as a challenge to both the medieval and modern audiences, as the discussion concerning *aglæca* suggests, is a network of correspondences linking the poem's heroes and its monsters, especially the dragon and Beowulf. It has often been recognized that the monsters in *Beowulf* are both similar and opposite to the human characters:[43] Grendel can be seen as a grimly parodic thane, an 'anti-thane' who comes to Heorot to feast on men; Grendel's mother is likewise an 'anti-queen' who exacts her own vengeance for the death of her son; and the dragon rules his barrow in a similarly grim parody of a king. Both the dragon and Beowulf are aged, solitary rulers: Beowulf has been *folces weard*, "the people's guardian" (2513a) for fifty years (and the dragon is fifty feet long); the dragon has been a *hordweard*, "hoard guardian" for three centuries. Beowulf distributes treasure, a virtue, while the dragon hoards it, a vice, but in truth both are hoarders, since it is the function of the king to guard and preserve the people's treasure: Hroðgar, who like the dragon is called a *hordweard* (1047), says that he expects Beowulf to become a good *hordweard* (1852) in the future.[44] One might even see the dragon, as Irving once ironically suggested, as the last in a dynastic line comprising Hygelac, Heardred, Beowulf, and the dragon.[45]

Moreover, the dragon's barrow is referred to as a *dryhtsele*, "retainers' hall" (2320a), as if it were in fact a king's hall. Like the Grendels' cavern under the mere, the barrow functions as an "anti-hall," to use Kathryn Hume's term, and may be "pictured as a negation of [the] normal hall characteristics, or as an internalization of the usual hall enemies."[46] As a grave mound, however, the dragon's barrow stands in direct opposition to the life-enhancing king's hall, making the dragon not merely a symbol of a bad king who hoards instead of distributing treasure, but a figure of death itself.[47]

Beowulf consistently uses the dual pronoun to refer to himself and the monsters: in reference to his fight with Grendel (2002b), with Grendel's mother

(2137a), and with the dragon (*unc* 2525b, 2526b; *uncer twega* 2532a). When he tells his retainers that *Nis þæt eower sið, / ne gemet mannes, nefne min anes,* "This is not your venture, nor is it right for any man, except me alone" (2532b-33), the earlier use of the dual emphasizes the implication of the lines: Beowulf and the dragon are akin, both of them set apart from the rest of humanity. Each receives the epithet *stearcheort* "stouthearted" (the dragon in 2288b and Beowulf in 2552a); both are referred to as *aglæcan* (2592a). After death the two lie side by side (3033–40) as Wiglaf *healdeð higemæðum heafodwearde / leofes ond laðes,* "in weariness of heart, holds death-watch over the loved and the hated" (2909-10a). And at the end of the poem, "a curious interchange is suggested: the dragon is pushed into the watery depths in which Beowulf had been so much at home—his element—and Beowulf, now a barrow-dweller, is consumed by the dragon's element."[48]

Beowulf is also linked in his death and burial to Scyld Scefing, whose funeral opens the poem as Beowulf's closes it, and to the nameless Last Survivor who first buries the dragon hoard (2232b–70a). Beowulf is himself a last survivor of a sort, since he dies heirless, lamenting the fact that he has no son (2729–32a). His only legacy is the treasure, which, as it was by the original Last Survivor, will be buried again in a barrow, *ðær hit nu gen lifað / eldum swa unnyt, swa hit æror wæs,* "where it now still dwells, as useless to men as it was before"(3168b–69). The final leader of the Geats will be yet another last survivor, Wiglaf, *endelaf usses cynnes / Wægmundinga,* "the last left of our race, the Wægmundings" (2813-14a).

Beowulf is additionally associated with another famous dragon slayer and *aglæca,* Sigemund, whose dragon fight is narrated in the first half of the poem by Hroðgar's *scop* as part of the Danish celebration after Beowulf's victory over Grendel (875–900). The implicit comparison between the two heroes raises Beowulf to the ranks of the celebrated heroes of Germanic legend and also provides ironic foreshadowing of the second half of the poem, in which Beowulf's victory over his dragon ends with his own death. The tale is linked through its diction to Beowulf's story in several ways: the dragon is to be found *under harne stan,* "under the grey rock" (887b; cp. Beowulf's dragon 2553b, 2744b); like Beowulf, Sigemund ventures alone to meet the monster (*ana geneðde,* 888b); and like Beowulf and his dragon, Sigemund is called an *aglæca* (893a). This dragon is apparently also a fire-breathing monster, since after its death it melts (897b), presumably in its own fiery heat, but possibly also because of the corrosive nature of the monster's blood—foreshadowing the ancient sword's blade melting after its contact with Grendel's blood.[49] The fights differ, however, in both resolution and tone: the exultation of Sigemund's victory over his dragon contrasts sharply to the mourning which follows Beowulf's. Nonetheless, in the immediate context Sigemund's victory over the dragon is linked to Beowulf's victory over Grendel, implying by the comparison that Beowulf's killing of Grendel is the thematic equivalent of a dragon slaying. Given that equivalence, it may be useful to look closely at all three of Beowulf's monster killings in the context of the Indo-European dragon slaying myth discussed in Chapter I. In particular, the variant of the Indo-European dragon myth dealing with monstrous or 'dragonish' guests and hosts will prove to provide a key to understanding Beowulf's relationship to the monsters.

HOSTS AND GUESTS IN *BEOWULF*

The first lines of *Beowulf* contain the story of Scyld Scefing's mysterious arrival in Denmark, his accession to the kingship, and his death and ship-burial: this opening 'digression' constitutes one of the most obviously mythic elements in *Beowulf*. It is an originary myth which attempts to legitimize the Danish royal line by positing a divine, or at any rate divinely sanctioned, origin for its founder. But by asserting divine approval for Scyld's accession to the kingship, the text sublates—that is, simultaneously negates and confirms[50]—yet another, earlier and more violent version of the succession which may still be seen in outline in the text. The narrative in effect attempts to deny what its own plot would seem to affirm, what Thomas D. Hill has called "the disturbing social truth that any magnate who possessed good luck and the prerequisite military skills could conceivably aspire to make himself king."[51]

Seen in this context, the Scyld Scefing story serves as the first in a series of many examples within the poem of an uninvited guest whose presence in a foreign hall constitutes a threat to the existing social order.[52] Although we have the story only in miniature, apparently Scyld first arrives at the oddly leaderless Danish hall as a helpless—*feasceaft*—foundling, having for some unknown reason been sent from an unnamed land *ænne ofer yðe umborwesende* "forth on the waves, a child alone" (46). In his position as an unexpected guest, he is utterly dependent on the kindness of his hosts until the time comes when he *weox under wolcnum weorðmyndum þah* "became great under the sky, prospered in honors" (8). In fact, Scyld's greatness originates in the fact that he effectively inverts the socio-political order of Danish society: he reverses his own position from guest to host by taking possession of the Danish throne in an act which simultaneously recreates his former hosts as his present guests. Scyld's deeds seem entirely beneficent only because they are unopposed within the discourse of the text: no living king of the Danes is mentioned before Scyld, despite the fact that Scyld is received into an already constituted and viable society. We are told only that God sent Scyld's *son*:

> folce to frofre;   fyrenðearfe ongeat,
> þe hie ær drugon   aldor(le)ase
> lange hwile (14–16a)

> [to comfort the people: He had seen the sore need they had suffered during the long time they lacked a king.]

By substituting an assertion of a divinely sanctioned succession *after* Scyld for a description of his own bid for power, the narrator is able to imply that Scyld was also sent *folce to frofre* "to comfort the people,"and that his accession to the kingship of an *aldorlease* "lordless" people was accomplished like his son's without dissent or violence.

Nevertheless, the description of Scyld's frequent (*oft*, 4a) behavior as king, when he :

> sceaþena þreatum
> monegum mægþum   meodosetla ofteah,
> egsode eorl[as] . . . (4b–6a)

> [deprived of their meadseats troops of enemies from many tribes,
> terrified the noblemen . . .]

paints a somewhat darker picture by refusing to specify just who Scyld's enemies were, just whose mead-benches he took away, just which nobles he terrified. Whether Scyld's actions as an uninvited guest in the Danish hall parallel his actions in those halls the narrator designates as belonging to "enemy bands," that is, whether they could have been interpreted by at least some of his erstwhile hosts as the monstrous actions of Hill's 'magnate' with nothing but 'good luck and the prerequisite military skills,' is a question the poem conspicuously avoids, but still suggests in its description of Scyld's violent behavior toward the *ymbsittendra*, "neighboring peoples, those who lived about him" (9b). The inherent duality of Scyld's actions should be apparent: only in the retrospective and always already politically motivated telling of the story is the heroism or monstrosity of the guest's behavior specified.

In the main plot of the poem, Beowulf (as hero) and Grendel and Grendel's mother (as monsters) are all uninvited visitors to the *gestsele* "guest-hall" (994a) of Hroðgar their host. Despite the fact that the narrative clearly delineates one as welcome and beneficial and the others as unwelcome and maleficent, each is in fact both heroic and monstrous in differing degrees.[53] That Grendel and his mother function as monstrous guests in Heorot scarcely needs to be argued; that the two play roles which are both parallel and opposite to those played out in heroic society, that they constitute in fact the "negative image"[54] of that society, has also long been recognized. What is most interesting about the theme of the monstrous guest in *Beowulf* is the way in which the roles of guest and host tend to reverse themselves, making guest into host, host into guest, and conceivably even monster into hero and *vice versa*.

For twelve years Grendel visits Heorot at night, where he hosts morbid banquets at which he *swefeð ond snedeþ* "puts to sleep and feasts on" (600a)[55] his unwilling guests. Likewise, when Hroðgar cedes control of Heorot to Beowulf— a welcome, if equally deadly, guest—for the night (655–60), in a somewhat ironic gesture since after dark the king no longer rules the hall, he reverses Beowulf's status from guest to host while at the same time changing Grendel's status back *to* guest *from* host. Beowulf, reporting his exploits to Hygelac, calls Grendel a *gæst* (2073b) in a context which implies that the hero with his men was the host: . . . *we gesunde sæl weardodon,* " . . . safe, we occupied the hall" (2075). And although Grendel arrives at Heorot as a hungry guest *wistfylle wen,* "[in] hope of full-feasting" (734a), he departs to become a different sort of guest to a different set of hosts: *se ellorgast / on feonda geweald feor siðian,* "the alien spirit [now also an 'elsewhere-guest' or guest elsewhere?] was to travel far off into the power of fiends" (806a–7). In the same way Grendel's mother and Beowulf exchange the roles of (monstrous) host and guest as they parallel each other's actions as avengers in the ensuing blood feud. Hroðgar in fact calls Grendel's mother a *wælgæst wæfre,* "restless murderous guest" (1331a)[56] after her deadly intrusion into Heorot; Beowulf is likewise a murderous guest (*gist* 1522b) and *selegyst,* "hall-guest"(1545a) when he intrudes into her underwater home.

It is perhaps less easy to see how the second part of the poem, the dragon slaying, pertains to this neatly articulated schema of host/guest relations gone awry. The dragon has inhabited its barrow for some three hundred years (2278b) and thus hardly seems a visitor or even an intruder into Geatland; its visit to Beowulf's hall is intended simply to burn the building down and contains none of the parodic echoes of normal hospitality that Grendel's or his mother's depredations have. And yet it is precisely in reference to the raid on Beowulf's home that the poet first calls the dragon a guest (*gæst,* 2312a). Obviously the word can here be translated as "stranger" or "foe," both of which aptly characterize the dragon's relationship to the Geats. But given the emphasis on host/guest relations in the first part of *Beowulf,* as well as the poet's repeated use of various forms of the element *gist* in compounds referring to the dragon (2560a, 2670a, 2699a), a closer look at the situation seems warranted.

The emergence of the dragon as a monstrous *gæst,* that is, "guest" *and* "stranger or foe" in Geatland requires Beowulf to play out the roles of both hero and host. But, just as in the first part of the poem, the roles of host and guest reverse themselves: in order to slay *his* monstrous guest, Beowulf and his men must seek out the dragon in its barrow, become "guests"(or what Watkins terms "anti-guests") in the dragon's "anti-hall." As the barrow's guardian, the dragon thus inadvertently becomes a monstrous host to its own, equally predatory, guests: not only does Wiglaf plunder the barrow after the monster is dead, but the thief provokes the dragon's hostility by entering the barrow and stealing a cup—certainly "dragonish" behavior in its own right.

At this point it may be useful to look at how the *Beowulf* poet uses the word 'guest' both as a simplex and in compounds throughout the poem, that is, at who is termed a 'guest' and under what specific circumstances. A problem immediately arises in that it can be difficult to differentiate the poet's usage of *gist,* "guest, stranger" from his usage of *gāst,* "ghost, spirit, sprite, or demon," given the scribe's frequent use of the spelling *gæst* for both words. In oral performance the two forms would be distinguished in pronunciation: *gæst* as a variant of *gist* or "guest"features a short *æ*, while *gæst* as a variant of *gist* or "ghost" has a long *æ*. In written form, the length of the vowel is impossible to determine, since *gist, gæst* has the same metrical value as *gāst, gǣst*. Semantic differentiation thus depends at times entirely upon the discursive context of the individual usage.

Relatively unambiguous usages of *gist* and its variant *gæst* include references to winter as a guest departing the land in springtime (*gist of geardum*, 1138a); to the sea-dragon killed by Beowulf's men at the Grendelmere (*gryrelicne gist*, "horrible guest/stranger" 1441a); to Beowulf in Grendel's mother's hall under the mere (*gist*, 1522b; *selegyst*, "hall-guest" 1545a); to Beowulf's retainers as they await his return from the underwater hall (*gistas*, 1602b); to Beowulf in Heorot (*gæst*, 1800b); to Beowulf and his men together as they return to their ship (*gæstas*, 1893a) as well as when they enter Hygelac's hall (*feðegestum*, "foot-guests" 1976a); and to the dragon when it attacks Beowulf's hall (*gryregieste*, "dreadful stranger/guest" 2560a). Unambiguous usages of *gāst* and its variant *gǣst* include four references to Grendel, either alone or with his mother (133a, 1274a, 1357a and *ellorgast*, 1621b); one to fire (1123a); one to the monstrous beings that arise after Cain murders Abel (*geosceaftgasta*, "fated spirits," 1266a) and one to the devil shooting arrows at unwary sinners in Hroðgar's sermon (1747b).

This leaves ten instances of the term ambiguous: all ten are spelled in the manuscript as *gæst*, either as a simplex or within a compound; all are in positions that do not definitively determine vowel length: *gæst* (102a, 2073b, referring to Grendel; 2312a, referring to the dragon); *wælgæst*, "murderous *gæst*" (1331a and 1995a, referring to Grendel's mother and to Grendel respectively); *ellengæst*, "powerful or bold *gæst*" (86a, referring to Grendel); *ellorgæst*, "alien *gæst*, a *gæst* living or going elsewhere" (1617a, referring to Grendel) and *ellorgæstas* (1349a, referring to Grendel and his mother); *inwitgæst*, "malicious *gæst*" (2670a, referring to the dragon); and *niðgæst*, "hostile *gæst*" (2699a, again in reference to the dragon).

An examination of Klaeber's lexical decisions shows that in general he prefers the reading *gāst*, "ghost, spirit, demon" for references to Grendel and Grendel's mother, whom he consistently regards as supernatural rather than natural (that is, human or bestial) creatures, and *gist*, "stranger, visitor, guest" for those usages referring to the dragon. However in two cases he seems to find this interpretive distinction impossible to maintain, and he therefore lists two occurrences of *gæst* (2073b, in reference to Grendel, and 2312a, referring to the dragon), as questionable under both terms in his glossary. Furthermore, although most translators and later editors follow Klaeber's lead in these ambiguous cases, his lexical decisions do not always match those of Bosworth and Toller, who tend to read "guest" or "stranger" in lines in which Klaeber glosses the word as "ghost, spirit, sprite, or demon"—thus Bosworth and Toller read an unambiguous "guest"for *gæst* in 2073b and 2312a, as well as in 102a, *se grimma gæst*, "the grim guest/ghost," referring to Grendel; and in the two occurrences of *wælgæst* at 1331a and 1995a, which refer to Grendel's mother and Grendel respectively. Both editors agree to read "spirit" for *ellorgæst* (1617a) and *ellorgæstas* (1349a), probably by analogy to the unambiguous usage of *ellorgast* (1621b). Both also agree to read *ellengæst* (86a), as "bold or powerful spirit," perhaps because of its stressed position in the line, but also perhaps because there are no unambiguous uses of *gist* which refer to Grendel in the poem, while the majority of unambiguous uses of *gāst* are references to Grendel. The same principle may be at work in the case of *inwitgæst* (2670a) and *niðgæst* (2699a), both referring to the dragon, since there are no unambiguous uses of *gāst* in reference to the dragon, as compared to a single unambiguous usage *gryregieste*, "dreadful guest/foe" (2560a). Finally, there is one usage of the simplex *gyst(e)*, "guest" in the reconstructed line 2227a. It is tempting to read this as a reference to the thief, an unexpected and uninvited "guest" in the dragon's earth-hall, but the manuscript is so damaged that any reading here is purely conjectural.

Neither Klaeber nor Bosworth and Toller take the possibility of puns or other wordplay into account in their readings. As glossators and lexicographers, these scholars obviously felt the need to make hard and fast lexical distinctions wherever possible. As literary critics, however, it is necessary for us to consider the possibility that the *Beowulf* poet has used the fortunate congruence of the variant spelling (and concomitant pronunciation) *gæst* for both *gist* and *gāst*, "guest" and "ghost," as a vehicle to allow him to pun on words that otherwise would be too far apart in their vowel sounds to allow for effective wordplay. It seems clear that a pun on *gāst* and *gist* would be missed by the majority of an Anglo-Saxon audience; a pun on *gāst* and *gæst*, however, or even perhaps on *gæst* and *gǣst*, would seem both possible and likely.

Thus, even though the *Beowulf* poet conceives of Grendel and his mother in the first part of the poem primarily as *gāstas*, i.e. "ghosts, spirits, sprites, or demons," as is evidenced by the four unambiguous usages of this term to refer to the monsters, given the clear theme of host-guest relationships as it appears in the opposition of Hroðgar's guest-hall to the anti-hall under the mere and in the ever-shifting roles of host and guest that Beowulf and his adversaries play out, surely the poet's usage of the variants *gāst* and *gǣst/gæst* to refer to his monsters carries with it the punning sense of "(monstrous) guest." Conversely, in the second part of the poem, the traditional Christian association of the dragon with the devil would make the explicit designation of the monster as a *gāst*, "spirit or demon," unnecessarily and perhaps undesirably specific, while the dragon's metaphoric role as a *gist* or "guest"is less self-evident and needs pointing out in specific usages of the word. Still, the predominant variant of the term used in reference to the dragon is not *gist* or *giest* but rather *gæst*, thereby allowing a pun on *gāst*, in a simple reversal of the wordplay found in the first part of the poem.

Also interesting for its paronomastic possibilities is the use of the compound *gastbona* (177a) in reference to the heathen idol to whom the Danes turn in their despair over Grendel: Klaeber glosses the word as "soul-slayer, devil," but this is an interpretive choice which privileges the Christian context of the narrator's remarks to the exclusion of all other possibilities. George Clark has recently pointed out that in a pagan context the term could be glossed "monster-destroyer," which he calls "an appropriate expression for Thor, whom Norse tradition describes as continually in battle with monsters and giants."[57] Such an interpretive gloss makes the poet's rejection of pagan practices more specific, and yet at the same time allows for a Christian pun on 'soul-slayer' or 'devil.' Surely there is also a possible pun on 'guest-slayer' here, since it is the Danes' desire, the *hæþenra hyht*, "hope of the heathens" (179a), that their idol slay Hroðgar's uninvited guest.

The theme of the monstrous host/guest is played out in such an intricate and elaborate way in all three monster fights in *Beowulf* as a means of establishing what I would assert is the poem's primary theme: the creation and maintenance of a civilized social order in the face of violent wars and blood feuds.[58] As we have seen, the Indo-European dragon slaying myth is essentially concerned with the establishment of cosmic order and/or with legitimating a prevailing cosmic regime. But in its variant of the 'dragonish' guest or host the myth tends to concern itself with questions of social rather than of cosmic order, and when the myth is transformed into a secular epic, the social characteristics become primary.[59] In *Beowulf* the dragon, like Grendel and like Grendel's mother, is represented as Beowulf's double, as the obverse image of his kingship, so that its slaying can function as Beowulf's final, perhaps futile, attempt to maintain the social order he has created.

To understand why the creation or maintenance of social order requires not only a double, but specifically a *monstrous* double of the hero, we need to turn back to René Girard's theory of violence and the role of the scapegoat in early human culture. One of Girard's major points is that while social order is based on the differentiation between human beings in terms of their social status, roles, rights, and privileges, reciprocal violence obliterates those differences, turning antagonists into twins:

> If violence is a great leveler of men and everybody becomes the double, or 'twin' of his antagonist, it seems to follow that all the doubles are identical and that any one can at any given moment become the double of all the others. (*VS*, 79)

The restoration of social order thus becomes a matter of the restoration of social difference, which myth (and heroic poetry) accomplishes through the designation of one of the twin antagonists as a monstrous double, a dragon or 'dragonish' character who can be killed in an act of unavengeable, unreciprocated violence by the other twin/antagonist, now designated the hero. The scapegoating inherent within the traditional combat myths, in the words of John P. Hermann, "allows the other within to be located without, differences within to be rewritten as differences between opposed categories."[60] The dragon slaying serves to sublate the monstrous double's identity with the hero as well as his or her ultimate origin in the leveling effect of reciprocal violence. Thus "doubles are always monstrous, and duality is always an attribute of monsters"(*VS*, 162). Moreover, the double must also be specifically designated as monstrous because of the inherent reversibility of the roles of the hero and his antagonist: the monstrous shape and/or dragonish behavior is detailed in the language of the text to place an *a priori* value judgment on the characters which can both differentiate the hero from the monster and determine the valuation of the ensuing violence in such a way that it cannot engender further, reciprocal violence:

> The direction must not be allowed to reverse itself; it has been fixed once and for all, and the expulsion [of the monstrous double from society] is always understood to have *already* taken place. (*VS*, 132, emphasis in original)

Thus those critics who see the similarities between Beowulf and the monsters as indicative of hidden evil on Beowulf's part[61] have missed the point: Beowulf is an untarnished hero precisely because in the retrospective viewpoint of the poem he has been split off from his doubles and designated as such, while the doubles have retrospectively been designated both evil and monstrous.

This is why the appearance of Grendel's mother as an avenging relative (and therefore as indisputable proof that the monster exists in and as part of the human community) is such an "unanticipated and shattering surprise," to quote George Clark's assessment of her nocturnal raid.[62] For if Girard is correct, monster killings exist in early myth and literature as culturally necessary sublations of the internal strife and violence that could, unchecked, destroy the social fabric; i.e., the fictional monster slaying sublates—simultaneously affirms and denies—the historical existence of "interfamily vendettas, or blood feuds" (*VS*, 14) in any given society. When Grendel's mother avenges her son's death, her action reveals what the text with its insistence on monsters and elliptical allusions to future events attempts to conceal: the historical existence of human blood feuds in Heorot.

Thus the poem's sublation of human violence in the existence of Grendel and his mother as superhuman, demonic monsters redirects our attention away from Hroðulf's threatening relation to Hroðgar and his sons and from Freawaru's ill-starred betrothal to Ingeld by substituting a special kind of socially sanctioned, peace-generating violence against a race of monstrous Others for the socially destructive reciprocal violence of a blood feud. In the same way the ravages of the dragon burning down Beowulf's hall in Geatland serve to keep us from focusing as clearly as we otherwise might on the historical reality of war between the Geats and the Swedes and Franks in a narrative strategy designed to sublate historical human violence into a mythic battle between the poem's last surviving *aglæcan*.

But of course the material of the Geatish wars cannot and does not stay in the margins of the dragon-fight, any more than the fact of Hroðulf's treachery could finally be excluded from Beowulf's visit to Denmark. Such absolute, monologic substitutions of what Girard would call 'sacred' violence for human blood feuds are possible only in myth. *Beowulf* is not myth, however much it makes use of mythic elements; it is a quasi-historical poetic fiction about the real ancestors of its Anglo-Saxon audience. Human history can never be completely subsumed into the superhuman and mythic. Although Beowulf and the dragon destroy each other in what is seemingly the end of an era, their historically situated position ensures that their battle cannot provide the restoration of social harmony Girard posits as the desired result of the killing of the monstrous double.

Consequently, the sublation of human violence into superhuman heroism that is the poem's *raison d'être*, although possible in the 'absolute past' of myth, remains incomplete; the monsters never quite succeed in displacing their human counterparts; the unilateral violence of monster-slaying never quite effaces the reciprocal violence of men. Seen in this context, W.P. Ker's comment that the *Beowulf* monsters push the relevant material into the margins is, perhaps, not quite so wrong-headed after all.

CHRONOTOPE AND CHRISTIANITY

Most readers will have noticed that the foregoing discussion conspicuously ignores the specifically Christian dimensions of *Beowulf*, its monsters, and its dragon battle, even though the nature and extent of the Christianity in *Beowulf* has, as the most cursory review of the critical literature makes plain, occasioned one of the largest critical controversies out of all the cruces and questions of the poem's interpretation.[63] Although my reading emphasizes the mythic context of the *Beowulf* dragon, to disregard the importance of Biblical and hagiographical intertexts for the poem's dragon and dragon slaying would be seriously to distort the medieval audience's horizon of expectations and reception of the poem. The precise role such intertexts played, however, remains a controversial question in contemporary *Beowulf* criticism.

In what is still one of the most notable attempts to resolve this controversy, J.R.R. Tolkien in 1936 asserted that the answer is intimately bound up with the poem's representation of and attitude towards human events as they are played out within Time; that is, with whether the *Beowulf* poet saw the events of the poem solely from the viewpoint of his own contemporary Christian era with its emphasis on eternal, spiritual victories and defeats, or whether in fact he saw them from "a pregnant moment of poise," a moment when "[h]e could view from without, but still feel immediately and from within, the old dogma."[64] Perhaps Tolkien's most important insight here lies in his insistence that the narrative discourse of *Beowulf* need not be limited to a single, monologic viewpoint, but rather that the poet's narrative stance could be dual, possibly even multiple, in its point of view.

In order to talk about the Christianity of *Beowulf* it will be useful to establish what Bakhtin would call the "chronotope"of the poem. Bakhtin uses the term "chronotope" (literally, 'time/space') to signify "a formally constitutive category" of literature which is determined by "the intrinsic connectedness of temporal and spatial relationships" as they are "artistically expressed;"[65] he adds that "in literature the primary category in the chronotope is time."[66] For Bakhtin, a work's chronotopic structure—that is, its characteristic depiction of temporal and spatial relationships—determines its genre. Each genre, he asserts, is distinguished by its own peculiar chronotope, and any change in chronotope is equivalent to a change in genre.

Genre classification of *Beowulf* has always been notoriously difficult. Scholars have variously termed the poem a "heroic and philosophical epic," a "wondertale . . . set in early heroic dress,"an "oral-derived . . . court poem," a "heroic elegy," a "heroic tragedy," and even an "autonomous saint's life."[67] Each of these generic classifications is based in a particular interpretation of the poem's chronotopic structures—that is, in its perceived representations of and attitudes toward time and space. Critical agreement concerning the genre of *Beowulf* can arise only out of a critical consensus concerning the nature of its chronotope. This is in turn difficult to come by in part because the poem has not one, but rather several chronotopes; more than one perspective on time and space is represented. Thus David Williams describes *Beowulf* as "bounded by the tropes of time as history and time as 'eschatophore,'"[68] while Tolkien, as noted above, sees the poem as originating in "a pregnant moment of poise"[69] between the pagan and Christian eras. But critical differentiation between chronotopes is not limited to such major distinctions as that between Christian and pagan attitudes; in practice, more subtle refinements regarding the representation of time and space can and must be made: "each such [major] chronotope," Bakhtin says, "can include within it an unlimited number of minor chronotopes; in fact . . . any motif may have a special chronotope of its own."[70] In a multi-layered poem like *Beowulf*, therefore, a mythic motif like the dragon slaying need not be included within the chronotopic purview of other, historical events narrated within the poem, even though it may, at first glance, be both contemporary with and contiguous to those events. A more subtle distinction regarding time and space is required.

Time in *Beowulf* is dominated by a nostalgic, almost thematic sense of the past. All of the poem's events take place *in geardagum* "in days of yore"(1b) and can be known only as a result of a present quoetioning of that past: the narrator's word for this is *gefrunon*, "learned, heard of" (2b), which in its root sense means "asked and received answers"or "learned by asking."[71] In looking at precisely how and by whom the past is questioned in *Beowulf*, however, one quickly discovers that there is more than one 'past' being questioned by more than one 'present' within the poem. In fact, John D. Niles has articulated six major time-frames which the contemporary reader of *Beowulf* can distinguish: three of these, the 'Mythic past' of the Creation, Cain and Abel, and the Flood, the 'Mythic future' of Judgment Day, and the medieval 'Present of the poem's performance' are specifically Christian; one, the 'Present of reading the text,' is obviously different for different readers. Framed by the Christian Mythic Past and Future are two specifically pagan categories: the 'Legendary Past' of Germanic heroes like Sigemund and the 'Historical Past' of the poem's narrated events, whether these are past, present or future in terms of the narration itself.[72] It is this layered temporal framework that allows the poem's pagan historical action to occur in a Christian text and yet to seem untouched by explicit Christianity.

Each of these temporal categories could be described in Bakhtinian terms as constituting its own chronotope. Each is necessarily separate from the others: neither the events of the Christian mythic past and future nor the attitudes of the present of the poem's performance have any place in the historical time of the poetic narrative, nor are Beowulf's superhuman deeds, while they remain within the world of the poem, as yet the stuff of 'timeless'[73] pagan legend. "The relationships that exist *among* chronotopes cannot enter into any of the relationships contained *within* chronotopes."[74] Still, all of the poem's chronotopes can and do interact with one another:

> Chronotopes are mutually inclusive; they co-exist, they may be interwoven with, replace, or oppose one another, contradict one another or find themselves in ever more complex interrelationships. . . . The general characteristic of these interactions is that they are *dialogical* (in the broadest use of the word).[75]

Because the dialogue between chronotopes—and thus between pagan and Christian viewpoints—does not take place *within* any one chronotope, it also does not occur *within* the fictional world created by the poem's discourse: "it is outside the world represented, although not outside the work as a whole."[76] Consequently, there is in *Beowulf* no overt discussion of, for example, the ontological status of dragons, nor are there any specific pointers as to the viewpoint we as the poem's audience are expected to take towards the spiritual status of its pagan heroes. Instead, for the contemporary medieval audience of *Beowulf* the polylogue among the poem's various chronotopes would have taken place during and as part of the reception of the poem's performance, while for the modern audience it occurs during and as part of the act of reading—a fact which also brings the equally chronotopic voices of the various audiences into dialogue with the narrative concerning time and the poem's significance.

This schema goes a long way towards articulating the relationships among various temporal strata within *Beowulf*, yet it makes no distinction between the deeds of purely historical characters and those characters and deeds which fall under the heading of 'the marvelous,' i.e., the poem's hero and its monsters and their superhuman battles. Beowulf's monster-quellings are seemingly classed within the same chronotopic heading as any other historically situated event of the poem. On one level this is as it should be: the poem presents, to paraphrase Tolkien once again, the war between men and monsters as it is acted out historically, in Time.[77] Certainly Grendel and his mother are neither pagan legends nor Christian myths to the inhabitants of Heorot, and an historically situated Beowulf could not fight a non-historical dragon. But on another level, it seems clear that the monster fights must be in some way chronotopically separate from the other events of the poem: although the time they occupy is historic time, their space within that time is constituted differently from the space of ordinary, historically situated human beings.

The space occupied by Grendel and his mother lies outside the possible habitation of human beings; it includes the *mistige moras*, "misty moors" (162a) where people don't go, but it is principally a region beyond human ken: *men ne cunnon / hwyder helrunan hwyrftum scriþað*, "Men do not know where hell-demons direct their footsteps" (162b–3). After Grendel's mother's raid on Heorot, Hroðgar disclaims any knowledge of the Grendels' habitat:

> 　　　　　　　　Ic ne wat hwæder
> atol æse wlanc　　eftsiðas teah
> fylle gefægnod. (1331b–3a)

> [I do not know by what way the awful creature, glorying in its prey, has made its retreat, gladdened by its feast.]

Once Beowulf has agreed to fight the monster, however, the Grendelmere is reported to be located not very far away *milgemearces*, "as measured in miles" (1362b); the implication may be that it is quite far away by other measurements, i.e., that it exists in a qualitatively different space than Heorot. It is reached by *uncuð gelad*, "unknown ways" (1410b). No one has ever explored it: *No þæs frod leofað / gumena bearna, þæt þone grund wite*, "Of the sons of men there lives none, old of wisdom, who knows the bottom" (1366b–67).[78] Similarly, the path to the dragon's barrow is *eldum uncuð* "unknown to men" (2214a) and leads to the same sort of otherworld—a place within but not of Beowulf's realm. Edward R. Irving Jr has articulated the distinction most clearly:

> . . . we can speak of two distinct worlds impinging on each other, occasionally invading each other, and always defining each other with an interface of sharp clear edges. . . . One is the world of man, *humanitas*, and the other is *draconitas*, the world of the alien and everlasting worm.[79]

When the spatial boundaries between the worlds are crossed, the poem's chronotope changes. *Draconitas* invades *humanitas* and the spatial change brings with it a concomitant temporal shift. Purely historical time is interrupted; in its place is the chronotope Bakhtin calls "adventuristic time":

> Adventuristic 'chance time' is the specific time during which irrational
> forces intervene in human life; the intervention of Fate (Tyche), gods, de-
> mons, sorcerers or . . . villains who as villains use chance meetings or fail-
> ures to meet for their own purposes: they 'lie in wait,' they 'bide their
> time,' we have a veritable downpour of 'suddenlys' and 'at just that mo-
> ments.'[80]

The monsters in *Beowulf* are introduced not by a 'suddenly,' but rather, at least
in the case of Grendel and the dragon, by the characteristic phrase *oð þæt an
ongan*, "until one began . . ." (100b, 2210b), while Grendel's mother brings
with her an instantaneous reversal of men's fortunes: *þa ðær sona wearð /
edhwyrft eorlum*, "change came quickly (*sona*) to the earls there"(1280b–1a).
The principle is the same; with the entrance of the monsters the chronotope
shifts from the historic to the marvelous.

It is precisely this primarily spatial distinction between chronotopes within
the historic past of *Beowulf* that divides the narrative, most noticeably in the
second half of the poem, into what have conventionally been called the 'main
plot' of the monster slayings on the one hand and the primarily historical 'di-
gressions' on the other. This division of the narrative in turn allows for the
temporary diversion of audience attention away from the historical, purely human violence of pending blood feuds in Heorot or of the seemingly unending
Geatish wars with all their concomitant moral ambiguities, and toward the relatively unambiguous morality of monster killing—a discursive strategy that allows the audience to suspend, for a time, the disturbing question of the state of
its pagan hero's soul as it unreservedly champions him in his fight against the
monsters. Historic time with its wars, its feuds, and its epochal shift from pagan
to Christian is sublated into the marvelous, adventuristic time of monsters and
heroes so that the poem's audience may wholeheartedly applaud the actions of
a pagan, and thus presumably damned, hero.

Rather than simply negating one chronotopic structure in favor of another,
however, the sublated chronotope is conserved within the discourse of the text.
This is why the sublation of *Beowulf*'s historical/human chronotope into an
adventuristic/marvelous chronotope splits the narrative rather than simplifying
it, and thereby ensures that the two time/space modes continue to exist in an
actively dialogic relationship rather than in a new, monologic text. When the
monster fights reach narrative closure through the deaths of their superhuman
antagonists, those questions about the relationships between pagan and Christian, past and present, myth and history, that had been deferred for a time by the
narrative's lateral shift into the marvelous are reopened with renewed dialogic
force, expanding into the discursive space that has been newly cleared by the
narrative closure reached in adventuristic time.

The dialogic relationship among the poem's various chronotopes is created
through their shifting juxtapositions, one to the other, within the narrative, or,
to extend Fred Robinson's suggested reading of the semantic elements of the

poem, through their apposition. Robinson points out that "the distinguishing feature of apposition (or variation) is its parataxis—its lack of an expressed logical connection between the apposed elements" (*BA*, 3). It is left to the reader/ audience to determine, for example, the precise relationship between the dragon fight and contemporary reality, or between the poem's Mythic Past and its Legendary Past, which in terms of the poet's chronotopic schema means in practice the relationship between Anglo-Saxon Christianity and pagan Germanic antiquity.

The apposition of the various structures of the poem, be they semantic, thematic, or chronotopic, forces the audience of *Beowulf*, in Robinson's words, to "exercise . . . [their] ability to entertain two simultaneous points of view"(*BA*, 13–14). The result is a strong sense of the poem's duality, a perception "that we are experiencing the narrative simultaneously from the point of view of the pre-Christian characters and from the point of view of the Christian poet"(*BA*, 31). This apposition in itself, Robinson asserts, "seems . . . to afford a means of resolving the Christian-pagan tension" (*BA*, preface).

Robinson is certainly right in his analysis of the poem's dual point of view and systematic use of apposition to allow a simultaneous Christian and pagan significance to the same words and poetic structures, but such apposition cannot supply the resolution of tensions he describes. In the admittedly "deeply Christian age" (*BA*, 13) of the Anglo-Saxon poet, the question of how to regard one's pre-Christian ancestors had theoretically been settled theologically and intellectually by consigning all of pre-Christian humanity to eternal damnation, but the evidence of the poem suggests that it was not yet settled emotionally. The appositions of *Beowulf*, far from resolving such "poignant cultural tensions" (*BA*, 14), rather reopen the disturbing question of how the righteous pagan is to be viewed in a specifically Germanic historical context.

By continuing with a Bakhtinian analysis of the dialogic relationship between the poem's chronotopes, we can see that the interaction between the apposed elements is necessarily more dynamic and thus less resolved than Robinson's description would seem to indicate: Christian and pre-Christian discourses do not passively coexist in static apposition to one another, much less produce a metaphoric synthesis in their apposition; rather the apposition produces an interactive dialogue between discourses; the language of *Beowulf* becomes "double-voiced," i.e., "directed both toward the referential object of speech, as in ordinary discourse, and toward *another's discourse*, toward *someone else's speech*."[81] Rather than resolving tensions between discourses, such double-voicing accentuates and develops them by allowing the meaning structures of one chronotope to penetrate the temporal and spatial boundaries of another.

A good example of the use of double-voiced discourse in *Beowulf* can be seen in the creation song the scop sings in Heorot at the beginning of the poem. While it is a critical commonplace to say that the song metaphorically equates the creation of Hroðgar's hall to the creation of the world, most scholars have seen this equivalence in terms of the Christian creation myth alone. Paul Beekman Taylor, however, pointed out a number of years ago that the creation metaphor is in fact double, its discourse pointing simultaneously both to the Biblical account of the creation in Genesis and to essentially pagan accounts such as that found in the Old Norse *Vǫluspá*.[82] The double-voicing occurs not in the fact of the metaphoric correspondences themselves,[83] but rather in the duality of the discursive referents the metaphor implicates in the poetic text and thus brings into metonymic, that is to say appositional, relationship: the culturally dominant Christian discourse provided by the chronotope of the 'Present of the poem's performance' and the simultaneous discourse of the chronotope of pagan Germanic myth in the poem's 'Historic Past.' While the poetic metaphor of the hall and the cosmos provides a synthesis, resolving the tensions in the gap between the building of the hall and the creation of the world as well as between the scop's song and the song of creation, the referential metonym opens a new, wider gap between chronotopic interpretations. This gap is not and cannot be resolved, since for a medieval audience both the Christian and the pagan accounts of the creation cannot be simultaneously correct, just as Beowulf cannot be equivalent both to the pagan hero-god Þórr, a false god whose worship brings damnation, and also to Christ, the source of all salvation. The metonymic gap between the two discursive referents created by the double-voiced metaphor opens up a new dialogic space within the narrative in which the two discourses battle for textual recognition and authority.[84]

By the second part of the poem, the habit of perceiving both discourses is so ingrained in the audience that no specific textual pointers are necessary for the duality to be perceived:

> [the poet] need only introduce a monster with well-established credentials in both worlds—a dragon—and trust that the audience will, without further prompting, see the creature in its full complexity. It is on one level of perception like the dragon Sigemund slew; on another it has those connotations of Satanic evil with which Bible and commentary had long invested it. (*BA*, 32)

There is no need for the narrative to designate the dragon, as it does Grendel, as God's enemy or the kin of Cain; nor is there a need to spell out the dragon's possibly human origins. Both Christian and pagan discourses are as active in the dragon fight as in the rest of *Beowulf*, compelling the audience to ponder, as no doubt the poet pondered, disturbing questions concerning the relationship between present and past, Christian and pagan, salvation and damnation.

The dialogic battle between discourses persists quite literally up to the last word of *Beowulf*. In fact, the poem's final word, *lofgeornost*, "most eager for praise" (3182b), has been rightly regarded as an interpretive crux ever since Tolkien revised his estimation of the compound from "the summit of the praise of the dead hero"[85] to "an ominous note" signaling Beowulf's vainglory and

apparently prompting Tolkien's odd mistranslation "too eager for praise."[86] Within
the double-voiced discourse of the narrative, *lofgeornost* provides an example
of a Bakhtinian "microdialogue," i.e., a single word so permeated by dialogic
exchange that within that one word a reader or listener perceives "a battle and
the interruption of one voice by another."[87] Again there is no synthesis of voices,
no resolution of opposing viewpoints; instead, the poem's dual reference creates a new, appositional metonym that forces the poem, even as it ends, to
remain unresolved on the disturbing question of whether Beowulf is to be considered Christlike and thus deserving of salvation, as the preceding adjectives
mildust ond monðwærust, "mildest and gentlest" (3181) could imply, or whether
he is in fact damned not only because he is a pagan but because of his vainglory
as well.

The *Beowulf* poet thus resists either condemning his pagan hero outright or
celebrating him uncritically by employing two sophisticated narrative strategies: first, he double-voices the narrative; that is, he brings the language of two
disparate discourses—that of orthodox Christianity and that of heroic poetry—
into an unresolved semantic dialogue with each other; and second, he manipu-
lates the chronotopes, or time-space structures, of the poem into an analogous
dialogic relationship which allows the struggle between Christian and pagan
world views to take place simultaneously on a macro and a micro level. Because the dialogue inheres in the language and structure of the poem rather
than in its plot, it resists synthesis or closure.

The dragon fight in *Beowulf* is the site of a textual sublation of human violence into sacred violence that simultaneously reveals and conceals the fundamental fact of human civilization that although the monsters may be slain the
wars continue, and it participates in an unresolved dialogic encounter between
Christian and pagan interpretations of Germanic antiquity. For a twentieth century audience the second point may have lost its importance outside of academic debate; the first retains its urgency as our leaders create ever new and
more frightening monsters for us to kill. The radical openness of the poem
defies traditional generic classification; it means that *Beowulf* will continue to
generate new interpretations and discard old ones as the perpetually renewed
chronotope of the reading present interacts again with the chronotopes of
Beowulf's pasts.

3

Fáfnir

But if the hero went at once for the soft parts, there would be no fight at all, and all the fun would be lost. (R.W. Chambers, *Beowulf: An Introduction*)

The story of the *Beowulf* dragon was told only once in the Middle Ages; by contrast, the story of Fáfnir, the dragon slain by Siegfried [O.N. Sigurðr, M.H.G. Sîfrit], was told repeatedly in both German and Scandinavian literature and thus has a more specific, albeit not necessarily a more extensive, intertextual matrix. The most complete Scandinavian version of Fáfnir's story is the Icelandic *Vǫlsunga saga*, written sometime between 1200 and 1270, but extant in a unique vellum manuscript (Ny kgl. Saml. 1824b, 4ᵗᵒ) dating from c. 1400, as well as in numerous post-medieval paper manuscripts, all of which apparently stem either directly or indirectly from the extant vellum. While a comprehensive examination of the saga's intertexts, sources, and analogues is impossible here,[1] it will be useful to glance briefly at two of the more important intertexts, including the saga's apparent source in the heroic poems of the *Poetic Edda*, and its manuscript companion and sequel, *Ragnars saga loðbrókar*.

Vǫlsunga saga is in large part a prose paraphrase of the Sigurðr material found in the thirteenth-century MS Codex Regius, the so-called *Poetic* (or *Elder*) *Edda*, although the author of the saga most likely used a different, now lost, manuscript with a slightly different version of the poems as his exemplar, and very likely made use of a lost *Sigurðar saga* as well. In addition, the saga chapters 24–31 include material that may have been derived from poems originally contained in what is now an eight-page lacuna in Codex Regius. By comparison to the Eddic poetry, the saga must inevitably be seen as lacking in poetic force and even literary quality, so the present discussion of *Saga* rather than *Edda* may require some clarification. Literary critics' low opinion of *Vǫlsunga saga* stems primarily from the fact that, in turning poetry into prose, the saga author makes his prose unescapably prosaic as well: he quite deliberately refrains from any use of poetic diction and style by deleting or rephrasing kennings and other forms of rhetorical embellishment found in the poetry and by concretizing the supernatural wherever possible.[2] The resulting prose narration does, however, bring the entire story into a single, unified version that, in one critic's words, "lacks neither a certain vigour, nor yet considerable consistency."[3] Because this narrative consistency allows individual motifs, such as Sigurðr's dragon slaying, to be traced out more easily than in the separate, sometimes fragmentary poems of the *Edda*, I have decided to use the saga, whatever its literary deficiencies, as my basic text for the study of Fáfnir.

The manuscript context of *Vǫlsunga saga* provides a second important intertext, in that the saga exists in both the vellum and the paper manuscripts only as a prelude to *Ragnars saga loðbrókar* (or, variously, *Ragnars saga* exists only as a sequel to *Vǫlsunga saga*). The two are connected most obviously by the fact that in his saga Ragnarr marries Áslaug, the daughter of Sigurðr and Brynhildr, but for my purposes the most important intertextual elements are first that Ragnarr himself is a dragon slayer, and second that two of the children of Ragnarr and Áslaug carry internalized signs of the dragons' presence in their parents' pasts.

Like Sigurðr in *Vǫlsunga saga*, Ragnarr is a young man, an adolescent of fifteen, when he kills his dragon. That monster is at first merely a small serpent given by Herruðr of Gautaland to his daughter Þóra as a present; she accordingly keeps the snake in a little chest which she furnishes with gold for it to sleep on (chap. 2). Unfortunately, the serpent first outgrows the chest, then the room, and finally lies encircling the house on a bed of gold that increases as the dragon grows larger and more dangerous (chap. 2). Herruðr promises both gold and daughter to the man who can slay the dragon, a feat Ragnarr accomplishes with the help of homemade protective clothing: i.e., a pair of shaggy trousers (hence his nickname, *loðbrókr*, 'shaggy breeches') and a cape boiled in pitch and covered with sand (chap. 3). The episode clearly exists within the saga as an initiatory sequence that establishes Ragnarr both as an adult capable of taking a wife[4] and as a formidable hero who can be compared to his predecessor in the manuscript and future father-in-law, Sigurðr the Vǫlsung.

More important for the saga as a whole is Ragnarr's second marriage to Áslaug and the births of their five sons. Áslaug has inherited her father Sigurðr's wisdom and his ability (gained, as *Vǫlsunga saga* tells us, from the dragon Fáfnir's blood) to understand the speech of birds (chap. 9). Her youngest son, Sigurðr ormr-í-auga, has a serpentine mark in or around his eyes (chap. 8), while the eldest, Ívarr beinlauss, is born entirely without bones (chap. 7). His resulting nickname—and the story of his birth—may refer to an earlier version of the saga in which he was indeed born *beinlauss*, i.e. 'legless,' in a serpentine or dragon-like form.[5]

The two sagas thus interact intertextually through what is a basic theme in each: the slaying of a monstrous serpent by an adolescent warrior in an act which defines each boy externally not only as a hero, but also as an adult member of society, and which leaves an internalized mark on each, one that manifests itself in Sigurðr's increased wisdom and ability to understand the language of birds and in the aforementioned peculiarities of Ragnarr's sons. The fact that Ragnarr wins Þóra by killing a dragon may set up a contextual horizon of expectations for dragon slaying that would link Sigurðr's waking and winning of Brynhildr to his killing of Fáfnir more closely than the text of *Vǫlsunga saga* alone would indicate. The internalization of the dragon's characteristics, on the other hand, serves as an intertextual reminder that dragon and dragon slayer are doubles as well as opposites: having been proven to be 'dragonish' already through their phsyical abnormalities, neither Ívarr beinlauss nor Sigurðr ormr-í-auga need slay a dragon in order to gain adult status (indeed, Sigurðr ormr-í-auga becomes a warrior at the tender age of three years old) or to become exceptionally ferocious fighters.

In addition, Fáfnir's story finds extra-literary intertexts in the numerous carvings and illustrations of his death found throughout medieval Europe,[6] and especially on Norwegian stave churches built from the late eleventh to the mid-fourteenth centuries.[7] All but three of the existing stave churches have carvings based on Sigurðr and Fáfnir, showing clearly that in the Scandinavian Middle Ages this dragon slaying "underwent a symbolic reinterpretation. [Sigurðr] became a transition figure who crossed, intact, the line between pagan hero and Christian protector."[8] Thus, while neither the Sigurðr poems of the *Edda* nor *Vǫlsunga saga* show explicit Christian influence,[9] such influence was undoubtedly present as part of the saga audience's horizon of expectations, for they would most likely have viewed the old pagan hero, in Jesse Byock's words, as "not quite a saint," but rather as a syncretic figure who could serve "a wide variety of religious and secular needs."[10] Although Fáfnir's story as it is told in *Vǫlsunga saga* is neither as enigmatic nor as multivalent as the *Beowulf* dragon's, still, like *Beowulf*, the saga interacts dialogically with both Indo-European myth and Christian doctrine, natural history and hagiography.

CHRONOTOPE IN *VǪLSUNGA SAGA*

When we turn from the dragon slaying in *Beowulf* with its complex temporal layering and consequent multiple chronotopes to the story of Sigurðr and Fáfnir in *Vǫlsunga saga*, we find a much simpler state of affairs with regard to the saga's perspective on time and space. As the prime example of the Old Icelandic *fornaldarsǫgur* (sagas of ancient times, legendary sagas), *Vǫlsunga saga* deals exclusively with heroes and events from Nordic myth and legend. It thus shows little of the explicit concern for historical depth and temporal precision which characterizes not only the earlier Old English poem, but also the roughly contemporaneous *íslendingasǫgur* (sagas of Icelanders, family sagas) and *konungasǫgur* (kings' sagas), which feature "elaborate networks of temporal and spatial frames of reference."[11] By contrast, time in the *fornaldarsǫgur* is treated as in folktales or *Märchen*—i.e., it is either entirely unstipulated or vaguely stated to be a far-off, historically indistinct past.[12]

Even if explicit time references are generally lacking in these sagas, however, certain implicit temporal—and therefore chronotopic and generic—distinctions can be perceived. Hermann Pálsson and Paul Edwards have argued that three distinct temporal strata exist in the *fornaldarsǫgur* as a whole:

> Basic to the genre is the viking ethos. . . Besides this, there is also the
> realization of the hero at a level . . . of an older, more savage and gro-
> tesque world . . . the third level [is] that of romance.[13]

Thus the *fornaldarsǫgur* occasionally contain episodes which show their heroes
in a "comic-grotesque"[14] light seemingly inappropriate to viking ideas of honor,
or ascribe anachronistic romance attributes such as *kurteisi*, "courtesy" and
hæfersku, "good manners" to legendary heroic figures like Sigurðr (*Vǫlsunga
saga*, chap. 23).[15] When the differences between the various strata remain distinct, multiple chronotopes resembling those found in *Beowulf* emerge. In most
sagas the juxtapositions are merely unsettling, while in others the disparities
between the different strata are exploited by the saga authors to good effect.
But this sort of temporal layering exists within *Vǫlsunga saga* only *in poten-
tia*—little of the Viking ethos enters into the saga, and what temporal strata do
exist are allowed to bleed into one another, creating a 'blurred' time scheme
that Pálsson and Edwards acknowledge is often "a striking feature of this literature."[16]

Space in the *fornaldarsǫgur* is likewise treated in a folk-tale manner: "although countries and cities are commonly named, they are merely ciphers for
exotic settings, not carefully detailed locations."[17] And while *Vǫlsunga saga* was
written by an undoubtedly Christian author about overtly pagan characters and
even gods, that author shows no interest in the pagan/Christian disjunction that
so clearly occupied the *Beowulf* poet; Christianity as such does not appear within
the saga, although as noted above Christian intertexts would have participated
in the saga's audience reception.

One important result of the saga's characteristically 'blurred' chronotope is
the absence of any firm distinction in the saga between the historic and the
mythic, and thus between the natural and the supernatural.[18] In *Beowulf* the
world of *draconitas* may be said to invade the world of *humanitas* because the
chronotope of myth stands in direct apposition to the chronotope of history; in
Vǫlsunga saga, because the two chronotopes are never fully distinguished, the
two worlds are the same. Consequently, the extraordinary beings and occurrences within the saga are treated with a directness and literalism that may
strike the modern reader as naive or even, to use Katharine Hume's words, as
suffering "from a failure of artistic imagination."[19]

As an example, one may compare the funeral of Scyld Scefing in *Beowulf* to
that of Sinfjǫtli in *Vǫlsunga saga*.[20] As we have seen in Chapter II, Scyld is part
of the poem's mythic substrate: he enters Danish history as a hero intruder from
an unknown land across the sea in order to found the Scylding dynasty; after his
death, his body is placed on a ship laden with treasure and returned. No one
knows, or apparently can know, *hwa þæm hlæste onfeng*, "who received that
cargo" (52b). The gap between mythic origins and historical reality, between

this world and the next, the living and the dead, is a wide one in *Beowulf*, and its very width creates the sense of mystery, of a seemingly numinous unknown, that applies to any reference to the supernatural within the poem.

In *Vǫlsunga saga*, Sinfjǫtli remains a part of the saga's 'natural' world despite his superhuman resistence to physical torture and his early tenure as a werewolf. When he dies, his body is also sent over the sea, but both the saga's author and his audience know well who receives the body and what its final destination shall be, since Óðinn, disguised as a ferryman, arrives to take Sinfjǫtli literally and directly from his grieving father's arms:

> Sigmundr ríss upp ok gekk harmr sinn nær bana ok tók líkit í fang ser ok ferr til skógar ok kom loks at einum firði. Þar sá hann mann á einum báti litlum. Sá maðr spyrr ef hann vildi þiggja at honum far yfir fjǫrðinn. Hann játtar því. Skipit var svá lítit at þat bar þá eigi, ok var líkit fyrst flutt, en Sigmundr gekk með firðinum. Ok því næst hvarf Sigmundi skipit ok svá maðrinn. (chap. 10)

> [Sigmund rose to his feet, almost succumbing to his grief, and he took the body in his arms and went to the forest, and eventually came to a firth. There he saw a man in a small boat. The man asked if he wanted to be ferried across the firth. He said he did. The boat was so small that it would not hold them, and the body was taken first, Sigmund walking alongside the firth. The next instant the ship vanished from Sigmund's sight, and with it the man.]

Sigmundr returns home without comment. Sinfjǫtli has been sent *at sœkja heim Óðin*, "to join Óðinn" (chap. 2), who has, to no one's surprise, come halfway to meet him. The reader feels and understands Sigmundr's grief, but as William C. Johnson points out, "the saga writer is not concerned that we feel or ponder any disjunction between this world and the next."[21]

The basis of the difference between the two funerals is a difference in attitude towards knowledge. The *Beowulf* poet is keenly aware of the limitations on human knowledge, using his multiple chronotopes to underscore the fact that human beings can know only what is possible and appropriate within their particular time/space parameters. Especially in the area of the supernatural, the poet uses these limitations "as a source of aesthetic emotion and moral implication."[22] In the saga, however, the absence of firm chronotopic distinctions works to ensure that virtually everything is at least knowable if not already known, including, in Johnson's words, "secret runic lore (presumably from gods), the minds of wolves and the language of birds, the messages of magic rings, and the future."[23] It is significant that Sigurðr's successes come as he gains knowledge; his death and the deaths of the Gjúkungar come as a result of his loss of knowledge through Grímhildr's potion.

The saga author does not, therefore, convey any sense of an otherworldly encroachment of *draconitas* onto familiar *humanitas* in his description of Fáfnir's habitat, as the *Beowulf* poet does with Grendel's mere and, to a lesser extent, with the dragon's lair. Unlike Grendel's mere, which is not very far away *milgemearces*, "as measured in miles" (1362a), but is very far from the natural knowledge of human beings, Fáfnir's lair, Gnitaheiðr, lies *skammt heðan á brott*, "a short distance away" (chap. 13) by any reckoning. Its only peculiarity is that the crag on which Fáfnir lies to drink is thirty fathoms high, but this is because Fáfnir is a very large dragon. The landscape is known and thus not mysterious; Fáfnir's habits are also known and thus Sigurðr (with the help of Reginn and Óðinn) is able to devise a successful plan to slay him, unlike Beowulf who must fight his dragon with insufficient protection and a sword which breaks, because he knows of no other way.

Both Beowulf and Sigurðr rely on divine assistance (as well as their own strength) in their monster slayings. In *Beowulf*, however, God is remote, at least on the temporal plane of the poem's historical past: although the poet may assure us that God ruled the world then *swa he nu git deð*, "as he still does now" (1058b), he is neither known nor fully knowable to the chronologically pre-Christian Danes. Sure knowledge of God can exist only in the present—that is, the historically Christian—chronotope of the poem's performance, although noble pagans such as Beowulf and Hroðgar can dimly discern God's presence and his divine will through naive faith and proper interpretation of the course of events. Consequently, even though Beowulf consistently attributes his victories over the Grendelkin to God's aid, only the fact of his success and his faith can substantiate the attribution. Perhaps the mysterious light that shines in Grendel's mother's cavern after Beowulf's victory should be interpreted as a sign of divine favor; no other interpretation is readily available. But it is uncanny, otherworldly. And when Beowulf perceives, again dimly, that he will die fighting the dragon, that fact is signalled only by his uncustomary *þeostrum geþoncum*, "dark thoughts" (2332a) and his fear that he has somehow angered God *ofer ealde riht*, "against the old law" (2330a).

By contrast, Odinic theophany occurs so often in *Vǫlsunga saga*—and in the other *fornaldarsǫgur*—as to be commonplace.[24] Óðinn sometimes appears in these sagas as a helper figure, part of his function as the divine patron of heroes and protector of the most famous warriors; at other times he appears as a far more sinister character, or even a figure of evil.[25] That evil stems in part from the fact that, as the leader of the slain heroes in Valhǫll, Óðinn is the god of death; one of his many names, *Sváfnir*, is also the name of a serpent that gnaws at the roots of Yggdrasill and means "one who puts to sleep, kills."[26] His appearance, therefore, often heralds a particular hero's death when the god decides it is time for that hero to join the *einherjar* in their preparations for Ragnarǫk, and this can look very much like a betrayal of the same hero he has protected in life.

Both the god's roles as helper and as betrayer are evident in *Vǫlsunga saga*. Óðinn acts throughout as the patron and protector of the Vǫlsungr family, directing his *óskmey*, "wish-maiden" to drop an apparently magic apple into the lap of King Rerir to ensure the conception of Vǫlsungr (chap. 1) and appearing in person to give Vǫlsungr's son Sigmundr a sword better than any other (chap. 3). In the next generation Sigurðr receives direct, unambiguous help from Óðinn, first in the matter of choosing his horse Grani (chap. 13), then in his battle against the sons of Hunding (chap. 17), and finally in his preparation for the dragon fight:

> Sigurðr gerði grǫf eina. Ok er hann er at þessu verki, kemr at honum einn gamall maðr með síðu skeggi ok spyrr hvat hann gerir þar. Hann segir.
> Þá svarar inn gamli maðr, "Þetta er óráð. Ger fleiri grafar ok lát þar í renna sveitann, en þú sit í einni ok legg til hjartans orminum."
> Þá hvarf sá maðr á brottu (chap. 18).

> [Sigurd dug a pit, and while he was about this an old man with a long beard came up to him and asked what he was doing there. He told him.
> "That's ill-advised," the old man then replied. "Dig other pits and let the blood run into them—you are to sit in one and stab the dragon to the heart."
> Then the old man vanished.]

Although in scenes such as these the god seems unambiguously helpful and even friendly, Óðinn nevertheless also appears twice in his function as the god of death in the saga, once when he arrives to receive Sinfjǫtli's body (chap. 10), and finally when he appears to signal Sigmundr's own death in battle against King Lyngvi:

> Ok er orrosta hafði staðit um hríð, þá kom maðr í bardagann með síðan hǫtt ok heklu blá. Hann hafði eitt auga ok geir í hendi. Þessi maðr kom á mót Sigmundi konungi ok brá upp geirinum fyrir hann. Ok er Sigmundr konungr hjó fast, kom sverðit í geirinn ok brast í sundr í tvá hluti. Síðan sneri mannfallinu, ok váru Sigmundi konungi horin heill, ok fell mjǫk liðit fyrir honum. (chap. 11)

> [Now when the battle had gone on for some time, a man who had on a black cloak and a hat coming down low over his face entered the fray. He had but one eye and in his hand he held a spear. The man advanced towards King Sigmund, raising the spear to bar his way, and when King Sigmund struck fiercely, his sword hit against the spear and snapped in two. After this the balance of the casualties shifted: King Sigmund's good luck had turned and his losses were heavy.]

Later, the dying king tells his wife, '*Vill Óðinn ekki at vér bregðum sverði, síðan er nú brotnaði. Hefi ek haft orrostur meðan honum líkaði*', "Odin does not want me to draw sword, for now it lies broken. I have fought battles while it was his pleasure"(chap. 12). There is no distancing of the divine will here, no need to ponder an *eald riht* to discover the pleasure of the god; Óðinn's desertion, like his assistence, is direct and unmediated.

The *fornaldarsǫgur*'s tendency to merge the natural world of humanity with the supernatural world of gods and monsters, or rather to make no fundamental distinction between the relative 'naturalness' of each, is sometimes seen as characteristic of a more archaic viewpoint than is evidenced by the *Beowulf* poet:

> [The] inability to imagine abstract spirit and the incorporation of the supernatural into the 'real' world form the distinguishing features of the prescientific mind as compared to the modern mind. . . . The characters in the sagas, at least, accept *fylgar, draugar*, and the continued existence of the dead in a matter-of-fact way as part of that unified perception of reality.[27]

But attempts to calculate the relative archaism of the thought behind the Icelandic sagas are fraught with dangers, not the least of which is the possibility of concluding that Icelandic society in the thirteenth century was somehow fundamentally more 'primitive' than, say, English society in the eighth or eleventh century, or that the writers of *fornaldarsǫgur* as a genre or of *Vǫlsunga saga* in particular were peculiarly unable to differentiate between the natural and the supernatural. What can perhaps be said is that the author of *Vǫlsunga saga* has not attempted to reinterpret the old stories that make up his material in such a way as to give his saga a more modern meaning, as the *Beowulf* poet with the leverage of his decidedly Christian viewpoint and sophisticated historical consciousness has done. Instead, the saga's author has retained the mythic tone and many of the logical inconsistencies of his sources and has refrained, perhaps deliberately, from direct commentary on them.[28]

The resulting chronotope of *Vǫlsunga saga* is therefore not to be equated with the 'adventuristic, chance time' that intrudes into the historical past of *Beowulf* through its sudden ("*oþ þæt an ongan . . .*") irruptions of the supernatural into the historical; in its merging of diverse chronotopic categories it is more closely akin to what Bakhtin has called with regard to classical instances "the *adventure novel of everyday life*":

> What strikes us first of all is the mix of adventure-time with everyday time—a quality we sought to express in our provisional designation of the type as an 'adventure-everyday novel.' Of course a merely mechanical mix of these two different times is out of the question. Both adventure- and everyday time change their essential forms in this combination, as they are subject to the conditions of the completely new chronotope created by this novel. Thus there emerges a new type of adventure-time . . . one that is a special sort of everyday time.[29]

Within that "special sort of everyday time" the supernatural manifests itself not as a sudden irruption from another world or as an occurrence peculiar to a past, irrecoverably mythic time ("*in illo tempore*"), but rather as the chronotopically thematic motif of "*metamorphosis (transformation)*—particularly human transformation."[30] Such metamorphoses may be marvelous, as when a person becomes a dragon or werewolf, or they may be as commonplace as the transformation of a child into an adult; in either case, the changes are at once internally motivated and thus belonging to 'everyday time,' and externally manifested, as if they were indeed a consequence of a sudden breach of or (ad)venture across the spatial and temporal borders of the human environment. Metamorphosis serves as

> a mythological sheath for the idea of development—but one that unfolds not so much in a straight line as spasmodically, a line with 'knots' in it, one that therefore constitutes a distinctive type of temporal sequence.[31]

Such transformations are endemic to the *fornaldarsǫgur*, in which characters are often *hamrammir*, "shapestrong," i.e., having the ability to assume an alien shape at will.[32] In *Vǫlsunga saga*, for example, Signý exchanges shapes with a seeress (chap. 7) and Sigurðr does the same with Gunnarr (chap. 29). Frequently the shape assumed is that of an animal: the dwarf Andvari lives as a pike in the river, and Hreiðmarr's son Otr, appropriately enough, takes the shape of an otter to hunt (chap. 14). Sigmundr and Sinfjǫtli live for a time as wolves (chap. 8), and finally, of course, there is Fáfnir, *miklu mestr ok grimmastr*, "the biggest and fiercest" of Hreiðmarr's sons, who *vildi sitt eitt kalla láta allt þat er var*, "wanted everything to be called his" (chap. 14) and who turns himself into a dragon to guard his ill-gotten gold.

In each case the metamorphosis serves to establish a new or at least newly represented identity of a particular character; the transformation is a 'knot' in the representation of linear time that delineates a crux in the character's development:

> Metamorphosis serves as the basis for a method of portraying the whole of an individual's life in its more important moments of *crisis*: for showing *how an individual becomes other than what he was.* . . . There is not evolution in the strict sense of the word; what we get, rather, is crisis and rebirth.[33]

Thus Signý's shape-change with the seeress symbolizes a spiritually if not physically irreversible transformation of her social status and her human identity as she abandons her self-defining roles as wife and sister to commit incest with her brother and thereby conceive a son strong enough to kill her husband, an act precipitated by the crisis of Siggeirr's murder of all but one of her blood relations (chap. 7). She quite literally becomes another woman, neither Siggeirr's wife nor Sigmundr's sister, in order to avenge their deaths; although her vengeance is successful, her transformation tragically recreates her as a woman whose actions leave her no place in human society and no choice but to die with her husband in the course of her revenge.

In much the same fashion, Sigurðr's exchange of shapes with Gunnarr (chap. 29)—even more so than the agency of Grímhildr's magic drink—graphically depicts the transformation of his relationship to Brynhildr. He is, again quite literally, no longer his former self: instead of the brash young Vǫlsungr who twice promised to marry the valkyrie (chaps 22 and 25), Sigurðr has become one of the Gjúkungar through his marriage to Guðrún. His change in physical appearance reflects his change in family affiliation, and he is even willing to conceal his deception once he remembers his past.

Less immediately crisis-ridden, but no less indicative of identity, are the transformations of Andvari into a pike and of Otr into an otter. Otr's shape reflects his characteristic behavior, since *hann var veiðimaðr mikill ok um fram aðra menn*, "he was a great fisherman and surpassed other men in this skill" (chap. 14). Andvari's transformation, on the other hand, is more problematic. He tells Loki, in a verse interpolated from *Reginsmál* 2, that:

> Aumlig norn
> skóp oss í árdaga,
> at ek skylda í vatni vaða.
>
> [A dismal Norn decreed in days of yore that I should wade in water.]
> (chap. 14)

Andvari possesses the hoard of gold that will entice Fáfnir to abandon his human shape for the more forbidding countenance of a dragon, and which first Andvari, then Loki, and finally Fáfnir himself claim will be the death of each of its future owners. It may not be farfetched to speculate that the 'dismal Norn' imposed this fated metamorphosis on the dwarf in connection with his ownership—or perhaps guardianship—of the hoard hidden behind the waterfall. The pike is, after all, a most ferocious fish, and would therefore not be an implausible guardian for gold hidden in a river; Andvari's transformation would then foreshadow Fáfnir's and add credence to the idea that greed for treasure can effect an unwelcome moral, and therefore in the saga also a physical, metamorphosis. Undoubtedly such an identification also adds a certain measure of characteristic sarcasm to Loki's first words upon catching the pike:

> Hvat er þat fiska
> er rennr flóði í,
> kannat sér við víti varask?
>
> [What fish is this that swims in the flood, and from punishment knows
> no protection?] (chap. 14)

But however we interpret Andvari's transformation, the metamorphosis of Otr's brother Fáfnir into a dragon is explicitly a transformation designed to enable Fáfnir to keep the gold he has stolen from his murdered father all to himself; it constitutes an important 'knot' in the everyday time of the saga as a temporal node at which ordinary physical and moral characteristics—Fáfnir's status as *miklu mestr ok grimmastr*, "the largest and fiercest"—are transformed into extraordinary indications of an inhuman, dragonish identity formed in the crisis of intentional patricide.

Consequently, while Fáfnir's lair differs from the barrow of the *Beowulf* dragon in that it is not literally a grave mound and the dragon is thus not as explicitly connected with death, Fáfnir does in effect inhabit his gold hoard on the grave of his father. In fact, Gnitaheiðr, with its hidden treasure and its high crag on which the monster lies to drink, is somewhat reminiscent of the *Beowulf* dragon's barrow, which is located high on a ness next to the sea (2241–3) and which features a cliff over which the dragon's corpse can be pushed into the ocean (3131b–2a).[34] It is also similar to the gravesites of the more usual saga inhabitants of such mounds, the *draugar*, the dangerous, often malicious corporeal ghosts of the buried dead whose barrows are frequently "set on a high headland looking out to sea . . . a favorite spot in particular for the graves of those who are thought likely to be restless after death."[35] Because of this similarity in setting, Hilda Ellis has concluded that "there is undoubtedly a link between the menacing dragon in his lair and the dead man transformed into a dangerous draugr."[36]

The similarities between dragon and *draugr* aptly illustrate the emphasis such metamorphoses place on the linked concepts of crisis and rebirth: more than a simple change, metamorphosis in the saga requires dying to one's previous life, literally and physically in the case of the *draugr*, in order to undergo a new birth and the creation of a new identity. The process is never undertaken without crisis, though it is frequently conscious and even intentional: often a *draugr* is reported to have entered a specially built barrow while still alive, with the expectation of living on as a ghost or of being reborn from the barrow.[37] Once complete, the transformation is irreversible, physically so in the case of the *draugr*, whose body dies with his old identity, and psychically so in all cases: Fáfnir remains a dragon with dragonish characteristics even after he has secured his treasure, and although Signý and Sigurðr do regain their previous shapes, neither can go back to what they were before the crisis of transformation.

INITIATION RITUAL IN *VǪLSUNGA SAGA*

Closely associated with the ideas of transformation, crisis, and rebirth is the concept of initiation, the ritualized process by which a child becomes an adult or (and in the sagas there is little difference between the two) by which a young man becomes a warrior. The process is conceptualized within the *fornaldarsǫgur* as a metamorphosis of the same type as the shape-changing transformations discussed above, and in fact can often include a symbolic transformation into an animal such as a wolf or a bear as part of the initiatory ritual. A process of initiation will thus involve crisis and rebirth in the same way and for the same reasons as physical metamorphosis:

> The content of [initiation] rites is not so much the symbolization of a transition as of a 'new birth.' The child dies and the man begins his life. They are, as it were, two different beings who at this moment separate within the same individual.[38]

Consequently, the central element of any initiation ritual always involves some sort of symbolic death and reawakening which simultaneously manifests itself both as an outward, corporeal change in the initiand or in his or her physical circumstances, and as an inner, spiritual or psychological change that marks the complete separation of past and future identities. As a temporal event, an initiatory sequence, like a physical metamorphosis, functions as a transformatory node of adventure time within the everyday time of the saga, a 'knot' separating the linear course of a character's life into a discrete 'before' and 'after.'

All initiations consist of three distinct segments, which anthropologists have designated as (1) a *preliminal* phase, or 'separation,' during which the initiand is symbolically or physically detached from his or her previous place in the social structure as preparation for the initiation proper; (2) a *liminal* or 'marginal' phase (from Latin *limen*, 'threshold'), during which the initiand has lost the characteristics of his or her previous social identity but has not yet gained those of the new and thus inhabits a marginal sociocultural space; and (3) a *postliminal* phase, 'reaggregation' or 'reincorporation,' in which the transition is completed and the initiand rejoins society in the role of his or her new social identity.[39] 'Liminality,' the ambiguous state of being on the threshold between states of being, or of inhabiting for a time the margins of a social and cultural structure prior to reentering that structure at a new point, is what gives rise to the recurrent ritual imagery of crisis, death, and rebirth; it is, in Victor Turner's words, "frequently likened to death, to being in the womb, to invisibility, to darkness, to bisexuality, to the wilderness, and to an eclipse of the sun or moon."[40]

The elements of initiation ritual embedded in the plots of the *fornaldarsǫgur* can also be roughly classified as falling into three corresponding categories: (1) separation from family or community and isolation with an "initiation master"[41] who imposes tests of strength and bravery which can include ritualized torture or participation in a real or mock battle; (2) mock death and reawakening, symbolized by physical transformation, outlawry or community ostracism, being devoured by a monster, or entering a grave mound alive; and (3) acquisition of the outward signs of a new identity, which can include symbolic objects, esoteric knowledge, a new shape, a new name, or even a new language.[42]

These elements are important for any consideration of Fáfnir's role in *Vǫlsunga saga* because the first and longest part of the saga, up through Sigurðr's betrothal to Brynhildr (chap. 22) and therefore including the dragon fight (chap. 18), is concerned almost exclusively with rituals of heroic initiation.[43] Both Sinfjǫtli and Sigurðr undergo such initiation; each instance illustrates a different aspect of the ritual. And while Sigurðr's dragon slaying stands as the climax of this series of events, it is Sinfjǫtli's earlier initatory sequence that most clearly exemplifies the ritual process.

Sinfjǫtli's preliminal separation from family and community occurs when his mother Signý sends him to Sigmundr as part of a series of explicit trials of strength and bravery, trials the boy survives only because he is a Vǫlsungr through both his maternal and paternal lines. Unlike his ill-fated half brothers, Sinfjǫtli does not hesitate to knead the *mesti eitrormr*, "huge poisonous snake" (chap. 7) into the batch of flour Sigmundr gives him to bake into bread, nor does he scream under Signý's torture of sewing his tunic to his arms and then ripping it off; despite his agony, Sinfjǫtli merely remarks, *Lítit mundi slíkt sárt þykkja Vǫlsungi*, "No Vǫlsung would think much of a pain like that" (chap. 7). His comment provides an important insight into the nature of change and transition in the *fornaldarsǫgur*: because change in the saga comes solely through meta-morphosis, characters do not learn or gradually develop heroic characteristics; an individual is either a potential hero from birth—in this case a full-fledged Vǫlsungr—or he is not.[44] It is in turn this representative absence of gradual development, of even the possibility of evolutionary change, that causes the transformative moment of metamorphosis to stand out so sharply as a 'knot' in the otherwise smooth flow of time in the saga.

The liminal phase of Sinfjǫtli's initiation is represented by animal transfor-mation and outlawry and contains within it two separate episodes of mock death and rebirth. Sinfjǫtli and Sigmundr are eking out a liminal existence on the margins of civilized human society—*fara nú um sumrum víða um skóga ok drepa menn til fjár sér*, "for some summers they roved far and wide through the forests and killed people for plunder" (chap. 8)—when they discover a pair of wolf skins which transform their wearers into wolves for ten-day periods. Were-wolves have a long history in Germanic literature and culture; historically at-tested Norse initiation rituals included the transformation of young men into *úlfheðnar*, "wolf-skin wearers," warriors who, by putting on the wolf's charac-teristics with its skin, became ferocious fighters whose battle-fury could be rivalled only by that of the more widely known *berserkir*.[45] Additionally, an outlaw in Germanic society was conceptualized as a *vargr*, 'wolf' and could be proclaimed such in "a magico-legal pronouncement which transformed the crimi-nal into a werewolf."[46] Sigmundr and Sinfjǫtli's physical transformation literalizes the liminal, outlaw status that the two heroes have temporarily adopted, and at the same time presages Sinfjǫtli's postliminal status as a particularly ferocious warrior. Because Sinfjǫtli is not only being initiated into adulthood, but is also being prepared to kill his stepfather and his two remaining half brothers in vengeance for Siggeirr's murder of the Vǫlsungar, his transformation partakes significantly of both conditions: he becomes a wolf in both its admirable and detestable manifestations; he is at the same time hero and outlaw, *úlfheðinn* and *vargr*.[47]

Sinfjǫtli's mock death and reawakening occurs when Sigmundr, who as stated earlier acts as the initiation master throughout the episode, bites him in the throat and then heals him with a magic leaf. This would seem to complete Sinfjǫtli's initiation, for immediately afterwards the two discard the wolf skins and resume their human shapes; we are told that *þá þykkist Sigmundr hafa reynt hann mjǫk*, "Sigmund believed that he'd tested him thoroughly" (chap. 8). But in a manner common to both folktale and mythic narrative, the motif of mock death and resurrection is reduplicated in the following episode when Siggeirr buries the two heroes alive in a *haugr mikinn*, "huge burial-mound" (chap. 8), from which they escape by cutting their way out with a sword smuggled into the mound by Signý; thus metaphorically 'reborn' out of the grave, they avenge themselves by burning Siggeirr and his household alive in the king's hall.

Sinfjǫtli's postliminal or reaggregative phase reveals his character as a formidable Vǫlsungr warrior. As was the case in the transformations discussed earlier, even though Sinfjǫtli regains his human shape before rejoining human society, his psychospiritual transformation into a wolf is irreversible: he demonstrates his wolvish nature by slaughtering the two little boys who are his remaining half-brothers in cold blood—a deed Sigmundr refuses to do because they are Signý's children—and he does not deny the appellation *vargr*, 'wolf, outlaw' (chap. 9) in his *senna* with Granmarr before the battle with Hunding's sons. In fact, Sinfjǫtli not only accepts Granmarr's allegation that he is a wolf, he also turns the accusation against the accuser in a characteristically hyperbolic sexual slander: *ek gat við þér níu varga á Láganesi, ok var ek faðir allra*, "in Laganess I begot nine wolves on you, and I was the father of them all" (chap. 9).

Sigurðr's initiatory sequence follows the same pattern of separation, liminality, and reaggregation, but its centerpiece is of course the slaying of the dragon Fáfnir. Like Sinfjǫtli and the rest of the Vǫlsungar, Sigurðr is, in Stephen Mitchell's apt phrase, a "neo-natal hero," and he is recognized as such at birth by King Hjálprekr, who remarks that *engum mundu líkan verða eða samjafnan*, "no one would be like him or a match for him" (chap. 13).[48] His liminal phase is signalled by his fosterage with the dwarf smith Reginn, who acts as one of the young hero's initiation masters; the other is the god Óðinn.[49]

Both Reginn and Óðinn are associated with magic and esoteric knowledge,[50] a fact which makes them particularly appropriate as mentors for the hero, since his initiatory process is far less concerned with trials of strength and martial prowess than it is with the acquisition of both esoteric and mundane knowledge and *íþróttir*, "gentlemanly accomplishments," to use Geoffrey Russom's translation of the term.[51] During Sigurðr's liminal residence with the smith, i.e., after his childhood at King Hjálprekr's court but before he joins Heimir's household as an adult, he is educated by a variety of tutors: Reginn teaches him *tafl ok rúnar ok tungur margar at mæla sem þá var títt konungasonum, ok marga hluti aðra*, "a board game, runes, and also how to speak many languages, as was then customary for princes, and much else besides" (chap. 13); Grípir, who *var framvíss ok vissi ørlǫg manna*, "had the gift of second sight and knew in advance what a man's fate would be" teaches him *ǫll forlǫg hans, eptir því sem eptir gekk síðan*, "his entire destiny, just as it afterwards came to pass" (chap. 16); Óðinn teaches him how to kill a dragon without danger to himself (chap. 18); the newly awakened Brynhildr teaches him runes and gives him advice about manners and everyday life (chaps 21–22). Even the dragon slaying is inseparable from Sigurðr's hero's education: from Fáfnir, Sigurðr learns the answers to two questions concerning mythological lore (chap. 18) and also, albeit indirectly through the dragon's blood, he learns to understand the language of birds (chap. 19).

Symbolic death and rebirth, the core of the initiation ritual, occurs as part of Sigurðr's encounter with Fáfnir as well. The affinities between the dragon in his lair and the *draugr* in his grave mound have already been cited; the hero's encounter with the dragon is structurally analogous to entering the world of the dead as it exists in a *draugr's* barrow. More striking in this context, however, is the peculiar manner in which Sigurðr kills his dragon, i.e., his crouching in a cavity in the earth until Fáfnir crawls across it and he stabs the dragon from below, followed by his emergence, arms covered with blood, from beneath the monster's body. His motions mimic those of initiands who are symbolically swallowed by a monster and then 'reborn,' often by cutting their way out from the belly of the beast.[52] The visual image of the dragon slaying graphically illustrates Sigurðr's passage from life to death and back again in a way that needs no prior association between dragon and *draugr*. The imagery is directly reminiscent of birth instead of resurrection; indeed, Mircea Eliade has pointed out that "entering the belly of a monster also carries a symbolism of return to the embryonic state."[53]

Sigurðr's reaggregation is signalled in the plot of the saga by his acquisition of the dragon's treasure and with it (in this case somewhat redundantly) the traditional accoutrements of a heroic warrior—a famous sword and fabulous armor:

> Sigurðr fann þar stórmikit gull ok sverðit Hrotta, ok þar tók hann ægishjálm ok gullbrynjuna ok marga dýrgripi. (chap. 20)
>
> [There Sigurðr found a vast store of gold, and the sword Hrotti, and there he took possession of the helm of terror, the gold hauberk and many valuables.]

Moreover, his rebirth and corollary return to human society are represented rhetorically as he rides away from his meeting with Brynhildr (chap. 23), his initiation and hero's education finally complete, by the saga's first full description of his physical appearance and personal characteristics.[54] This description might seem somewhat belated, since the usual saga practice (made possible by the fact that evolutionary change or development is absent throughout these sagas) is to state all that will ever be told about a character at his or her first entrance into the saga, preferably at the time of birth.[55] The narrative placement of Sigurðr's description emphasizes the fact that his initiation/transformation is here complete: he has been (re)born as a new hero with a new name, *Fáfnisbani*. And that name, the saga tells us, *gengr í ǫllum tungum fyrir norðan Grikklands haf, ok svá mun vera meðan verǫldin stendr*, "is current in all the languages

spoken north of the Greek Ocean, and so it will be for as long as the world
endures" (chap. 23).

A Dialogue with the Dragon

Sigurðr's enduring fame as the slayer of Fáfnir suggests that the medieval audience of *Vǫlsunga saga* would have had an extraordinarily specific horizon of
expectations in regard to the dragon fight itself, and probably would have ob-
jected vehemently to any overt, controversial innovations by the saga's author,
who therefore avoids thwarting his audience's expectations by adhering closely
to his Eddic sources. There are no surprises in the saga's plot or in its characterization of the dragon: as the audience would have known, the dragon Fáfnir,
originally a man (or giant or dwarf), Reginn and Otr's brother, secretly murdered their father Hreiðmarr to gain the gold extorted from the gods as weregild
for Otr's death (chap. 14) and then metamorphosed into a dragon to guard the
treasure. He leaves the treasure only to crawl to his thirty-fathom crag to drink;
when he moves the earth shakes violently (chap. 18). Both the height of the
crag and the violence of the earthquakes testify to his enormous size, which is
further if ironically emphasized by Reginn's repeated protests to Sigurðr that
Fáfnir is not all *that* big, even though both his reputation and his tracks belie
Reginn's words (chaps. 13; 18). As Fáfnir moves he breathes poison, but he
does not belch fire, nor is there any mention of wings. He does have legs, since
Sigurðr stabs him *undir bœxlit vinstra*, "under the left shoulder" (chap. 18). He
seems altogether more reptilian than the *Beowulf* dragon, except that Fáfnir
retains his ability to speak.

Indeed it is necessary that Fáfnir speak, because the conversation between
Sigurðr and the dragon is what fills the gap left by the absence of a physical
fight between the two. While many scholars have commented on the oddity of
this conversation, only a few have seriously attempted to ascertain its thematic
point or value for the saga as a whole.[56] Critical commentary ranges from expressions of disappointment that the dialogue is "filled out with conventional
lore questions"[57] to admissions that "one is totally unprepared for Sigurðr's
asking . . . general questions" about such lore.[58] This scholarly perplexity seems to
stem in part from confusion over genre, for as discourse, the conversation between
hero and dragon does not easily conform to any one of the Old Norse discursive
subgenres, but is instead constituted by a second intertextual interaction, a conversation, as it were, among the coded conventions of three separate forms of traditional discourse in Germanic literature: the *senna*, the death song, and wisdom
poetry. This intergeneric exchange adds new interest and even some suspense to
the narrative by challenging the horizon of expectations of the audience with regard to rhetorical genre rather than to plot or characterization.

That one participatory genre in this discursive polylogue is a flyting or *senna* would have come as no surprise to its medieval audience, although the dialogue between Fáfnir and Sigurðr has seldom been recognized as such in modern criticism.[59] A flyting is a stylized battle of words which typically either precedes or replaces physical violence on the part of its (almost always) male participants[60]—its occurrence after Fáfnir has already been stabbed to the heart in a markedly unexciting dragon fight might have been regarded as just compensation for the fact that the hero "went at once for the soft parts" and thereby lost "all the fun."[61] But a verbal battle is also singularly appropriate in the saga's initiatory context, for one of the *senna*'s societal functions has historically been to enable young men to establish, through a verbal struggle made up of a series of ritualized challenges and insults, the cultural norms of proper social and sexual behavior as well as to define their own individualized psychosexual identities within those norms[62]—one is reminded of the sexually suggestive insults traded by Sinfjǫtli and Granmarr earlier in the saga. Moreover, a *senna* between a man and a monster, as Karen Swenson has recently demonstrated, serves to allow the hero to define himself as a human subject against an inhuman, objectified other:

> The structure of the *senna* is . . . like that of a transitive sentence in which the subject acts upon the object and, by doing so, asserts himself as the subject. 'I am I, and I define you as It,' or, more symbolically, 'I kill the dragon.' 'I' defines the dragon as that which he kills, but the dragon does not act upon or actively define 'I.'[63]

This is clearly both the situation and the basic structure of Sigurðr and Fáfnir's dialogue, although that structure must repeatedly reassert itself against rival discursive formulations.

The first challenge to the *senna*'s anticipated structure occurs even before the *senna* has been firmly established, when Sigurðr initially refuses to identify himself by his proper name and patrimony to Fáfnir, a reticence explained in a prose passage of *Fáfnismál* by the conjecture that he is afraid of falling victim to a deathbed curse. His unwillingness to name himself openly is also, however, a rhetorical convention belonging to a second subgenre of Old Norse literature, for participants in the wisdom dialogues of the Edda often conceal their true names from their interlocutors, usually until the end of the conversation. Óðinn, for example, habitually describes himself as a wanderer and frequently assumes an alias, taking the name *Gagnráðr*, 'useful advice,' in *Vafðrúðnismál,* and *Vegtamr*, 'road-tamer' in *Baldrs Draumar.* In *Fáfnismál* and *Vǫlsunga saga,* Óðinn's protégé Sigurðr renames himself *gǫfugt dýr*, "noble beast" and further asserts that *'á ek engan fǫður né móður, ok einn saman hefi ek farit'*, "I've neither father nor mother, and I've journeyed alone" (chap. 18). His cryptic alias serves to set up a second audience expectation of a catechetical dialogue in direct opposition to the initial expectation of a *senna*, an expectation bolstered by the fact, well-known to an audience versed in Eddic and saga literature, that barrow-dwellers, be they dragons or *draugar*, can have esoteric knowledge to impart,[64] and that Sigurðr, like Óðinn in the Eddic poems, is at least partially engaged in a quest for knowledge.

The exact significance of the term *gǫfugt dýr* remains unclear: several scholars have attempted to read it as an onomastic pun on the name Sigurðr or its alternative form Sigrøðr;[65] it may also be a reference to the hart, a "noble beast" to which Sigurðr is compared in the *Edda* and which plays a definite, albeit rather obscure, symbolic role in many of the extant versions of the Sigurðr/Siegfried story.[66] It is possible, but less likely, that it is simply a metaphor for "human being."[67] In the context of the saga, however, Sigurðr's denial of his proper name and family and his mention of travelling alone refer literally to his status as an orphan, and are also pertinent reminders of his liminal condition outside of the human community until his initiation is complete. Such liminality is, as the example of Sinfjǫtli's initiation confirms, sometimes signified by a physical transformation into an animal. Although Sigurðr undergoes no such physical metamorphosis, he is in the process of a transformation into an adult human being and warrior, and he has not yet accomplished that feat; hence, while 'noble,' he is still merely a 'beast.'

The *senna* structure reasserts itself with Fáfnir's accusation that Sigurðr is a liar, a contention which quickly elicits the hero's name and his father's name. The dialogue continues in the standard flyting sequence of accusation and denial, threat and counterthreat, until Fáfnir asserts enigmatically that *'drukna muntu ef þú ferr um sjá óvarliga, ok bið heldr á landi unz logn er'*, "if you're careless in crossing the sea you'll be drowned: better wait on shore until it's calm" (chap. 18). Although clearly containing an implied threat, this remark seems to refer neither to Sigurðr's current situation nor to his well-known future fate, and its departure from standard flyting form signals the re-emergence of the wisdom dialogue into the conversation's discursive structure.

Rather than replying directly to the dragon's mysterious warning, Sigurðr proceeds to ask Fáfnir two specific questions concerning mythological lore. His questions retain some of the outward form of the flyting since he initially frames them as challenges to the dragon, prefacing them with *'Seg þú þat, Fáfnir, ef þú ert fróðr mjǫk . . .'*, "Tell me, then, Fáfnir, if you are so wise . . ." (chap. 18), almost as if he intends to stump the dragon and thereby prove his superiority in mythic lore. But the adversarial aspect of the questions pales beside their sheer contextual oddity. The first question, *'hverjar eru þær nornir er kjósa mǫgu frá mæðrum?'* "who are the Norns that deliver mothers of their sons?"[68] elicits the reply:

> "Margar eru þær ok sundrlausar. Sumar eru Ása ættar, sumar eru álfa ættar, sumar eru dœtr Dvalins."
>
> ["They are many and varied. Some belong to the Æsir, some belong to the elves, and some are Dvalin's daughters."]

Fáfnir's answer is reminiscent of several gnomic passages in the *Edda* which enumerate the attributes of the various races;[69] and like the question itself, the structure of his answer belongs to the subgenre of catechetical dialogue rather than to that of the *senna*. While this exchange is often interpreted as a reference to the norns' offering some sort of obstetrical aid to women in childbirth, a more relevant implication may be that the norns, being "many and varied," would bring similarly varying fates to humanity: good luck from the Æsir, a mixed fate from the elves, and bad luck from the dwarfs.[70] Sigurðr's second question, *'Hvé heitir sá hólmr er blanda hjǫrlegi Surtr ok Æsir saman?'* "What is the name of the islet where Surt and the Æsir will shed each other's blood?" is answered, *'Hann heitir Óskaptr'*, "It is named Oskapt," a designation most often translated either as the "ill-fated"[71] or "uncreated"[72] place. The reference is evidently to the ultimate destruction of all created brings in Ragnarǫk, the final battle between gods, men, and monsters which will end the world with their mutual defeat.

What is happening here is that first Fáfnir, then Sigurðr, transfers the dialogue from the personal, *ad hominem* level of a typical *senna* to a cosmological, mythic level that still retains symbolic resonance for the personal situations of both hero and dragon. While the discourse of the dialogue itself is non-narrative in that nothing either participant says advances the diegetic flow of the plot, the words contain what Frederic Amory has called, in reference to the narrative component of skaldic kennings, a "narrative precipitate"[73] which relies on the intertextual knowledge of the audience for its significance. Thus Fáfnir's warning about crossing the sea, as Alv Kragerud has recently argued, may be a reference to a version of the Ragnarǫk myth based on *Fáfnismál* 15 in which the last battle is envisioned as a kind of *hólmganga* between gods and monsters (an idea reinforced by Sigurðr's designation of Óskaptr in the saga as *hólmr*), in which the gods are initially victorious, but are destroyed by drowning when the rainbow bridge *Bifrǫst* (*Bilrǫst*) breaks under their feet as they return from the "ill-fated" island.[74] Hence, Fáfnir's warning can in fact be interpreted as an allusive reference to Sigurðr's current situation: he too has defeated a monster, but he's not home free yet. Because Sigurðr will remain in a liminal, fluid state until his hero's education is complete, he could still perish in his rebirth out of his personal *Óskaptr*, the 'uncreated,' liminal space of his initiation, depending on what sort of fate the norns who preside over his (re)birth assign to him.

Seen in this light, Fáfnir's gnomic information about the norns tells Sigurðr nothing useful about his particular destiny; it is instead simply another threatening warning. The hero's second question, meant perhaps as a pointed reminder to the dragon of the monsters' future destruction in Ragnarǫk, backfires in its turn: the narrative precipitate, instead of suggesting the dragon's immanent demise, serves rather to underscore Fáfnir's earlier prediction of death by water: like the gods and monsters, Sigurðr is also fated to die, whether by the agency of the cursed treasure or not is no matter.

Fáfnir at this point appears to have won the *senna*, for Sigurðr is silent despite the fact that by right it is his turn to speak. Given this discursive opportunity, Fáfnir continues speaking what can only be construed as the opening lines of a *Sterbelied* or 'death song,' a subgenre of Germanic literature first defined by Andreas Heusler and Wilhelm Ranisch and most recently discussed by Joseph Harris.[75] As is the case in other examples of this subgenre, Fáfnir speaks of his impending death and the legacy he leaves behind him; he attempts to justify his behavior and his reputation and alludes ominously to the fated nature of his treasure. But he is not permitted to finish, for Sigurðr—and on a discursive level the unfinished *senna*—once again interrupts. Sigurðr drives home his physical victory over the dragon by disputing the martial efficacy of Fáfnir's *ægishjálmr*, "helm of terror," and in so doing elicits yet another threat from the dying dragon. The dialogue ends, not with the dragon's curse on the hero, but with the hero's curse on the monster: *'En þú, Fáfnir, ligg í fjǫrbrotum, þar er þik Hel hafi.' Ok þá deyr Fáfnir,* "'But you, Fáfnir, lie in your death-throes until Hel takes you.' And then Fáfnir died" (chap. 18).

The saga author's deliberate intertextual mythologizing of Sigurðr's seemingly straightforward dragon slaying through the use of cryptically allusive narrative precipitates embedded in a catechetical dialogue places the scene squarely in the context of the Indo-European cosmological dragon myth examined in Chapter I. There the dragon serves as a symbol of the chaos upon which all created order is predicated, a cosmic liminality directly analogous to Sigurðr's marginal initiatory state.[76] The external sign of Fáfnir's status as a chaos monster is the *ægishjálmr*, the helm or "crest of terror" he claims as the source and symbol of his power, boasting that, *'Ek bar ægishjálm yfir ǫllu fólki . . . en allir váru hræddir við mik,'* "I raised a crest of terror above all men . . . and they were all afraid of me" (chap. 18).[77] The terror of the *ægishjálmr* in *Vǫlsunga saga* is more than the fear of death; it is the terror of non-Being—of dissolution or of remaining trapped in the liminal, dragonish place on the threshold of identity. But having conquered the dragon physically, Sigurðr can be at least outwardly scornful of its power; he takes possession of the helm along with the dragon's cursed treasure in token of the fact that he has faced and accepted the inevitablility of his own end:

> 'Heim munda ek ríða, þótt ek missta þessa ins mikla fjár, ef ek vissa at ek skylda aldri deyja, en hverr frœkn maðr vill fé raða allt til ins eina daga.' (chap. 18)

> ['If I knew I'd never die, I'd ride back . . . even though I were to forfeit all the wealth. But every valiant man desires to have wealth until that day comes.']

Also analogous to the Indo-European dragon myth is the fact that in both the cosmic and the initiatory dragon slayings destruction and creation are the result of a single act: Sigurðr is symbolically 'reborn' from the dragon's belly at the same moment he deals Fáfnir his death blow. By killing the dragon, Sigurðr (re)creates himself as a warrior and hero over and against the uncreated absence represented by Fáfnir's monstrous form; he thus gains the 'hallowed illusion'[78] of ontological presence for himself and to himself through the mediation of the dragon.

Finally, like the hero and dragon of the creation myths, Sigurðr and Fáfnir are 'monstrous doubles' in Girard's sense of the term, distinguished as hero and monster only retrospectively from the viewpoint of the written text. Their status as doubles may be uncovered by comparing their actions: Fáfnir kills his father Hreiðmarr in an unprovoked attack to gain his gold; Sigurðr kills Fáfnir in a similarly unprovoked attack for the same reason. In addition, each 'internalizes' the other: Fáfnir symbolically devours Sigurðr as he crawls over the pit in which the hero is hiding; Sigurðr quite literally ingests the dragon's roasted heart. In order for Sigurðr to be designated a hero, he and his 'good' violence must be differentiated from Fáfnir and his 'evil' violence, even though there is seemingly little to distinguish the two. This is done rhetorically, in the text's definition of Fáfnir as a literal, vanquished dragon and of Sigurðr as a victorious hero; even so, Sigurðr carries his double—his always present absence—within himself in the form of the eaten heart.

The mythic scenario is thus familiar, almost to the point of banality. What saves it as literature is again the dialogue. For in order for a text to designate one double as 'monstrous' or 'dragonish' and his violence as 'evil' in contradistinction to the other's 'good' heroic violence, it is necessary to reduce the victim of the hero's violence to a mute object whose nature can be monologically defined by the text at will. No voice is ever raised in defense of the chaos monster of myth. Yet the Fáfnir of *Vǫlsunga saga* insists upon defining himself as a speaking subject within the text, turning the monologic pseudo-discourse of heroic violence into the dialogic exchange of a *senna* and wisdom dialogue and then, almost, into the monologue of a valedictory *Sterbelied*. Sigurðr's attempts to win the *senna* and thereby silence the dragon with words are, as we have seen, ineffective at best; Fáfnir's death song may be interrupted, but the dragon is silenced only by his wounds. His death reenacts the violence of the saga's narrative strategy of differentiation by forcing Fáfnir into his textually determined role as a mute victim of justifiable heroic violence. Without the dialogue, the saga's teasing sublation of the dragon's point of view would be lost; with it, Fáfnir comes very close to subverting the saga's retrospective designations of hero and monster.

The difficulty in (re)writing the story of the most famous dragon and dragon slayer of heroic legend lies in challenging the audience's horizon of expectations without violating that audience's sense of the 'rightness' of the traditional text. If audience expectations are fulfilled to the letter, the story loses its interest; if the text transgresses the boundaries of what the audience regards as acceptable variation, it risks losing its audience. *Vǫlsunga saga* retains the traditional plot of Sigurðr's dragon slaying while transgressing genre boundaries in the dialogue with the dragon to create simultaneous conflicts on two distinct discursive levels: the verbal debate between hero and dragon is intensified and augmented by a subtextual debate among the various subgenres of Old Norse literary discourse. Through that debate Sigurðr defines himself as a hero and subject in contradistinction to Fáfnir, but as the various subgenres of the dialogue battle for discursive dominance, Fáfnir very nearly succeeds in similarly defining himself as subject as well. Thus while there can be no doubt that Sigurðr will indeed slay Fáfnir and survive, the saga author uses the dialogue with the dragon to raise subtextual questions concerning the underlying nature of heroes and dragons, the twin adversaries of myth and legend, their simultaneous (re)creation as heroic subject and monstrous object in the violence of the dragon slaying, and their ultimate fate in the destruction of this world. Like the *Beowulf* poet and the poet of *Fáfnismál*, the saga author understands that heroes and dragons create each other, and although dragons may be defeated, they cannot be destroyed without the destruction of the hero and of the heroic world as well.

4

Sîfrit

> . . . the Others are no longer monstrous beings, just different men. As for the monsters, they are internalized: their place is no longer 'out there,' but in the depths of the very soul. (Paul Zumthor, *Speaking of the Middle Ages*)

The most striking fact about Sîfrit's dragon in *Das Nibelungenlied* is its unimportance in and relative absence from the plot. It is mentioned only twice, first when Hagen tells Sîfrit's history to Gunther and his court (3, 100),[1] and second when Kriemhilt betrays Sîfrit's one vulnerable spot to Hagen (15, 899). The obvious question of why the Nibelung poet chose to all but omit the dragon slaying from a narrative concerning the most famous dragon slayer in Western history is one that will occupy us for most of this chapter.

Das Nibelungenlied is an epic-length heroic poem written in southern Germany or Austria by an anonymous poet around the year 1200. It exists in three different redactions and a large number of manuscripts; in each complete manuscript it is followed by the *Klage*, an inferior verse 'sequel' that has as its primary purpose the association of the longer work with the city of Passau and the seat in that city of Bishop Wolfger, a possible patron of the poem. *Das Nibelungenlied* tells roughly the same story as *Vǫlsunga saga* and *Þiðreks saga af Bern*: that is, it tells the story of Sîfrit's youth, marriage, and murder in the first part, and the destruction of the Burgundians by Etzel's Huns in the second. But the Nibelung poet's treatment of this story differs both chronotopically and materially from Norse versions of the tale. While some differences may be attributable to variations in source material, the majority would seem to be a direct result of the poet's distinctive incorporation of courtly romance elements into the precourtly, heroic material of his sources. The precise relationship between courtly and 'non-courtly' or heroic elements has occasioned a great deal of critical commentary on the poem, and holds the key to understanding the surprisingly large role that dragon slaying plays, after all, in this seemingly dragonless text.

HEROISM AND ROMANCE

The assumption that the *Nibelungenlied* poet sought to modernize the story of Siegfried, here called Sîfrit, by revising his sources in light of late twelfth-century fashions in courtly romance literature has never been in doubt. What has been disputed is twofold: first, scholars have attempted to ascertain the exact nature and content of the poet's written and/or oral sources to arrive at as complete an idea of Germanic literary history as possible;[2] and second, they have tried to gauge the impact of the poet's modernization on the Nibelung material itself as a guide to the interpretation and evaluation of the poem's thematic concerns.[3]

Through comparison of *Das Nibelungenlied* with the extant German and Scandinavian intertexts—primarily the Eddic poems, *Þiðreks saga af Bern*, and the thirteenth century German *Dietrichs Flucht* and *Rabenschlacht*—scholars can, with some degree of certainty, posit the existence of an earlier version of the fall of the Burgundians and make a fairly detailed estimation of that version's contents. This hypothetical source poem was assigned the name 'Ältere Not' by Andreas Heusler and is still referred to by that title.[4] The hypothetical sources underlying the first part of *Das Nibelungenlied* are more complex, but they may include, among others, a German 'Brünhildenlied' containing the story of Sîfrit's youth.[5] Such a 'Brünhildenlied' version of the dragon slaying would most likely have paralleled that found in *Þiðreks saga af Bern*, in which the young hero, orphaned and raised outside of aristocratic society by a smith, is sent to burn charcoal in the forest; when attacked by the dragon, he summarily clubs the monster to death.

This story is generically closer to folktale and *Märchen* than to chivalric romance, and thus could have no place in the *Nibelungenlied* poet's reconceived, courtly version of his tale; it is therefore supplanted by a new, updated version of Sîfrit's aristocratic youth at his father's court in Xanten. Sîfrit is described as *eins edelen küneges kint*, "a royal prince"[6] (2, 20), who *Man zôch . . . mit dem vlîze, als im daz wol gezam*, "was reared with all the care that befitted his high station" (2, 23). His childhood is in fact somewhat sheltered: he is not allowed to ride out alone (2, 25), being always in the care of *wîsen, den êre was bekant* "experienced men, well-versed in matters of honor" (2, 25). The dragon battle is accordingly displaced from its position in the Norse versions as the young man's initiatory trial, to be replaced by a more conventional, courtly *Schwertleite*, as well as by the wooing of Kriemhilt. Sîfrit thus receives his inheritance and his sword along with four hundred other young men (2, 29–30) in an elaborate ceremony during which he gives away *lant unde bürge* "land and cities" (2, 39) as part of the festivities, but declines the crown of the Netherlands since his father and mother are yet alive (2, 43). Instead, following the fashion of the twelfth century bridal-quest romance,[7] Sîfrit decides to seek out love, and resolves that only Kriemhilt of Burgundy will do (3, 47). His wooing of Kriemhilt includes a year spent waiting for a single glimpse of her (3, 138) and is made dependent upon his service to Gunther (6, 333), thereby providing an entirely new set of fashionable, because 'courtly,' initiatory trials. Whereas Sigurðr's initiation into adulthood in *Vǫlsunga saga* culminates in his betrothal to Brynhildr as a direct result of the dragon slaying, Sîfrit's ends in his marriage to Kriemhilt as the result of a protracted period of *minnedienst*.[8]

When juxtaposed to this narrative version of Sîfrit's chivalric *enfance*, Hagen's description of Sîfrit's early adventures seems to come from another story entirely. In this heroic version of Sîfrit's youth, the young man rides out to find adventures *al eine* "alone" (3, 88), something the courtly knight from Xanten is expressly said never to do. He comes across the princes Scilbunc and Nibelunc as they are engaged in dividing their treasure (3, 91), and is offered Nibelunc's sword Balmunc as a reward for dividing the treasure for them (3, 93). He fails in this task, but succeeds in killing the princes and twelve giants, subduing seven hundred warriors, who yield their lands to him (3, 94), and overcoming the dwarf Albrîch (3, 96), thereby winning the hoard and *tarnkappe* (3, 97). It is this adventure that provides Sîfrit with his second home in Nibelungenland, a location which serves as a heroic counterpart to the courtly Xanten. Moreover, in an apparently unrelated incident:

> Einen lintrachen   den sluoc des heldes hant.
> er badet' sich in dem bluote: sîn hût wart hurnîn.
> des snîdet in kein wâfen;   daz ist dicke worden sîn.
> (3, 100)

> [This hero slew a dragon and bathed in its blood, from which his skin
> grew horny so that no weapon will bite it, as has been shown time and
> time again.]

Later, Kriemhilt reveals to Hagen that Sîfrit's invulnerability is not total: a leaf fell on his back, shielding one spot from the dragon's blood (15, 902) and leaving him vulnerable to anyone who knows his secret. The dragon and dragon slaying are never described in greater detail in the poem.

The contrast between the poem's two versions of Sîfrit's youth underlies the critical commonplace that Sîfrit has a double nature: "Er hat ein zweifaches Dasein";[9] "Siegfried hat ein doppeltes Gesicht";[10] he is a "courtly gentleman and . . . supernatural strongman"[11] all at the same time. One view of this duality considers it a flaw in characterization that emblemizes the imperfect fusion between the poet's traditionally heroic sources and the new romance fashions he wished to follow. A.T. Hatto, for example, states that "[w]hen the plot demands it, the leading characters follow old ways. Otherwise they follow the new."[12] His view reflects that of Friedrich Neumann, who has written that

> die Gestalten des *Nls* behalten ihre alte Art, soweit dies durch die Grundfabel
> verlangt wird. Sie nehmen die Haltung der höfischen Ritter und Ritterdamen
> an, wenn ihnen die Kernhandlung nicht die Gebärden vorschreibt.[13]

The poet's presumed inability to rewrite the Nibelungen material so that old and new fuse smoothly has in its turn been attributed to the idea that a medieval poet must necessarily remain tied to "what he perceived to be his obligations to tradition."[14] In Neumann's words, "wenn ältere Dichtung gesprochen hat, ist man in der Erfindung nicht mehr frei."[15]

This explanation of the *Nibelungenlied* poet's treatment of his source material has been challenged by Edward R. Haymes, who points out that the formal structure of the poem—which is composed in the strophes of the traditional oral heroic epic instead of the couplets of the newer courtly romances—would tend to indicate that the poet was interested in more than simply modernizing his traditional tale.[16] Rather, Haymes sees the organization of the poem as more complex than earlier critics had portrayed, emphasizing that its generic structure is in fact triple rather than double. On the first level, the everyday workings of late twelfth century life are represented in a realistic, historically-oriented fashion that may be illustrated by the poem's pragmatic concern with the political stability of Gunther's realm. Layered on top of this 'realistic' foundation are elements from courtly romance literature such as Sîfrit's stylized wooing of Kriemhilt, while truly heroic elements such as Sîfrit's traditional encounter with the dragon and his winning of the Nibelung hoard provide a third level.[17] Each layer contains components that are the *Nibelungenlied* poet's inventions; it is not a simple matter of the medieval poet's addition of incompatible courtly material to an earlier uncourtly tradition. In fact, Haymes argues that those scenes in which Sîfrit shows his 'uncourtly' side most clearly—examples are Sîfrit's initial encounter with the Burgundian court (*Aventiure* 3) and his journey to Nibelungenland to summon his thousand knights (*Aventiure* 8)—are not taken directly from heroic sources at all, but instead are part of the poet's *courtly* innovations. Thus, when Sîfrit challenges Gunther to a battle for Kriemhilt and the Burgundian crown, he is not acting in a fashion characteristic of heroic poetry, but is instead

> clearly allied with the heroes of the romances, whose political fortunes are based on the possibility of finding the opportunity to win a castle, a wife and a realm by a successful passage through various tests of their knightly prowess.[18]

Furthermore, Haymes views Sîfrit's journey to Nibelungenland as well as his participation in the Saxon wars as examples of feudal *auxilium*, or service, to Gunther, undertaken by Sîfrit as part of his new role as a courtly lover in quest of Kriemhilt's hand in marriage.[19] That such behavior leads only to disaster in the context of the poem would therefore also indicate that the poet, far from simply modernizing an archaic character, is in fact holding the new ethical standards of the literary romance heroes up to question.[20]

Haymes' view of the *Nibelungenlied*'s generic structure thus ascribes far greater literary sophistication and control to the Nibelung poet than most earlier scholars allowed. His analysis falls short of a fully dialogic reading of the poem, however, in that he declines to explore the narratological consequences of the poet's juxtaposition of generic possibilities beyond noting the resulting commentary on chivalric behavior in regard to Sîfrit and a similar commentary on heroism in regard to Hagen.[21] Far from producing a monologic critique of literary ethics, however, the multiplication of generic models in *Das Nibelungenlied* creates a corresponding multiplication of 'voices' that compete dialogically for precedence in the narrative structure of the poem, resulting in a generic polylogue between the realistic, the chivalric, and the heroic points of view. This interaction among the poem's generic voices can best be examined through an investigation of the poem's specific chronotope in comparison to the extant Norse versions of the tale and to the dragon episode of *Beowulf*.

As is the case with its heroic predecessors in the Old English and Norse traditions, the temporal/spatial structure of *Das Nibelungenlied* conforms to Bakhtin's category of 'adventure time,' and is therefore characterized by the sudden intrusion of the unexpected or the uncanny into the everyday world of ordinary life. Without such intrusions, time in the poem is static,

> the world remains as it was, the biographical life of the heroes does not change, their feelings do not change, people do not even age. This empty time leaves no traces anywhere, no indications of its passing.[22]

Accordingly, in *Das Nibelungenlied* the Burgundians do not grow older despite the decades that pass between major episodes of the poem: Gîselher retains his characteristic epithets of *der junge* "the young" and *daz kint* "the child" throughout;[23] Kriemhilt remains youthful and beautiful despite the thirty-six years that pass after her marriage to Sîfrit.

Within individual episodes, however, the passing of time is "organized from without, technically" into discrete "segments that correspond to separate adventures"[24]—adventures prompted, as indicated above, by a sudden intrusion or unexpected change in situation. That is, each segment is chronotopically structured by the poet to conform to the conventions of heroic literature or to those of chivalric romance; some segments may contain a combination of competing elements that interact dialogically as the episode unfolds. Moreover,

> the link between space and time has, as it were, not an organic but a purely technical (and mechanical) nature. . . . The contingency that governs events is inseparably tied up with space, measured primarily by *distance* on the one hand and by *proximity* on the other.[25]

In other words, space is organized in *Das Nibelungenlied* in such a way that a change in location seems automatically to inaugurate a chronotopic shift as well, and thus a sudden change in circumstance or the abrupt beginning of an episodic adventure. At the same time, any chronotopic change—that is, any shift from the everyday into the heroic or chivalric—appears to necessitate a locational change as well. This spatial component of 'adventure time' combines in the *Nibelungenlied* with the two versions of Sîfrit's youth to produce a situation in which there appear to be two worlds occupying different but proximate spaces, and possibly different but proximate times as well. These two worlds have been differentiated in varying but related ways by different students of the poem.[26] Walter Johannes Schröder's 1954 description is one of the most explicit:

> Nibelungenland und Isenstein liegen im hohen Norden, zeitlich gehören sie der grauen Vorzeit an. Siegfried gewann hier den Hort und die Tarnkappe, hier und damals erschlug er den Drachen und badete in dessen Blut. . . . Dem mythisch-märchenhaften Norden steht der geschichtliche Süden gegenüber.[27]

More recently, Winder McConnell has referred to the unspecified location of Sîfrit's youthful adventures, his home in Nibelungenland, and Prünhilt's home in Isenstein, as parts of an otherwise unidentified "Other World"[28] of supernatural creatures and events. This 'Other World' of the *Nibelungenlied* is analogous to the monstrous world of *draconitas* in *Beowulf*, which encroaches upon the everyday world of *humanitas* first in the form of Grendel and his mother and then as a literal dragon. In *Das Nibelungenlied*, however, Sîfrit's dragon slaying notwithstanding, the encroachment is not primarily one of monsters, but rather of human and sometimes superhuman beings who act as hero intruders from one world into another, as 'dragonish' guests whose incursions, by the end of the poem, have engendered the destruction of both the Burgundian and Hunnish societies.

The analogy with *Beowulf* is possible because the two poems, different as they are, share the common chronotopic structure of adventure time. It is this chronotope which sets *Das Nibelungenlied* off from the 'pure' chivalric romances its surface content sometimes imitates, because the chronotope peculiar to chivalric romance, although admittedly similar to adventure time, contains what Bakhtin calls "a radically new element . . . which in turn pervades everything in its chronotope."[29] In the chivalric romances, invasions of *draconitas*, sudden changes in circumstance, and unexpected irruptions of the uncanny are 'normalized':

> The whole world becomes miraculous, so the miraculous becomes ordinary without ceasing at the same time to be miraculous. Even 'unexpectedness' itself—since it is always with us—ceases to be something unexpected. The unexpected, and only the unexpected, is what is expected.[30]

This is the chronotope of Arthurian romance, of the Breton *lai*, of many of the *fornaldarsǫgur*, and indeed (to look ahead for a moment) of *Þiðreks saga af Bern*. It is not, however, the primary chronotope of *Das Nibelungenlied*, whatever chivalric elements the Nibelung poet may have incorporated into his poem.

Nevertheless, if *Das Nibelungenlied* does not share the chronotope—and thus the genre—of chivalric romance, its temporal/spatial structure within the chronotope of adventure time is not precisely the same as that in *Beowulf* either. The difference here lies in the poet's treatment of and attitude toward the supernatural. In *Beowulf* the invasions of *draconitas* are deadly serious: the monsters are terrifying and dangerous; Beowulf's superhuman strength is necessary to combat them and is thus likewise taken seriously. In *Das Nibelungenlied*, by contrast, manifestations of the otherworld tend to take on a farcical, even slapstick quality, whether they occur in Isenstein, Nibelungenland, or Worms.

The journey to Isenstein to win Prünhilt as Gunther's bride in *Aventiure* 7 is a good example. Prünhilt's extraordinary strength marks her as a denizen of that heroic otherworld in which the ordinary rules of merely human society are challenged by the supernatural and superhuman. In contrast to Sîfrit's mannered and ritualized courtship of Kriemhilt in the courtly world of Worms, in Isenstein Gunther is expected to woo and win his wife through an athletic contest which consists of throwing spears, casting boulders, and a standing broadjump. Prünhilt enters into the competition with gusto. The situation is in itself comic, and the comedy only intensifies as Gunther, far too weak to compete with his intended bride, must rely upon Sîfrit—cloaked and invisible in the *tarnkappe*—to perform the deeds while Gunther merely pantomimes them.

Even more farcical are the events of Gunther and Prünhilt's wedding night in the tenth *Aventiure*, when Prünhilt not only forcibly evicts the hapless Gunther from her bed, but also leaves him to spend the night dangling helplessly from a nail on the wall. Some of the same burlesque quality likewise characterizes Sîfrit's behavior on the hunt—catching and then loosing a bear in the camp (16, 948–62)—and in his battles with Albrîch and the doorkeeper in Nibelungenland (8, 489–99), activities which he seemingly undertakes simply for the sport of it all.

Hagen's encounter with the *merwîp* in the second part of the poem is treated far more seriously than other incursions of the supernatural, yet some of the comic tone persists even here. The image of an armed warrior holding several water-nixies at bay by stealing their clothing (25, 1534)—whatever larger significance 'clothing' has taken on as a symbol in the poem—is in itself ludicrous. Moreover, Hagen's attempt to verify the *merwîp*'s conflicting statements by trying to drown the chaplain (25, 1575–80) has some of the same grimly humorous quality that the earlier contests between Sîfrit and Prünhilt, or Sîfrit and Albrîch, have.

The effect of this comedy is twofold. Its initial impact is to change the spatial aspects of the poem's chronotope by diminishing the perceived distance between this world and the otherworld, bringing the supernatural and uncanny up close where they can be examined and even laughed at. In *Beowulf*, by way of contrast, the felt distance between the human world of Heorot and the monstrous otherworld of the Grendelmere or the dragon's lair is made as wide as possible by the poet's insistence on the limitations of human knowledge. Thus there is irony in *Beowulf*, but no true comedy, for,

[a]s a distanced image a subject cannot be comical; to be made comical, it must be brought close. Everything that makes us laugh is close at hand, all comical creativity works in a zone of maximal proximity.[31]

In *Das Nibelungenlied*, the proximity between worlds facilitates what Bakhtin would call the "uncrowning" of the poem's superhuman characters and events; in this case, the reduction of the power of the otherworld and its denizens to a level that need inspire neither dread nor reverence: "Laughter demolishes fear and piety before an object, before a world, making of it an object of familiar contact."[32] Hence neither Sîfrit nor Prünhilt inspires the awe and terror their superhuman strength might arouse in another context; even the *tarnkappe*, invariably linked as it is with the otherworldly and farcical episodes, loses the numinosity which its counterpart in Norse versions of the tale, the *ægishjálmr*,[33] carried with it, becoming in *Das Nibelungenlied* merely an instrument to help Gunther achieve a goal of which he is unworthy. As I argued in Chapter III, the terror produced by the *ægisjhálmr* is the possibility of ontological obliteration, of non-Being. By comparison, the *tarnkappe* merely obliterates its wearer's visual presence while at the same time increasing his physical strength; it is consequently never used to destroy, but rather to carry out pranks and petty deceptions.

In sum, the *Nibelungenlied* poet's use of the heroic narrative material that traditionally surrounds the figure of Siegfried/Sigurðr, when set in a realistically portrayed late twelfth century milieu and combined with poetic innovations based in courtly romance literature, produces a version of the Siegfried story in which the truly supernatural and mythic elements—i.e., the dragon, the awakening of Brynhildr, the Odinic theophanies of *Vǫlsunga saga*—are eliminated or downplayed in favor of the merely superhuman. This is in turn 'uncrowned,' stripped of its numinosity and power through comedy. The result is a poetic narrative in which the adventure-time incursions of *draconitas*, although foreshadowed by Hagen's brief tale of Sîfrit's actual dragon slaying, take place on a human rather than a monstrous level. And as our earlier discussion of dragon slaying in Indo-European myth and legend would indicate, such sociopolitical incursions manifest themselves within *Das Nibelungenlied* as part of a complicated nexus of guest-host relationships.

DRAGON AND DRAGON SLAYER

Virtually all of the events in *Das Nibelungenlied* take place within a carefully prepared context of visits, friendly and unfriendly, expected or unexpected, from one location to another. Sîfrit woos and wins Kriemhilt as an uninvited guest of the Burgundians; Gunther wins Prünhilt as an unexpected visitor at Isenstein. Likewise the quarrel of the queens and the resultant murder of Sîfrit take place after Prünhilt insists on inviting Sîfrit and Kriemhilt to Worms; the destruction of the Burgundians is carried out by Kriemhilt under the guise of inviting them for a visit to Etzel's court. Because the Indo-European dragon slaying myth, once having descended into a societal rather than a cosmic sphere, most often takes the form of a guest-host dispute, it may be useful to explore each of these visits in terms of that myth.

Sîfrit arrives at Worms in the guise of a hero intruder,[34] an uninvited, 'dragonish' guest who single-handedly threatens the destruction of the entire realm if he is not granted Kriemhilt's hand in marriage. His appearance initiates a momentary change in the poem's chronotopic structure from simple adventure time to what Bakhtin calls "the chronotope of *threshold* . . . the chronotope of *crisis* and *break* in a life."[35] Obviously akin to the literally transformatory chronotopic structures discussed in relation to initiation ritual in *Vǫlsunga saga*, the threshold chronotope in *Das Nibelungenlied* recurs as the characters move from one geographical location to another, and most acutely when the move may be construed as one from the otherworld to the everyday world or vice versa. Each threshold crossing inaugurates a moment of 'crisis time' which is resolved when the intruding character's status as either a hostile foreign invader or a welcome guest is established. Sîfrit's challenge presents an obvious crisis for the Burgundians in *Aventiure* 3, albeit one laced with disbelief and uncertainty: knight-errantry notwithstanding, that Sîfrit could possibly expect to be able to win Kriemhilt by force seems ludicrous, an early example of the farcical nature of otherworldly incursions in the poem—until one remembers the fate of Scilbunc and Nibelunc. Gunther and his court are understandably incredulous. Violence seems imminent. But as A.T. Hatto points out, "Siegfried's love for Kriemhild . . . soon tames him."[36] At the very thought of his love, *wart der herre Sîvrit ein lützel sanfter gemuot* "Lord Siegfried was somewhat appeased" (3, 127). The crisis is resolved; Sîfrit crosses the cultural threshold into Burgundian society as an honored guest instead of a monstrous intruder in a virtually instantaneous transformation of his status that demonstrates the underlying similarities between the two roles and the relative ease with which one metamorphoses into the other.[37] But Sîfrit is still far from being totally 'tamed' by Kriemhilt, as is shown by his trip to Nibelungenland (*Aventiure* 8), by his callous behavior toward Prünhilt in both Isenstein and Worms (*Aventiuren* 7 and 10), and by his sheer high spirits in the bear episode on the hunt (*Aventiure* 16). In Carl Singer's words, Sîfrit "lapses into [his] natural behavior" here, showing his strength and indulging in "pointlessly repeated triumph[s] . . . for [their] own sake."[38] In other words, Sîfrit retains his initial character as a possibly dragonish hero intruder, in spite of his transformation in status to a guest and the courtly overlay of his wooing of Kriemhilt.

The potential for violence inherent in Sîfrit's arrival at Worms is recalled when he returns to Nibelungenland to fetch his thousand knights in *Aventiure* 8, but it is here played out as slapstick rather than as truly threatening behavior. Once again Sîfrit assumes the role of a hero intruder at the threshold of a city and challenges its inhabitants to battle: disguising his voice, he identifies himself simply as *ein recke* "a soldier of fortune" (8, 488) and proceeds to engage in life-threatening (8, 491, 495) physical combat in order first to enter and then ostensibly to conquer the realm. His first opponent is the giant doorkeeper, who functions within the episode as what Joseph Campbell would call a "threshold guardian"[39] and whom Sîfrit handily defeats and binds; the second is the dwarf Albrîch, who receives much the same treatment, but who suffers the additional indignity of being pulled to and fro by his beard (8, 497). There is no little irony in the narrator's comment that Sîfrit refrains from killing the dwarf when *er schônte sîner zühte, als im diu tugent daz gebôt* "[he remembered] his good breeding, as decency required" (8, 496), as if Sîfrit's behavior were in keeping with the courtly manners of a guest rather than the violence of a hero intruder.

Throughout each of these episodes Sîfrit is referred to as a *gast*, a term normally translated as 'stranger,' but one which, in Middle High German as in Old English, may also mean 'guest':[40] *gast* "stranger" (3, 105; 3, 106; 3, 128); *der hêrlîche gast* (8, 490), *disen gast vil edelen* "the noble stranger" (8, 493); *der wœtlîche gast* "the handsome stranger" (8, 495). The word is a straightforward designation in the third *aventiure*, but ironic in the eighth for the same reason that the fights are comic: Sîfrit is neither stranger nor guest but rather lord and host in Nibelungenland. No doubt Haymes is right that the episode serves as an example of Sîfrit's feudal *auxilium* to Gunther and is accordingly part and parcel of his wooing of Kriemhilt; it also clearly parallels the events of Sîfrit's arrival at Worms in *Aventiure* 3 and by doing so differentiates Sîfrit's behavior in the otherworld from his actions in the everyday or courtly world. And although Sîfrit engages in no such casual violence or meaningless deception in Worms, his behavior in Nibelungenland is a reminder of the violence intrinsic to the function of a hero intruder, even when transformed into the more benign role of guest.

This has of course already been manifested, if in a less overtly violent fashion, in the Isenstein venture of *Aventiure* 7, wherein Sîfrit and Gunther together play the combined roles of hero intruders and monstrous guests. The latent physical violence of their intrusion is sublimated into the psychological violence of deceit and the physical competition of sports: in order for Gunther to win Prünhilt, he must first convince her that he is a worthy opponent, which he does by allowing Sîfrit to pose as his vassal to give credence to his claim of superiority, and then defeat her in athletic contests that are comically 'uncrowned' substitutes for the military victory of a conquering hero. The moment of 'crisis time' that occurs as the Burgundians disembark, on the threshold, as it were, of Prünhilt's land, is tacitly resolved by the deceitful expedient of having Sîfrit hold Gunther's horse for him and thereby demonstrate publicly his feigned social inferiority and the corresponding absence of danger to Prünhilt's unmarried state that this implies (7, 396). More immediately crisis-laden is the dialogue at the literal threshold of Prünhilt's castle, where the strangers are asked to surrender their weapons and in so doing to demonstrate their status as friendly guests rather than hostile invaders (7, 406). Although Hagen's initial refusal is countermanded by Sîfrit's assurances that this is the custom of the realm, Hagen's compliance remains *ungerne* "much against his will" (7, 407) and clearly constitutes a break in his usual behavior. Both moments of crisis time serve to underscore the Burgundian duplicity, the dragonish element in their visit, even as we remember that Prünhilt herself is also a monstrous host, since she will kill any suitor who loses at her games.

Gunther is of course too weak to win his bride honestly, so the Burgundian deception extends from the vassalage ruse to the games themselves. The absurd nature of the contests as a means of wooing a wife, coupled with the image of an invisible Sîfrit carrying a terrified Gunther through what must have been the performance of his life, tends to obscure the truly monstrous nature of the Burgundians' behavior in this scene. It is a dragonish guest indeed who can defeat his host at her own games, acquire her realm, and bind her to himself for life through simple fraud. This characterization is reinforced by the sheer rudeness of the Burgundians after Gunther's dishonest victory, as when Sîfrit remarks:

> "Sô wol mich dirre mære,"   sprach Sîfrit der degen,
> "daz iuwer hôhverte   ist alsô hie gelegen,
> daz iemen lebet, der iuwer   meister müge sîn."
> (7, 474)

> ["I am delighted to hear that your pride has been lowered in this way," said brave Siegfried, "and that there is someone alive who can master you."]

Nonetheless, the real brutality underlying Prünhilt's defeat is deferred until the return to Worms, where the game turns serious when Sîfrit beats Prünhilt into submission in order to allow Gunther to rape her. Even there, the farcical quality of Prünhilt and Gunther's wedding-night wrestling match and her initial victory in the bedroom mask the viciousness of the men's actions against her; moreover, because Prünhilt becomes *niht sterker dann' ein ander wîp* "no stronger than any other woman" (10, 682) with her loss of virginity, the rape in itself ensures that she can have no physical revenge against her conquerors.

Prünhilt's only recourse is in once again playing the role of a monstrous host, which she does a full ten years later when she conceals her real reasons for inviting Sîfrit and Kriemhilt to the festivity at Worms. And it is this festivity, in its turn, that provides the impetus for the societally rather than mythically constructed dragon slaying that is at the center of *Das Nibelungenlied*.

Sîfrit's behavior as a hero intruder on his visits to Worms, Isenstein, and Nibelungenland establish him firmly in the role of a potentially dragonish guest, an alien visitor with a penchant for violence and deceit whom Gunther may use politically, but who may also turn suddenly and unaccountably wild, as he does on his arrival in Nibelungenland and in his pranks on the hunt. He is even physically dragonish: he is preternaturally strong; he owns a magic talisman, the *tarnkappe*, which not only renders him invisible but increases his strength twelvefold; he is the owner and guardian of a golden treasure; his horn-hard skin, gained through bathing in a literal dragon's blood, marks him as having internalized the characteristics of the dragon while retaining his human form. That Sîfrit could change from a literal dragon slayer into a metaphorical dragon in the course of the narration should not be surprising, for as we have seen in Chapter I, the two are doubles, differentiated into hero and monster, dragon slayer and dragon, only retrospectively, in the telling of the story. But although Sîfrit's physical attributes reveal him to be the double of the dragon he has killed, once the dragon is dead, his situation at Worms re-creates him as the double of Hagen, who as Sîfrit's murderer thus becomes the more important dragon slayer in *Das Nibelungenlied*.

That Hagen and Sîfrit may be seen as doubles and opposites within the poem has to some degree already been recognized: Sîfrit may be designated a 'bright' hero, while Hagen is 'dark,' but a hero nonetheless.[41] Each serves Gunther in an advisory capacity; each has at least some knowledge of and experience in dealing with the otherworld. It should be remembered that Hagen recognizes Sîfrit on sight and is able to tell the story of his youthful adventures to the Burgundians, even though there is no reason to believe Hagen has ever seen Sîfrit before. Hagen is Gunther's vassal, while Sîfrit poses as such, thereby erasing the social differentiation between their respective ranks. D. G. Mowatt and Hugh Sacker's controversial suggestion of homosexual tension between the two heroes is off the mark,[42] but nonetheless captures a sense of the affinity that exists between the two as doubles and yet antagonists, host and guest, dragon slayer and dragon.

The reason Hagen kills Sîfrit has often been debated, with most recent commentators concluding that the murder has at best no obvious motivation within *Das Nibelungenlied* as we have it. Theodore M. Andersson states explicitly that "the failure to explain Siegfried's murder persuasively is the chief blemish in the work,"[43] while Haymes asserts that "there is no clear overriding reason for the act."[44] If we look at Sîfrit's murder as an instance of Girardian sacred violence, however, and thus as an example of the guest-host pattern of the Indo-European dragon slaying myth, an explicit motivation becomes unnecessary: Sîfrit is the requisite scapegoat/victim, his murder a political rather than religious sacrifice designed to reestablish the social differentiation that has been blurred by the vassalage deception and by so doing to end the dissension within Burgundian society as it is emblemized by the quarrel of the queens. His often cited guilt for his own murder, whether that guilt is attributed to his *übermuot* in presenting Prünhilt's ring and girdle to Kriemhilt, or to his failure to fulfill his destiny by winning and wedding Prünhilt himself,[45] is established in retrospect by the fact of his death, just as the dragons of myth and legend are rendered monstrous by their deaths in the retrospective, monologic retelling of the myths in which they occur. By making Sîfrit their scapegoat, the Burgundians can cut through the tangled web of degrees of guilt and innocence, truth and deception, that has led to the argument between the queens; they can prevent the warrior society at Worms from taking sides and broadening the dissension to the point of unstoppable reciprocal violence; and they can restore the social order by reinterpreting the figure of Sîfrit as an outsider, an alien, monstrous intruder who can be killed with impunity. Sîfrit's actual status—as a king, as Gunther's brother-in-law, as an invited guest in Worms—is thus immaterial:

> Human behavior is determined not by what really happened but by the interpretation of what happened. The double transference guides such interpretation. It transforms the victim into something radically other than, and transcendent to, the community. . . . In general, then, the victim will appear to be more foreign than native; as in many myths, the victim is a *visitor* that has come from an unknown world.[46]

With Sîfrit dead and Prünhilt effectively neutralized by the loss of her virgin strength, only Gunther and Hagen will be left to tell the tale of the journey to Isenstein and its aftermath. In the same manner the solitary nature of the victim in the mythic dragon slaying, as Girard has demonstrated, assures the victor that only one version of the story describing the killing survives, that of the god or hero who has made himself ruler of the cosmos. As a politician, Gunther too must insist upon maintaining monologic discourse about his victories as King of Burgundy, but Sîfrit's presence has opened the possibility of a second version of the Isenstein venture that could lead to an interpretation of those events unfavorable to the Burgundian regime. It is this *potential* challenge to Gunther's royal power, and not any real threat to or concern for Prünhilt's honor, that provides the rationale for Sîfrit's murder.

The murder itself is structurally reminiscent of a literal dragon slaying, which as we have seen most often takes place in the wilderness, sometimes, as in *Beowulf*, after the dragon has invaded and ravaged the human world, and sometimes, as in *Vǫlsunga saga*, while the monster is intent on drinking from a river. In his role as a monstrous—i.e. dragonish—guest, Sîfrit is not represented as inflicting any significant physical damage to Burgundian society or property; like other incursions of the supernatural in the poem, his behavior is 'uncrowned' and made comic in the Isenstein and Nibelungenland journeys, but more importantly in the immediate context of the hunting expedition. Far from intending violence or serious destruction to his hosts, Sîfrit resolves simply to provide *guoter kurzewîle* "good entertainment" (16, 888) for them, and does so by capturing a bear, setting it loose to rampage through the Burgundian encampment in what is almost a parody of a dragon's attack, and then recapturing and finally killing it in a farcically redundant demonstration of his qualities as the strongest and best huntor. The irony of these events should be apparent: Sîfrit's role is in fact not that of a hunter or dragon slayer, but rather that of the prey or dragon, to be run down and slaughtered by Hagen.

His murder confirms the irony: having agreed to race Hagen to the river, Sîfrit handicaps himself not only by carrying his arms and hunting gear, but also by beginning the race literally on the ground, lying like an armored serpent—that is, like a dragon—face down in the grass at Hagen's feet (16, 975–76). Despite these handicaps, Sîfrit's speed makes the race resemble a pursuit rather than a contest between equals, and the *hêrlîche gast* "magnificent [stranger /] guest" (16, 980) easily arrives first at the river. The use of the word *gast* in these lines, despite its frequency in the poem as a whole and the by now trite double meaning it carries, attains for an instant the status of a Bakhtinian 'microdialogue' as Sîfrit stands on the threshold of his death, his position as guest or stranger once again in doubt in a chronotopic moment of 'crisis time.' We see him, briefly, for the final time in his role as 'guest' as he courteously waits for Gunther to catch up and drink before stooping to the water himself; then the moment passes, and Sîfrit becomes once and for all a 'stranger,' a metaphorical dragon to be slain by the poem's dark hero, Hagen:

> Dâ der herre Sîfrit   ob dem brunnen tranc,
> er schôz in durch das kriuze,   daz von der wunden spranc
> daz bluot im von dem herzen   vaste an Hagenen wât.
> (16, 981–3)

> [Then, as Siegfried bent over the brook and drank, Hagen hurled the spear at the cross [marking Sîfrit's vulnerable spot], so that the hero's heart's blood leapt from the wound and splashed against Hagen's clothes.]

The parallel with Fáfnir, killed on his way to a river to drink, by a similar thrust to the 'soft' and thus vulnerable parts of his dragon-hard body, would be hard to miss, were it not for our expectation that Sîfrit must be the hero rather than the dragon, and our belief, reinforced by countless monologic retellings of mythic encounters between hero and monster, that the two are not the same.

HAGEN SÎFRITSBANE

The dragon slayings of Indo-European myth, of course, allow for no confusion between monster and hero. Myth is monologic discourse, in which events are interpreted once and for all to ensure the monstrosity of the victim and the divinity of the victor in a fashion that allows no dissenting second voice, no questioning of the predetermined meaning of the narrative. But *Das Nibelungenlied* is fiction, not myth, and is in fact even less mythic in its content and structure than *Beowulf,* making the murder of Sîfrit problematic in a way that the killing of Grendel or the *Beowulf* dragon could never be. The popularity of the Siegfried legend in the Middle Ages would in any case naturally work to prohibit the drastic challenge to audience expectations that would be produced by an explicit reinterpretation of the story to make Sîfrit openly dragon-ish and Hagen unambiguously heroic, even if the poet of *Das Nibelungenlied* had desired to reinterpret his tale in that way. As it is, the poem's enigmatic characterization of Sîfrit is produced by the poet's manipulation of the audience's horizon of expectations concerning Siegfried in juxtaposition to the mythic horizon of expectations concerning dragons and dragon slaying. The result, as we have seen, is a dialogic inquiry into the nature and ethics of the poetic representation of heroism, in the context of historical, heroic and chivalric literature.

In *Das Nibelungenlied* there is thus no possibility of an absolutely monologic interpretation of events. Nevertheless, while the immediate outpouring of grief for Sîfrit's death is described in detail within the poem, the influence of the Indo-European dragon slaying myth is indicated by the fact that most of *Das Nibelungenlied*'s characters maintain a curious silence with regard to blame or revenge for the murder, treating Sîfrit's violent death as if it were an inevitable, albeit tragic, occurrence, best forgotten quickly.[47] In *Das Nibelungenlied* as in *Beowulf*, it is the victim's only surviving female relative, whose existence and voice have been disregarded by the male characters, who avenges the murder.

As a dragonish victim herself, Grendel's mother is presented in *Beowulf* as not only monstrous but, like Grendel, as a literal monster; her function is merely to provide a delay in the hero's ultimate victory in Heorot. Kriemhilt is not so easily reinterpreted. Just as Sîfrit never fully becomes the slain dragon his murder would seem to require, Kriemhilt is only partially demonized within the poem's discursive structure. Her treacherous behavior towards her brothers at Etzel's court marks her as a particularly monstrous host, and there are hints within the narrative that she is no longer to be regarded as fully human: the narrator limits himself to the comment that the *übel vâlant* "foul fiend" (23, 1394) caused her to turn against her brothers, but Kriemhilt is called *vâlandinne* "she-devil" by Dietrich (28, 1748) and again by Hagen (39, 2371). Her death resembles the extermination of an animal rather than the execution of a human being: she is brutally *ze stücken . . . gehouwen* "hewn in pieces" (39, 2377) by an outraged Hildebrant.

But despite the textual indications of her monstrosity, Kriemhilt remains the representation of a human woman whose husband has been treacherously murdered by her brother's henchman, a woman for whom one may have some degree of sympathy even without condoning her later actions. That audiences from the Middle Ages to the present have in fact been sympathetic to Kriemhilt is shown by the sheer number of her apologists, from the anonymous redactor of the 'C' version onward.[48] Likewise, Hagen is never fully reinterpreted from the villainous murderer of an innocent victim into a dragon slayer, despite the text's best efforts to do so.

This is not to say that Hagen has never been recognized as the hero of at least the second half of *Das Nibelungenlied*.[49] Rather, as a 'dark' hero Hagen remains in the shadow of Sîfrit's brightness throughout the poem. Just as Sîfrit's image can never be divorced from his unambiguously heroic status as a dragon slayer, Hagen's image is always colored by his ambiguously represented murder of Sîfrit. What Sîfrit accomplishes seemingly without effort, Hagen attains to only with difficulty and with sometimes disastrous repercussions. His actions are parallel to but different from Sîfrit's, once again providing a dialogic rejoinder to the conventional narrative of Sîfrit's heroism.

The immediate result of Sîfrit's dragon slaying is the hero's acquisition of the dragon's horn-hard skin and with it the monster's virtual invulnerability in battle. This physical transformation marks Sîfrit as a dragon slayer, externalizing his resemblance to his monstrous double and indicating that he has, as mentioned above, internalized the dragon's characteristics. Such a literal change is of course impossible for Hagen to achieve, even though we are told that at his death Sîfrit's heart's blood *vaste an Hagenen wât* "splashed against Hagen's clothes" (16, 981–3). But in a curious way Hagen is also marked as Sîfrit's slayer by his adversary's blood:

> Daz ist ein michel wunder;   vil dicke ez noch geschiht:
> swâ man den mortmeilen   bî dem tôten siht,
> sô bluotent im die wunden,   als ouch dâ geschach.
> dâ von man die schulde   dâ ze Hagene gesach.
> (17, 1044)

> [Now it is a great marvel and frequently happens today that whenever a blood-guilty murderer is seen beside the corpse the wounds begin to bleed. This is what happened now, and Hagen stood accused of the deed.]

The moral distinctions to be drawn here are obvious: the effects of the dragon's blood mark Sîfrit as a hero forever to be admired; Sîfrit's blood just as blatantly reveals Hagen to be a criminal.

The moral differentiation blurs, however, as the narrative continues and its discursive interpretation of Hagen's actions becomes more positive than negative. When the Burgundians arrive at Etzel's court in *Aventiure* 28, for example, the Huns are as curious about Hagen as Gunther's court in *Aventiure* 3 and Prünhilt's court in *Aventiure* 7 had been about Sîfrit. And just as the Burgundians listen to Hagen's tale of Sîfrit's youth and dragon slaying in growing fear and admiration, the Huns listen to the stories of Sîfrit's killing and are eager for a glimpse of Hagen:[50]

> dô wunderte dâ zen Hiunen   vil manegen küenen man
> umbe Hagen von Tronege,   wie der wære getân.
> Durch daz man sagete mære   (des was im genuoc),
> daz er von Niderlande   Sîfriden sluoc,
> sterkest aller recken,   den Kriemhilde man.
> des wart michel vrâge   ze hove nâch Hagene getân.
> (28, 1732–33)

[. . . many a brave man among the Huns was most curious to know what
Hagen of Troneck looked like. Because of all the many tales told about
his slaying of Kriemhild's husband Siegfried of the Netherlands, the
strongest of all warriors, numerous questions were asked at court
regarding Hagen.]

The Hunnish curiosity is clearly mixed with a healthy measure of respect, and
even admiration for Hagen's ability to kill the *sterkest aller recken* "strongest of
all warriors," whatever the moral implications of the deed.

Yet the parallels between Sîfrit's actions and Hagen's do not end with the
similarities between the two killings and their immediate consequences. Sîfrit,
as we have seen, plays the role of a hero intruder three times during the first
part of the poem: seriously and openly when he arrives at Worms in *Aventiure* 3,
ironically, as the real power behind Gunther's facade on the trip to Isenstein in
Aventiure 7, and farcically in his journey to Nibelungenland in *Aventiure* 8. In
Part II of the poem, even though the Burgundians are invited guests at Etzel's
court, Hagen himself clearly considers his passage to and arrival in Hungary to
be the journey of a hero intruder,[51] and his actions may be usefully compared to
Sîfrit's in the earlier episodes.

In particular, Sîfrit's trip to Nibelungenland in *Aventiure* 8 provides a striking parallel to Hagen's encounter with the ferryman and *merwîp* in *Aventiure*
25, an episode that Gottfried Weber has described as "von der Dunkelheit und
Wildheit übernaturlicher Krafte durchzogen,"[52] beginning with Hagen's encounter
with the *merwîp* and ending with his attempt to drown the priest. The same
words could aptly describe *Aventiure* 8. Sîfrit is trying to get a thousand Nibelung
warriors to accompany him to Isenstein; to do so, he must cross a liminal boundary that separates the otherworldly realm of Nibelungenland from the everyday
world. This threshold is guarded by a giant doorkeeper who must be placated or
fought to gain entrance; the realm is overseen by the dwarf Albrîch, a powerful
and supernatural creature whose associations with the hoard and *tarnkappe* are
clear, although never explicitly defined in the text. Both are formally subject to
Sîfrit, who therefore disguises himself to avoid recognition as he indulges in a
successful, albeit playful and unnecessary, battle with them.

Hagen in *Aventiure* 25 is similarly trying to take a thousand 'Nibelung' warriors[53] to Etzel's land, but is faced with the liminal boundary of the Danube, which
functions here as a chronotopic threshold between the everyday, historical world
of Worms and the chronologically distant world of Etzel's Huns, a world which
exists, in A.T. Hatto's words, in "a distant past . . . a place grown shadowy and
remote."[54] Hagen too must deal with a recalcitrant and violent threshold guardian
in the person of the ferryman, and he too resorts to a disguise, although for precisely the opposite reasons as Sîfrit: rather than impersonating a stranger in order
to avoid recognition as a returning friend, Hagen impersonates a returning friend
in order to avoid recognition as a stranger. The resulting violence is serious rather
than slapstick, and ends in Hagen's murder of the ferryman (25, 1562).

Corresponding to the giant and Albrîch as representatives of the otherworld are the *merwîp*. Hagen's encounter with the bathing water-nixies is the only supernatural event within *Das Nibelungenlied* that is not explicitly connected with Sîfrit, a fact that in itself may indicate the underlying similarity between the two characters. The comic elements of the encounter have already been mentioned; they stand in ironic counterpoint to the *merwîp's* grim prophecy that the Burgundians' journey to Etzelnburc is destined for disaster:

> ez muoz alsô wesen,
> daz iuwer deheiner kan dâ niht genesen,
> niwan des küneges kappelân, daz ist uns wol bekant.
> der kumet gesunder widere in daz Guntheres lant.
> (25, 1542)

> [It is fated that not one of you shall survive there apart from the King's chaplain . . . as is well known to us. Only he will get back to Burgundy alive.]

Hagen's futile attempt to prove the prophecy false (and thus commit another murder) by drowning the chaplain retains its darkly humorous tone only because of the chaplain's apparent inability to be killed. In frustration, Hagen destroys the ferry once all are across the river: his gesture is not only "fatalistic,"[55] it is also a sign of Hagen's anger at his own failure to control events.

The same sort of parallel may be seen with regard to the Isenstein venture in *Aventiure* 7, where Hagen's resistance to Prünhilt's demand that the Burgundians lay aside their weapons is countered by Sîfrit's cheerful compliance. When an identical moment of 'crisis time' presents itself to Hagen at Etzel's court in *Aventiure* 28, he defies Kriemhilt's order to surrender his arms, and in so doing ensures not only that the Burgundians will be prepared for violence, but that violence will in fact erupt.

The structural parallels between the *aventiuren* serve to point up the differences as well as the similarities between Hagen and Sîfrit. Both heroes encounter threshold guardians and otherworldly creatures on their journeys, but whereas Sîfrit functions well when dealing with the liminal and supernatural, Hagen does not. Sîfrit succeeds, through his playful fights with the doorkeeper and Albrîch, in reinforcing their respect for him and gaining their assistance; he then departs with his thousand warriors to return to Isenstein. Hagen fails to gain the ferryman's support and so must kill him and play the ferryman himself for the thousand warriors, knowing he can never return. Sîfrit can surrender his weapons to Prünhilt because he knows he is both powerful enough and shrewd enough to subdue her without them; Hagen must refuse Kriemhilt's demand, since his only power lies in his willingness to allow the slaughter of thousands of men, including all the Burgundians, to thwart Kriemhilt's plans for revenge and her desire for the Nibelung hoard.

MIMETIC DESIRE AND THE HOARD

Like the figure of the dragon, the idea of a hoard of some kind is common to all four works considered in this study. In *Beowulf* and *Volsunga saga* the hero's acquisition of the hoard is a result of the dragon slaying; the treasure itself is relatively unimportant except as a measure of the dragon's avarice. In *Das Nibelungenlied*, however, the hoard has been detached from the monster and assumes a more significant role in the action of the poem. Instead of acquiring the hoard in his dragon slaying, Sîfrit obtains his treasure by force from the princes Nibelunc and Scilbunc after failing in his task of dividing it for them, even though he has already been handsomely paid for the division in the form of Nibelunc's sword Balmunc (3, 93): this story suggests that the princes (like dragons) were too avaricious to divide the gold equitably between themselves and were thus forced to resort to asking a stranger. Moreover, Sîfrit's curious inability to divide the treasure implies that the hoard should be considered as a single unit, indivisible by nature.

In itself, the hoard is made up *niht anders wan gesteine unde golt* "entirely of gems and gold" (19, 1123),[56] and comprises so much treasure that:

... zwelf kanzwägene   meiste mohten tragen
in vier tagen und nahten   von dem berge dan.
ouch muose ir ietslîcher   des tages drîstunde gân.
(12, 1122)

[It was as much as a dozen wagons fully loaded could carry away from the mountain in four days and nights coming and going thrice a day!]

The *tarnkappe*, which Sîfrit wins from Albrîch in the course of his fight with the princes (3, 97), is separable from and thus apparently not part of the hoard. Sîfrit himself seems to regard both the cloak and sword more highly than the hoard proper, as is evidenced by the fact that he keeps and uses them himself (19, 1119), but magnanimously gives the hoard to Kriemhilt as her *morgengâbe* (19, 1116).

If Sîfrit is relatively indifferent to the hoard, however, Hagen is decidedly not. He dwells upon the sheer size of the treasure when relating Sîfrit's history to Gunther (3, 92), and begins to speculate about the possibility of bringing it to Burgundy as early as *Aventiure* 12, after Prünhilt has convinced Gunther to invite Sîfrit and Kriemhilt to the festivity at Worms:

Er'n kundez niht verswenden,   unt sold er immer leben.
hort der Nibelunge   beslozzen hât sîn hant.
hey sold er komen immer   in der Bergonden lant!
(12, 774)

[Were [Sîfrit] to live for ever he could never squander all that he owns, for he holds the Nibelungs' hoard in his power. Ah me, if that were to come to Burgundy!]

Hagen's strong desire for the hoard at this point in the poem is yet another sign of his status as Sîfrit's rival and double. As Gunther's vassal, Hagen has no real need for the treasure as money, and of course even when he steals it from Kriemhilt after Sîfrit's death it technically becomes Gunther's, not his. Hagen wants the hoard in *Aventiure* 12 simply because it is Sîfrit's; his desire is of the kind René Girard has termed "mimetic," i.e., as originating in ontological rivalry rather than in the intrinsic value of the desired object itself:

> Man is subject to intense desires, though he may not know precisely for what. The reason is that he desires *being*, something he himself lacks and which some other person seems to possess. The subject thus looks to that other person to inform him of what he should desire in order to acquire that being (*VS*, 146).

Moreover, as we have seen in Chapter 1, the Indo-European dragon slaying myth can also be interpreted ontologically as an assertion of the human desire for Being as it is symbolized by the dragon's treasure. Consequently, it would seem that by desiring the hoard Hagen wants more than simply to emulate Sîfrit: he wants to acquire the sense of ontological presence that Sîfrit has apparently gained through his dragon slaying and that is exemplified by Sîfrit's understanding of and ease in dealing with the poem's otherworld and its inhabitants. The parallels between Hagen's behavior in Part II of the poem and Sîfrit's in Part I emphasize the fact that their relationship is structurally mimetic. But, as Girard points out, "mimesis coupled with desire leads automatically to conflict" (*VS*, 146), conflict that can and often does result in violence. Thus, when the quarrel between the queens threatens to degenerate into violence between the warriors loyal to each, i.e., into the kind of undifferentiated reciprocal violence that, unchecked, could destroy the Burgundian regime and society and that must therefore be averted at all costs, Hagen's mimetic desire for the hoard intersects with Sîfrit's status as a foreign and hence 'sacrificeable' guest in Worms to result in the seemingly unmotivated murder of his (retrospectively) monstrous rival and double.

Upon Sîfrit's death the hoard passes, not to Gunther or Hagen, but to Kriemhilt, who leaves it far from the reach of the Burgundians in Albrîch's care in Nibelungenland. Hagen once again expresses his desire for the hoard, counselling a reconciliation between Gunther and Kriemhilt for the sole purpose of acquiring it:

> Möht ir daz tragen an,
> daz ir iuwer swester   ze vriunde möhtet hân,
> sô kœme ze disen landen   das Nibelunges golt.
> des möht ir vil gewinnen,   würd' uns die küneginne holt.
> (19, 1107)

[If you could succeed in winning your sister's friendship . . . we could
bring Nibelung's treasure here to Burgundy. If only the Queen were well-
disposed towards us you could possess yourselves of much of it.]

Kriemhilt does bring the hoard to Burgundy, and uses it to win allies through
largesse (19, 1127) until Hagen, with Gunther's help, steals it from her (19,
1132). A new mimetic rivalry arises between Hagen and Kriemhilt, each of
whom want the hoard initially because it was once Sîfrit's, but each of whom
also, by the end of the poem, desire the hoard simply because the other, hated
rival also desires it. Neither has any desire or need for the hoard as money:
Kriemhilt, we are told, would be willing to forego the treasure entirely if she
could regain Sîfrit (19, 1126), and even after Hagen steals the hoard she still
anticipates winning new friends by distributing gold among the Huns (20, 1271).
Hagen, of course, is willing to sink the entire treasure in the Rhine simply to
keep it from Kriemhilt: *er wând' er sold' in niezen: des enkunde niht gesîn*
"[he] imagin[ed] he would make use of it some day: but this was not destined to
happen" (19, 1137). There is no question here of *dividing* or sharing the hoard
between Kriemhilt and her brothers: although gold and jewels can be shared,
the hoard as an object of all-consuming mimetic desire is indivisible, as the
princes Scilbunc and Nibelunc had already discovered in their encounter with
Sîfrit.

The conflict arising out of Hagen and Kriemhilt's mimetic desire for the
hoard quickly escalates into the ultimate Girardian nightmare of societal destruction through unstoppable, ever-escalating reciprocal violence. For, once
the hoard is indeed out of reach at the bottom of the Rhine, the desire for
violence replaces the desire for the hoard in both antagonists: "[a]t the very
height of the crisis violence becomes simultaneously the instrument, object,
and all-inclusive subject of desire" (*VS*, 144). This is why Hagen deliberately
provokes Kriemhilt by refusing to stand in her presence (29, 1781), and also
why Kriemhilt is willing to bring her young son to the feast, apparently knowing that it will incite Hagen to murder (31, 1912). Only violence can resolve the
crisis produced by mimetic desire. That violence may, however, be
"reciprocal . . . [and] wholly destructive in nature" or it may be "ritual . . . [and]
creative and protective in nature" (*VS*, 144); that is, it may be the violence of
war and blood feud, or it may be the violence of a peace-generating blood
sacrifice, retrospectively interpreted as a monster slaying.

In *Das Nibelungenlied*, nothing but a cessation of desire—for the hoard, for
violence, for ontological presence—on Hagen's side or on Kriemhilt's, can prevent the catastrophic destruction of society; no obvious scapegoat/sacrificial
victim is available upon whom the violence can be deflected. Nevertheless, the
textual hints that Kriemhilt is to be regarded as a demon, when coupled with
the presentation of Hagen as a dark hero, show the lines along which a mythic
solution to the mimetic crisis—that is, a narrative sublation of communal violence by sacrificial violence—might have been found. Kriemhilt, herself a foreign guest in Etzel's court, has already been partially reinterpreted in the text

itself as an alien outsider, as a demonic—dare one say dragonish?—intruder;
she is also Sîfrit's widow and thereby already associated with a figure whose
dragonish characteristics have been well established within the poem; moreover, her desire for the hoard mimics Hagen's and thus characterizes her as his
twin and his antagonist. Her death, followed by a retrospective narrative transformation into monstrous form, might have sufficed to avert the mimetic crisis
discursively, had *Das Nibelungenlied* been myth rather than fiction, its characters gods or demigods rather than human beings, its discourse monologic rather
than dialogic. The progressive literalization of the murders within the poem,
from the initial, wholly mythic dragon slaying by Sîfrit, tenuously connected as
it is to the apparently mimetic desire of Scilbunc and Nibelunc for the hoard, to
the second, metaphoric dragon slaying of Sîfrit by Hagen in response to the
quarrel of the queens, and finally to the sheer carnage of the mimetic conflict
between Hagen and Kriemhilt, parallels the descent of the narrative mode from
myth into fiction. Sîfrit's actions as a dragon slayer establish him as an undis-
puted and indisputable hero, with any merely human violence underlying the
story of the dragon having been entirely suppressed in the telling of the tale. By
contrast, Hagen's dark heroism in his murder of Sîfrit is contingent upon the
incomplete transformation of a political killing into a dragon slaying, a narrative stratagem that is unable to attain to a full reinterpretation of either victor or
victim in the text as we have it. Finally, the violent destruction of Burgundian
and Hunnish society in Kriemhilt's revenge admits of no strategies of sublation,
although one can see the beginnings of a discursive alternative to the violence
in the poem's representation of a heroic Hagen and a demonic Kriemhilt.

To say that Sîfrit's dragon slaying plays no significant role in *Das
Nibelungenlied* is therefore to miss the point of the Indo-European dragon myth
as it is transmuted into the socially and politically motivated fiction of the high
Middle Ages. At the heart of both the myth and the poetic fiction is the question
of how society can avoid the most destructive effects of the seemingly universal
human desire for violence, whether that violence is represented as occurring
between heroes and monsters, guests and hosts, or professional warriors dedi-
cated to the service of opposing feudal lords.

5

A Wilderness of Dragons

... there is a kind of potted history here, which suddenly bursts its boundaries and breaks into a world of mythical events and ancient, vaguely remembered customs. (Hermann Pálsson and Paul Edwards, *Legendary Fiction in Medieval Iceland*)

The final work to be considered in this study, *Þiðreks saga af Bern*, is a
thirteenth-century Norwegian translation out of German sources of a
compilation of tales and legends centered around the character of Þiðrekr
af Bern (M.H.G. Dietrich von Bern), who is a legendary hero loosely based on
the historical figure of Theodoric the Goth, ruler of Rome from 493–526.[1] The
earliest manuscript of *Þiðreks saga* dates from the middle of the thirteenth
century; the saga was most likely compiled in Norway during the reign of King
Hakon IV (1217–63), that is, sometime around the year 1250.[2] *Þiðreks saga* is
intertextually connected with both the German and Icelandic versions of the
Siegfried story: it probably had as an immediate source a written German epic
of the twelfth century which also served as a source for *Das Nibelungenlied*;[3]
additionally, a chapter of the saga has found its way verbatim into the extant
version of *Vǫlsunga saga*. Unfortunately, the literary quality of *Þiðreks saga*
pales by comparison to its more famous analogues; nevertheless, it may stand
as an example of the large number of *fornaldarsǫgur*, "sagas of ancient times,"
lygisǫgur, "lying sagas," and *riddarasǫgur* "courtly romances" in which marvels and monsters abound and dragon slaying is a common and thus not particularly significant activity of heroes.[4] W.P. Ker almost certainly had some of
these tales in mind when he spoke of the commonplace nature of dragons in the
passage cited in Chapter II with regard to *Beowulf*; these sagas contain the
"wilderness of dragons" which R.W. Chambers wanted to trade for a single
well-told story about Ingeld.[5]

It is thus not surprising that, like many of the Norse romances, *Þiðreks saga*
has not fared particularly well in the eyes of literary critics. Although it deals
with Siegfried and Dietrich, two of the great heroes of Germanic legend, the
saga does not, in Hilda Ellis' words, carry the "heroic stamp";[6] R.G. Finch calls
it an example of "the typical *fornaldarsaga* where the . . . heroic spirit degener-
ates into mere heroics and literary qualities count for little."[7] And yet the dragons and dragon slayings of *Þiðreks saga*, although pallid by comparison to
those of *Beowulf* and *Vǫlsunga saga*, are actually better conceived than many of
the monsters and monster fights found in Scandinavian romance—which is to
say that they are described in some detail, are set in at least a rudimentary

context, and have, in hindsight at any rate, some motivation for their existence.

However, these dragons carry none of the faintly numinous aura of the supernatural unknown that characterizes the *Beowulf* dragon and which is transferred in large part to Sîfrit in *Das Nibelungenlied*, nor do they embody the mythic conception of greed and esoteric wisdom that characterizes Fáfnir in *Vǫlsunga saga*. Instead, the saga's presentation of both its monsters and its heroes takes place within a new chronotopic context that implies a perception of the supernatural on the part of the saga author which is radically different from the attitudes we have previously encountered.

As we saw briefly in Chapter IV, *Þiðreks saga* takes place within a distinctive chronotope peculiar to chivalric romance, a chronotope Bakhtin describes as creating "*a miraculous world in adventure-time.*"[8] Within this chronotope, irruptions of the uncanny or the supernatural into ordinary life are 'normalized' and thus become "something generally applicable, in fact, almost ordinary. The whole world becomes miraculous."[9] It is therefore misleading to speak of an ordinary 'this world' and a supernatural 'other world' in the context of chivalric romance. Heroes are not those who, like Beowulf and Sîfrit, can most effectively deal with otherworldly incursions; rather the heroes themselves are as marvelous as the world they inhabit:

> In this world the hero is 'at home' (although he is not in his homeland); he
> is every bit as miraculous as his world. His lineage is miraculous, as are
> the conditions of his birth, his childhood and youth, his physique, and so
> forth. He is flesh of the flesh and bone of the bone of this miraculous
> world, its best representative.[10]

The Girardian scenario of the monstrous double is likewise out of place here, for just as there is no duality of worlds, there is no duality of hero and double: the monsters are not slain in order to sublate and thereby conceal-while-revealing a narrative of communal violence; rather, "in this miraculous world heroic deeds are performed by which the heroes *glorify themselves*, and *glorify others* (their liege lord, their lady)."[11] Such a change in chronotope mandates a concomitant change in the function of the dragon. Because dragon slaying has traditionally been the preserve of only the most exceptional heroes, glorifying them as no other action could, in the romances the major function of a dragon slaying becomes, as Kathryn Hume has pointed out, simply a means to distinguish a saga's greatest hero from other, lesser heroic figures.[12]

But this function presents a problem in *Þiðreks saga af Bern*, since by this measurement the saga's account of Siegfried, who is here called *Sigurðr sveinn*, or 'Young Sigurðr,' and who is the most famous dragon slayer of Germanic legend, could easily overshadow that of the saga's titular hero, Þiðrekr. This problem is solved in part by making Sigurðr sveinn Þiðrekr's vassal, but also and more effectively by giving Þiðrekr two dragons—as well as three baby monsters—to conquer for Sigurðr sveinn's one, by making those dragons more powerful and dangerous than the one Sigurðr kills, by turning Þiðrekr into a more courtly hero than Sigurðr, and finally by playing down the heroism involved in dragon slaying in general and in Sigurðr sveinn's dragon slaying in particular.

"A MIRACULOUS WORLD IN ADVENTURE TIME"

The first indication of how the saga audience is expected to view the extraordinary world of *Þiðreks saga af Bern* comes quite explicitly in the saga's *Formáli* or Prologue. The anonymous author of the prologue takes great care to set the scene of the narrative, first in a known historical context, and then in the context of what might be termed the belief structures of his audience. He is careful to assure his readers that the events of the saga, fantastic though they may be, are nonetheless to be believed, given the time of their occurrence, the nature of the protagonists, and the proof of the saga's veracity in old poems and stories.

The saga takes place, he tells us, *í þann tíma, er Konstantinus konungr inn mikil var andaðr* "at the time when King Konstantin the Great had died," and when Christianity was still struggling against the Arian heresy (*Formáli* 5).[13] Such comparative historical precision is striking when juxtaposed to the mythic time of *Vǫlsunga saga*, the hazy *on geardagum* "days of yore" of *Beowulf*, and the *Nibelungenlied*'s vague reference to *alten mæren* "old tales." It implies a concern for a rationalized setting on the part of the prologue's author which has been missing in the works we have looked at so far, and which in turn reflects an uneasiness about the credibility of the saga contents which the remainder of the *Formáli* makes explicit.

Í þann tíma, we are told, human beings with superhuman abilities were still alive. The author's explanation for this is a well-known medieval topos: after Noah's flood, *váru menn svá stórir ok sterkir sem risar* "men were as large and as strong as giants" (*Formáli* 5), but as time went on the human race diminished, leaving only a few men whose size and strength could match that of their ancestors. Such men could easily wield weapons so large and heavy *at ekki fekk ein ósterkr maðr magn til upp at valda af jörðunni* "that a weak man would not have the strength to lift it from the ground" (*Formáli* 6), and therefore these heroes were often able to kill hundreds of ordinary men single-handedly and to strike so hard that their swords cut through iron (*Formáli* 6). Only foolish people, the prologue's author continues, will doubt something merely because they haven't seen it themselves; a wise man will recognize that his own experience is limited and will accept some things that are beyond his immediate understanding. After all, *þat þykkir í öðru landi undarligt, er í öðru er títt* "what seems in one land wondrous is ordinary in another" (*Formáli* 7).

If this is not enough to settle any doubts about the saga's credibility, there is also the evidence of older sagas and poetry to consider. The same tale is told by the Norwegians, Danes, and Swedes, albeit with some changes (*Formáli* 3–4), but this version is based, we are told, on the telling of the Germans, and the proof of its veracity can be found both in the uniformity of the story throughout Germany and in the fact that it is based on ancient poetry:

> Ok þó at þú takir einn mann ór hverri borg um allt Saxland, þá munu þessa sögu allir á eina leið segja, en því valda þeira in fornu kvæði (*Formáli* 4).

> [Even if you were to take one man from each town in all of Saxony, they would all tell the story the same way, and this is because of their old songs.]

Obviously, the prologue's author is greatly concerned that the saga be credible—or the audience credulous—and this in turn may suggest that he assumes the events of the saga will not easily be believed, and that the question of belief is important. As Michael Curschmann has pointed out, the prologue is remarkable for "the degree of detachment, the intellectual distance [it exhibits] from the very tradition on which the saga itself rests . . . we are in the presence of self-conscious writing".[14] One of the major components of this self-consciousness is the attention paid to the problem of audience reception, a matter which takes on new importance in light of the avowed purpose of the story telling. *Þiðreks saga*, although it uses as its source material the stories and legends of Germanic tradition, is not a paraphrase of archaic material in the manner of *Vǫlsunga saga*, nor is it a reworking of such material to create new literature which has contemporary thematic or mythic significance *à la Beowulf* or *Das Nibelungenlied*. Instead, *Þiðreks saga* is a compilation of tales collected and retold purely for their entertainment value. As the prologue points out, *sagnaskemmtan eðr kvæða er með engum fékostnaði eðr mannhættu* "the entertainment of tales or poems involves neither expense nor danger to life" (*Formáli* 7).

It is only when stories like those of *Þiðreks saga* are offered as pure entertainment that the question of audience belief, or more precisely of the tale's credibility, becomes important.[15] For without the larger themes stated or implied in such works as *Beowulf* or *Das Nibelungenlied*—themes that provide a truth-value which arises from, but is not wholly dependent upon, the events described—all that remains are the adventures themselves. And what good are adventure stories if they are not only untrue, but unbelievable? We are far from a Sidneyesque 'Defence of Poesy' here; the prologue's author can only insist that the events of *Þiðreks saga* are not as preposterous as they first appear, and thus may be, indeed ought to be, believed.[16]

Yet such insistence upon literal belief brings problems of its own, for in thirteenth century Europe the supernatural was not an unknown quantity, but existed in an established Christian framework which demanded adherence to orthodox belief, not mere credulity. The authors of the romances wanted to provide adventures, and what better focus for an adventure than a dragon? Yet at the same time they most often wished to avoid evoking the Christian complex of ideas and themes which could surround the figure of the dragon in medieval Europe. In Kathryn Hume's words,

> What had been a potent sublayer in the better *fornaldarsögur* and in some *íslendingasögur* [sagas of Icelanders] could not, as time went on, be handled in detail without undermining the adventures themselves, for in a Christian context, the goals of the heroes might have to be condemned. Viewed theologically, the eagerness of many heroes to lay hands on the dragon's treasure is *cupiditas*.[17]

Therefore the compiler of *Þiðreks saga*—who may well have been a cleric himself[18]—does not for the most part attempt to touch the actual belief structures of his audience; he tries only to provide the fantastic without straining the common sense of his readers too severely. Like a modern science fiction or fantasy writer, he includes only what might have existed or occurred, long ago or far away.

One cannot, however, automatically assume that the attitude towards the saga and its marvels which is shown by the author of the prologue is the same attitude which prevails throughout the saga itself, because some evidence exists to suggest that the prologue's author may not be the author of the saga.[19] How then are the marvellous characters and events of *Þiðreks saga* actually presented within the story?

To begin with, there is no indication within the saga that the marvels are actually miracles, i.e., that divine intervention plays a direct role in human affairs. Although extraordinary characters may claim elves or *sjókonur* 'mermaids' as ancestors, they are never literally descended from the gods, as are, for example, the Vǫlsungar of *Vǫlsunga saga*, who are ultimately descendents of Óðinn. The saga's major characters are conceived of as (Arian) Christians, but while they may occasionally swear by the name of God or invoke his aid, there is in fact little more than surface Christianity in *Þiðreks saga*: its heroes are interested in glory, honor, and worldly power, and these aims are neither condemned nor compared unfavorably to the theologically more important Christian virtues and aspirations. Reception theorist Hans Robert Jauss makes a similar distinction in describing the 'wonderful' elements of Arthurian romance:

> The wonderful in the Arthurian novel stands in direct opposition to the wonderful in Christian legend: in the former, an event in the real world is not a sign of a transcendent, higher reality. Indeed, whatever happens in the *aventure* unfolds according to the principle underlying the fairy tale, where the wonderful...no longer represents an exception but the rule.[20]

In addition, truly magical objects are either excluded from the saga or rationalized: neither the *ægishjálmr* of *Vǫlsunga saga* nor the *tarnkappe* of *Das Nibelungenlied* exist here; Velent has a *fjaðrham* "feather-cloak" which enables him to fly (chap. 77), but he constructs it through technical skill, not magic. Similarly, the best weapons, such as Sigurðr sveinn's sword Gramr, are the best because they have been forged by the most skillful smiths rather than through any specifically magical properties.

Of course many characters, *berserkir* and trolls, elves and *sjókonur*, are marvelous in their own right, and there is no lack of these in the saga. Þiðrekr

and Hildibrandr fight and kill a *berserkr*, Grímr, who has the strength of twelve
men, as well as his wife, Hildr, who is *fjǫlkunnig ok mikit troll í sinni náttúru*
"skilled at magic and had much troll in her nature" (chap. 17). Högni's father is
an elf, Velent's grandmother a *sjókona*. But these characters are simply extraordinary creatures living in a marvelous world; they are not otherworldly or supernatural. Like Hildr's status as a troll, their abilities are 'in their natures,'
although they might not be natural to any of the other characters. Herein lies
the difference between the chronotopic structure of *Vǫlsunga saga*, which
correponds to Bakhtin's category of the "adventure novel of everyday life," and
that of *Þiðreks saga*, a "miraculous world in adventure time": in the former no
distinction between natural and supernatural is made; in the latter all the characters are 'natural,' albeit fantastic, while the truly supernatural stands outside
the saga in the realm of theology, which the saga author does not try to enter.

The one exception to this rule is the mysterious black horse which appears,
saddled and ready, to carry Þiðrekr off to his death at the end of the saga (chap.
438). Unlike the other extraordinary creatures of the saga, this horse is clearly
demonic, a Satanic intruder from the otherworld of the Christian supernatural.
Þiðrekr is unable to move to dismount once he realizes his mistake in riding the
horse; his hunting dogs refuse to follow the creature. His only chance at salvation is a religious hope born of his calling on God and the virgin Mary for help.
But this is the end of the saga, as it is the end of Þiðrekr, and the horse,
otherworldly as it is, constitutes an anomaly, born of a different and singular
chronotope that contrasts sharply with the temporal/spatial structure within which
the rest of the fabulous creatures and events of the tale have their existence.

Because the romance chronotope 'normalizes' the marvelous elements of
the saga, its extraordinary objects and characters frequently take on a curiously
flat and often crude quality, even although they are intended to arouse wonder
and to intensify the excitement of the adventures. The dragons Þiðrekr encounters are large, unusual animals; Sigurðr sveinn's dragon, although as in *Vǫlsunga
saga* originally a transformed man, seems to retain no human characteristics.
The *sjókonur* Högni (M.H.G. Hagen) meets, obviously related to the *merwîp* of
Das Nibelungenlied, lose the mythic significance as liminal guardians of the
otherworld they carried in the German poem: Högni, elf's son that he is, quickly
elicits the information he wants, then kills the *sjókonur* without a second thought
(chap. 364). Even the hoard, divorced from both *tarnkappe* and *ægishjálmr* and
no longer the object of mimetic desire, loses its indivisible integrity and is here
nothing but money which Attila can count by reckoning up its sources:

> Ek veit, frú, at Sigurðr sveinn átti mikit gull, þat fyrst, er hann tók undan
> þeim mikla dreka, er hann hafði drepit, næst þat, er hann fekk í hernaði, ok
> þar með þat, er hans faðir hafði átt, Sigmundr konungr (chap. 359).

> [I know, lady, that Young Sigurd owned much money. First there was what
> he took away from the giant dragon when he killed it. Next there was what
> he gained in raiding, and finally that which his father King Sigmund had
> left him.]

The hoard as such plays very little role in the saga, and none at all in the dragon slaying. The first mention of the Niflung (Nibelung) hoard, in fact, comes almost as an afterthought, long after Sigurðr sveinn's actual fight with his dragon (chap. 359).

Whatever significance the dragons of *Þiðreks saga* have will thus stem from their nature as extraordinary creatures at home in an extraordinary world: they are not Christian allegorical figures, nor representatives of a world of *draconitas* inalterably opposed to *humanitas*, nor the retrospectively conceived monstrous doubles of the saga's heroes. Indeed, these dragons do not even seem to be the 'doubles' of each other, for there is clearly more than one type of dragon in the saga, and each dragon in its turn exemplifies a different tradition of *draconitas*.

"A WILDERNESS OF DRAGONS"

A conception of the dragon as the most powerful and fearsome creature on earth is apparently the only feature that unites all the dragons of *Þiðreks saga*, and this feature spills over into a number of allusions to dragons outside of the saga's narration of specific dragon fights. Þiðrekr's vassal Studas Studasson, for example, is said to resemble a dragon in personality and habits, and he therefore:

> Týnt hefir hann sínu nafni réttu, því at einn ormr heitir svá ok er grimmari en aðrir ormar, ok við hann eru allir ormar hræddir, þeir sem nær koma hans byggð. (chap. 18)

> [lost his real name and was called Heimir, because one particular dragon has that name and he is more vicious than all other dragons, and all other dragons are afraid of him if they come near his lair.]

Viðga wears a helmet with a dragon decoration, *þat merkir kapp Viðga ok grimmleik hans* "showing [his] bravery and his grim courage" (chap. 81); Ekka has a sword welded in such a way that:

> Ef þú setr odd hans niðr á jörð, þá sýnist sem ormr renni frá oddinum ok upp til hjaltanna, litr sem gull. En ef þú heldr honum upp, þá sýnist sem sá inn sami ormr renni undan hjöltunum ok upp á oddinn. Þat bragðar allt, sem kvikt sé, sá ormr. (chap. 98)

> [if you put the point on the ground, then it looks as if a dragon were running up from the ground to the hilt, bright as gold. If you hold it up, then it seems that a dragon is running up from the hilt toward the point. The dragon moves as if it were alive.]

A good number of characters are said to lose their lives to dragons, among them King Ísungr and his sons (chap. 353), Þéttleifr the Dane (chap. 354), and King Hernið (chap. 417). Moreover, particularly ferocious fighters may also be termed 'dragons' metaphorically, as when Elsungr refers to Samson as *inn digrhálsaði ormr* "a thick-necked dragon" (chap. 12).

In each of these cases, the term used for 'dragon' is the Norse word *ormr*, which more usually carries the denotation 'serpent,'[21] but which as we have seen in *Vǫlsunga saga* can also refer to a dragon. Those dragons in *Þiðreks saga* which are consistently called *ormr* seem to be particularly serpentine in character; i.e. they apparently lack wings and do not belch fire, although they may be poisonous. The Latin derived term *dreki* also occurs in the saga, but most often as part of the compound *flugdreki* "flying dragon," and appears to designate a slightly different type of creature: these dragons are winged, clawed, predatory, and dangerous, yet they are neither poisonous nor fiery.

Some characters are able to change themselves into flying dragons at will. Queen Ostasia of Vilkinaland

> [s]vá mikit gerði hún af sér í fjölkunngi ok trollskap, at hún sciddi til sín margs donar dýr, leóna ok björnu ok flugdreka stóra. . . . Svá segir í kvæðum þýðerskum, at hennar herr væri líkr fjöndum sjálfum. Hún sjálf var ok sem einn flugdreki. (chap. 352)

> [carried out such great spells of magic and trollship that she conjured up many kinds of beasts, lions and bears, and great flying dragons. . . . It is said in the poems of the Germans that her army was like the devil himself. She herself was like a flying dragon.]

Ostasia's dragons and dragon-shape are presented as if they are to be considered on the one hand as parallel to 'real,' naturally occurring animals such as lions and bears, and on the other hand as if they are supernatural, the product of magic and *trollskapr* "trollship." This dual nature of Ostasia's dragons splits with regard to the more important dragons in the saga: those slain by Þiðrekr are predatory animals carrying no hint of magic about them, while Sigurðr sveinn's dragon, like the *Vǫlsunga saga*'s Fáfnir, is a product of magical shapeshifting.

The first dragon to appear in *Þiðreks saga* is encountered by Þiðrekr and his companion Fasold as it carries its human prey, a knight named Sistram, off to its lair. The two heroes have just ridden out of a forest when the monster makes its dramatic entrance:

> Í munni sér hefir hann einn mann ok hefir sólgit fotunum ok allt upp undir hendir. En ór munninum út stóð höfuðit ok herðarnar. Hendrnar váru í neðra keftinum, ok enn lifir maðrinn (chap. 105).

> [He held a man in his mouth and had swallowed his legs and everything up to his arms. The head and shoulders still protruded from the mouth. The hands were on the lower jaw, and the man was still alive.]

This dragon is described as *einn mikinn flugdreka . . . bæði langr ok digr* "a huge flying dragon . . . both long and stout" (chap. 105). Despite its size, however, it is not quite large or strong enough to fly while carrying a human victim: when Þiðrekr and Fasold first see it, the dragon is half-flying, half-running, *ok hvervitna sem klær hans taka jörðina, þá var sem með inu hvassasta járni væri höggvit* "and everywhere his claws touched the earth it was as if the sharpest iron had struck it" (chap. 105). Later the narrator explains that the dragon is severely hampered by the weight of the man and his weapons, so much so that *komst hann eigi á loft at fljúga ok eigi sik at verja, svá sem hann væri lauss* "he could not get aloft to fly or defend himself, as he would have if he had been free" (chap. 105). No mention is made of fiery breath or even poison—if the dragon's victim dies, he will have been crushed to death in the monster's jaws.

The two heroes have a difficult time with the dragon from the start, for although Þiðrekr's sword is sharp enough to wound the monster *nokkut* "somewhat" (chap. 105), Fasold's sword is virtually useless. Ironically—since they are supposed to be rescuing him—Sistram comes to their aid. He instructs them to reach down into the monster's jaws and draw out his (Sistram's) sword, which he knows has a good chance of cutting through the dragon's hide, and then tells them exactly how and where to strike:

> Högg varliga. Mínir fætr eru harðla langt komnir niðr í háls drekans, ok skaltu varast þat, at eigi vil ek hljóta sár af sjálfs mín sverði (chap. 105).

> [Strike carefully. My legs are very far down into the dragon's throat, and you should be careful since I do not want to receive a wound from my own sword.]

Sistram not only retains his presence of mind while in the dragon's maw, he is positively chatty. His calm explanations and suggestions contrast humorously with the grim silence of his rescuers, although it is finally difficult to say whether or not the juxtaposition was intended to be funny.[22] In any case, the tale is constructed in such a way that the most memorable human character is the victim Sistram,[23] not Þiðrekr, nor even Fasold, who seems to show the most courage in that it is he who retrieves Sistram's sword from the monster's jaws. Additionally, it is Sistram who adopts a dragon as his heraldic device (chap. 178), although it is more usual for the dragon slayer to do so.

The vocabulary used to describe the dragon throughout the episode is for the most part straightforward, yet certain ambiguities remain. The dragon is consistently referred to as *dreki* or *flugdreki*, never as *ormr*. It is also called, by Sistram, *andskoti* "adversary, opponent" (chap. 105);[24] later, Sistram thanks his rescuers for saving him from *inum illa fjánda* "the evil fiend" (chap. 106). Both words can signify demonic opponents, but neither need do so: *andskoti* is sometimes used in reference to Satan, while *fjánda*, cognate with Modern German *feind* 'enemy' and Modern English 'fiend,' could have developed the same demonic connotations the English word carries. Words with specifically Christian associations like *andskoti* and *fjánda* most likely became standard terminology for describing dragons as a result of the common medieval equation of dragons with the devil, and their usage here might tend to increase Þiðrekr's prestige by a subtle analogy with hagiographic dragon tales, even though these dragons behave like animals, not devils. Neither word is used to describe Reginn,

Sigurðr sveinn's dragon, who, although he is *allra manna verstr*, "the worst of all men" (chap. 163) seems to carry no demonic connotations.

Obviously, if one function of dragon slaying in *Þiðreks saga* is to distinguish the saga's greatest heroes, the Sistram episode is no way to upgrade Þiðrekr's status to match that of Sigurðr sveinn. However, his second dragon slaying presents Þiðrekr in a much better light, and it is accordingly prepared for and developed more fully than the first dragon episode.[25] This dragon is stronger and more dangerous than Sistram's monster, a fact graphically impressed upon the audience by the dragon's earlier slaying of King Herniðr, who has foolishly gone into his forest alone to attack the monster and *annathvárt vinna frægð eða fá bana* "either gain fame or be killed" (chap. 417). Unlike Sistram, who had been taken unawares by his dragon while he slept, Herniðr knows that a dragon inhabits the forest, and he is armed and ready to encounter it. But whereas Sistram's dragon had scarcely been able to fly while carrying its prey, this dragon easily lifts Herniðr *ok flygr með hann í einn djúpan dal, ok þar er eitt berg ok einn hellir mikill* "and carrie[s] him to a deep valley where there [is] a mountain with a large cave" (chap. 417). In the cavern three young dragons eat the king's corpse while the adult dragon, far from coveting the gold and silver-plated armor, tidily *rótar í brott öllum hans vápnum ór sínu bæli* "rooted out the armor from its den" (chap. 417).

In itself, the second dragon seems much like the first: it has claws and wings, but does not seem to breathe fire, and like other animals it apparently cannot speak. Its main concern is feeding its young, and it accordingly hunts in the same forest as King Herniðr and, later, Þiðrekr. It is called both *dreki* and *ormr*, and the young dragons are referred to once, significantly, as *dýranna* "animals" (chap. 418).

When Þiðrekr encounters the dragon, the monster is fighting a lion. This is a common enough type-scene in the *riddarasǫgur* and owes its existence primarily to Norse translations of Chrétien de Troyes' *Yvain*.[26] Usually, however, when the knight enters the fray on the side of the lion, together they are able to defeat the serpent/dragon, and the lion becomes the constant companion and champion of the knight. One might expect something of the sort to occur here, especially when Þiðrekr remembers that he carries a lion as his heraldic device and decides to intervene, even calling upon God to aid him in the battle (chap. 418).

But Þiðrekr is not carrying his best sword, and the sword he does have fails him: the blade breaks off at the hilt, while the dragon, lifting the lion in its mouth, kills it. As Þiðrekr prepares to defend himself with *eitt mikit tré* "a large tree," which he has torn up by the roots, the dragon wraps its tail around him and flies off to its lair, carrying both Þiðrekr and the lion's body. There the lion functions as a distraction for the baby dragons, which devour it and go to sleep, leaving Þiðrekr unharmed. Thus he is able to escape long enough to find Herniðr's sword, which he uses to destroy the monsters.

The saga author describes at some length the 'hoard' Þiðrekr finds: Herniðr's jewelled and plated armor and his horse, which Þiðrekr must tame before he can ride. He successfully subdues the horse, even though the saga's author states hyperbolically that *þetta máttu eigi tólf menn gera at taka þenna hest* "twelve men would not have been able to take that horse" (chap. 419). The parallels here are not with the emblematic type-scene which began the dragon fight, but rather with the dragon slaying of Sigurðr sveinn, narrated earlier in the saga.

Sigurðr Sveinn's Dragon

As in *Vǫlsunga saga*, young Sigurðr's dragon slaying in *Þiðreks saga af Bern* functions as a rite of passage, separating his life into a distinct *before*—comprising his birth and the circumstances surrounding his parents' death, his early childhood in the forest and his adolescence as an apprentice smith—and an *after*, his adult life as a hero and knight. The differences between the two dragon fights (like the differences from Sîfrit's dragon fight in *Das Nibelungenlied*) stem largely from the sagas' differing accounts of his youth. In both sagas he is orphaned, and in both he is raised by a smith. But whereas in *Vǫlsunga saga* he is fully aware of his parentage and is fostered by Reginn as part of his education, in *Þiðreks saga* he has no idea of who he is or who his father is, and he meets the smith, here called Mímir, by chance. Both his birth and his upbringing before meeting Mímir are marvelous in a way that owes more to folktales and *Märchen* than to heroic poetry: born in a forest to a treacherously disgraced and dying mother, he is placed in a *glerpott* "glass vessel" (chap. 160), which is then accidentally kicked into a river. The jar drifts downstream, breaks open, and young Sigurðr, who in the manner of many folk heroes has been growing larger by the minute, is rescued by a hind, which suckles him with her own young (chap. 162).[27] A year or so later, when Sigurðr sveinn is as large as a boy three times his age, Mímir finds him in the forest, naked and speechless, and decides to adopt him (chap. 164), naming him, in what must have been a careless conflation of source materials, 'Sigfreðr,' although this name occurs only three times within the text (chap. 164).

Sigurðr sveinn's liminal status in the saga is thus almost a literalization of Sigurðr's characterization of himself in *Vǫlsunga saga* as a noble beast (*gǫfugt dýr*) with neither father nor mother: his second, parentless birth from the *glerpott* and his upbringing as a hart in the forest place him effectively on the margins of human society both literally and metaphorically. He is also marginalized by his behavior in Mímir's smithy, for as a boy Sigurðr is uncontrollable, sullen, and violent. Mímir's apprentices are afraid of him, and with good reason: at the age of nine he beats Ekkihnrðr, the oldest of the apprentices, and drags him out of the smithy by the hair (chap. 165). His enormous strength bars him from ever becoming a great smith like his master: when he strikes the iron, he breaks the anvil-stone and drives the anvil into the ground. One is reminded of the 'wildness' of Sîfrit stripped of all its playfulness and instead acted out with deadly seriousness.

Mímir, as one familiar with *Vǫlsunga saga* would expect, has a brother, here, again perhaps through a confusion of sources, named Reginn:

> Hann var mikill fyrir sér ok allra manna verstr, ok honum var þat ok goldit, at hann fekk swá miklar gerningar ok kynsl, at hann varð at ormi. Ok nu gerðist svá, at hann var allra orma mestr ok verstr, ok nú vill hann hvern mann drepa, nema vel er hann við bróður sinn . . . (chap. 163).

> [He was very strong and the worst of all men. This was repaid him in that he took so much to sorcery and magic that he became a dragon. He was the greatest and the worst of all dragons and he set out to kill any man he met, except for his brother.]

This description is somewhat reminiscent of the description of Fáfnir in *Vǫlsunga saga*, who is called *miklu mestr ok grimmastr* "the largest and grimmest" of his brothers and who of course also transforms himself into a dragon. But Fáfnir is not said to be particularly friendly with his brother, and rather than wanting to kill every man, Fáfnir *vildi sitt eitt kálla láta allt þat er var* "wanted everything to be called his." No mention is made in *Þiðreks saga* of greed for gold being a motive in Reginn's transformation into a dragon; in fact, a hoard as such is not mentioned until after Sigurðr sveinn's death. And, most important of all, unlike Fáfnir, Reginn does not speak in the saga, although he apparently retains the ability to understand human language.

But if Reginn is different from Fáfnir in some ways, he also differs from the two "natural" dragons Þiðrekr encounters in the saga. Unlike those monsters (but like Fáfnir), Reginn does not appear to fly nor even to have wings. He is never referred to as *dreki*, always as *ormr* or *linnormr*. He seems less powerful than the flying monsters and his attack appears to present a somewhat smaller danger to Sigurðr sveinn than the dragons encountered in the rest of the saga. Nevertheless, he is intelligent in a way that Þiðrekr's monsters are not: his motivation in attacking Sigurðr sveinn is not simple hunger; he is acting on his brother Mímir's orders to kill the boy.

On his side, Sigurðr sveinn expresses three different motives for killing Reginn: self defense, a desire to prove himself as a warrior, and hunger, since he has in one day already eaten the food Mímir told him should last at least nine (chap. 166). Reginn himself is quickly dispatched: Sigurðr takes *it mesta tré* "the largest beam" (chap. 166) from his fire and clubs the dragon to death. Remembering his hunger, he decides to cook and eat the monster. When he burns his hand in the hot broth, he puts his finger into his mouth and, as in *Vǫlsunga saga*, finds himself able to understand the language of the birds, who tell him that the dragon was Mímir's brother and advise him to kill the smith (chap. 166). Additionally, in a conflation of the various motifs of the Siegfried story, Sigurðr sveinn bathes in the dragon's blood, thus turning his skin horn-hard except between the shoulder blades. He then returns to Mímir's smithy, carrying the dragon's decapitated head instead of a hoard of gold (chap. 166). In fact, if Sigurðr sveinn gains anything resembling a hoard as a result of his dragon slaying, it consists of the horse Grani and the armor and sword that Mímir gives him, in part to atone for his own role in the dragon's attack, in part to appease the anger of his dangerous foster son:

> Ek mun gefa þér hjálm einn ok einn skjöld ok eina brynju. Þau vápn hefi ek gert Hertnið í Hólmgarði, ok eru allra vápna bezt. Ok einn hest vil ek gefa þér, er heitir Grani, sá er í stóði Brynhildar, ok eitt sverð, heitir Gramr; þat er allra sverða bezt (chap. 167).

> [I shall give you a helmet and a shield and a byrnie. The weapons I have made for Hertnid in Holmgard [Novgorod], they are the best of weapons. And I shall give you a horse named Grani from Brynhild's stud farm and a sword named Gram that is the best of swords.]

But if Mímir expects to buy his own safety through these gifts, he is sadly mistaken: Sigurðr sveinn accepts them, arms himself, then draws the sword and kills the smith (chap. 167).

In all of this, one can dimly see the remnants of the mythic significance the dragon slaying exhibits in other versions of the Siegfried story: Sigurðr sveinn, like Sîfrit, demonstrates unquestionably 'dragonish' behavior in his actions toward the other apprentices, toward Mímir, and even toward Reginn himself. Like Sîfrit, and like Sigurðr in *Vǫlsunga saga*, he internalizes the dragon's characteristics, here by both eating the monster's body and bathing in its blood. Nonetheless, Reginn and Sigurðr sveinn are not mythic doubles and the dragon slaying is not an instance of Girardian sacred violence, for the killing does not take place within a context of incipient reciprocal violence that threatens to destroy a community, as a substitute for and sublation of the violence that is retrospectively cast as a dragon battle. This dragon slaying occurs simply as part of an abortive attempt to rid Mímir of an unruly apprentice; Sigurðr sveinn's self defense is no more than one would expect under the circumstances.

Nor is Sigurðr sveinn's dragon slaying portrayed, as Sigurðr's is in *Vǫlsunga saga*, as an ontological assertion of his own humanity against the monstrosity of the dragon and thus a symbolic metamorphosis, a (re)birth from his liminal status as a child/beast to the fully human status of an adult warrior. While indeed marking Sigurðr sveinn's passage from a liminal childhood to a heroic manhood, the dragon slaying in *Þiðreks saga* serves mainly to provide a reason for young Sigurðr to leave Mímir's smithy and an opportunity for the penniless apprentice to gain the horse and armor necessary for his further exploits.

Sigurðr sveinn's arrival at Brynhildr's city to claim the horse Grani (chap. 168), although clearly an example of the hero-intruder theme discussed by W.T.H. Jackson and recognizably parallel to Sîfrit's arrival in Worms in the eighth *aventiure* of *Das Nibelungenlied*,[28] has no importance in the overall plot or structure of the saga beyond Sigurðr's acquisition of a horse to match the one Þiðrekr found as part of his 'dragon hoard.' This is true even though Sigurðr sveinn actually breaks down the iron gates of the city and needlessly kills seven knights before Brynhildr ends the violence by welcoming him despite his behavior (chap. 168). In *Das Nibelungenlied* Sîfrit challenges Gunther to a duel for Worms; his arrival is a political and military threat to the prevailing regime that is averted only by Sîfrit's meekness when he remembers his love for Kriemhilt. By contrast, the violence Sigurðr sveinn exhibits is in keeping with his childish temper tantrums at Mímir's smithy: it is crude, unexpected, and entirely gratuitous. It functions merely to demonstrate Sigurðr sveinn's extraordinary strength and to add one more marvel to his list of accomplishments.

By this time at least some of the parallels between Sigurðr sveinn's dragon slaying and that of Þiðrekr should be apparent. Both encounter dragons while alone in a forest; Sigurðr sveinn has no sword, while Þiðrekr's sword breaks, forcing each hero to defend himself with a large (*mesta* or *mikit*) *tré* 'tree, log;' neither obtains a traditional dragon's hoard, but instead each receives armor, a sword, and a horse as a result of killing the dragon. Each hero needs to tame the horse before he can ride it: Þiðrekr manages to subdue his horse by the unlikely expedient of tripping it (chap. 419), even though we are told hyperbolically that twelve men would have been unable to capture the horse; Brynhildr actually sends twelve men out to bring Grani to Sigurðr sveinn, but they fail (chap. 168). Sigurðr then tries alone, and Grani, seemingly recognizing his master, obediently comes *at móti honum* "to meet him" (chap. 168).[29] In addition, Sigurðr sveinn gains certain `dragonish' characteristics as a result of his dragon slaying, the ability to understand the language of birds and his horn-hard skin. For his part, Þiðrekr also exhibits at least one dragonish trait: we are told that Þiðrekr becomes so angry in his battle with Högni *at eldr flýgr af hans munni* "that fire flew out of his mouth" (chap. 398), so much fire that Högni is forced to remove his armor and surrender rather than burn.[30]

The formal parallels between the episodes would indicate that the two dragon slayings are themselves to be considered parallel and equivalent, or at least comparable. If anything, Þiðrekr appears as the greater hero, in part because the saga gives much more space and attention to his adventure (cp. almost three pages to Sigurðr sveinn's one). In addition, his motive in helping the lion is the more honorable of the two; his method, using Herniðs sword instead of a club, is the more knightly; and his accomplishment, performed in the dragon's own lair and including the three young dragons as well as the large one, is the more prestigious.

But if a comparison between Þiðrekr and Sigurðr sveinn is implicit in the two dragon slayings, that comparison is made explicit in chapters 219–22, in which Sigurðr and Þiðrekr fight in single combat for three days—a fight which is undertaken more as a contest of skill than as mortal battle. The two are evenly matched in the duel, even given Sigurðr sveinn's obvious advantage of horn-hard skin. As long as Þiðrekr fights with Ekkisax, his own sword, the outcome seems likely to be delayed indefinitely; it is only with Viðga's sword Mímungr that Þiðrekr can even hope to wound Sigurðr (chap. 221), a fact Sigurðr is apparently aware of, since he insists that Þiðrekr swear an oath not to fight with Mímungr (chap. 222). Þiðrekr nevertheless does use Mímungr on the third day of the duel, cleverly wording his oath to deceive Sigurðr: driving the sword into the earth past the point and letting its hilt rest against him, he swears

> at eigi veit hann Mímungs odd fyrir ofan jörð ok eigi veit hann hans meðalkafla í nokkurs manns hendi (chap. 222).
>
> [that he did not know of Mímung's point being above the earth and he did not know of any man's hand being on its hilt.]

Sigurðr is satisfied with the oath and the combat resumes until he finds himself wounded five times in short order. Realizing that he is indeed outmatched, he surrenders his weapons and himself to Þiðrekr (chap. 222). Although at this point in the saga Þiðrekr has yet to slay his second dragon, the import of the scene is clear: despite Sigurðr sveinn's accomplishment of killing a dragon in his youth, he is and will remain a secondary hero within the saga. If Þiðrekr has not yet equalled or surpassed Sigurðr's remarkable deeds, it is only a matter of time before he does so.

To slay a dragon has traditionally been the greatest accomplishment of only the greatest heroes. This single deed wins everlasting fame and honor for anyone who can perform it: traditionally, it gives Sigurðr his epithet of *Fáfnisbani* 'Fáfnir's bane' and ensures that

> hans nafn gengr í öllum tungum fyrir norðan Grikklandshaf, ok svá mun vera, meðan veröld stendr (chap. 185).[31]
>
> [his name is known in all tongues north of the Greek Sea, and will be known as long as the world lasts.]

If the name of Sigurðr sveinn is not to overshadow that of Þiðrekr af Bern in his own saga, then not only must Þiðrekr accomplish the same feat more heroically and more often, but the deed itself must be diminished in significance, played down so that Þiðrekr's life and legend can assume paramount importance. A dragon slaying must become simply one heroic accomplishment among many, not the heroic measure par excellence. In *Þiðreks saga af Bern*, as the dragons die, *draconitas* as a concept suffers what is nearly its own death blow. Its echoes remain in the remnants of a greater tradition of heroic literary motifs, as well as in the linguistic and emblematic reminders that dragons in another tradition can be demonic as well as draconic. Not until the nineteenth century in Wagnerian opera will a new dragon and a new Siegfried arise to rival the old.

6

Conclusion

One would like to say 'Dragons will be dragons' and be done with it.
(Howell D. Chickering, *Beowulf*)

What, then, remains to be said about the dragon in Germanic heroic literature? I would like to stress that, despite the thematic role or function of any one monster in any one text, all the dragons discussed in this study are 'real'; that is, they cannot be reduced to allegorical personifications or to symbolic constructs; they are not meant to point our attention to something beyond themselves. On the contrary, they are designed to draw our attention *to* themselves, away from the merely human, reciprocal violence their presence replaces and conceals. They may have been retrospectively designated as monstrous, i.e., as dragons, in a discursive sublation of human violence, but that is simply to say that there have been no literal dragons in human history. Once the retrospective designation has been made, a dragon remains a dragon within the literary text.

Additionally, the dragons of Germanic literature do not represent an evolutionary progression, chronological or otherwise. They are not steps on a developmental ladder leading to a more refined, mature conception of *draconitas*, nor do they degenerate from an early, mythic and most likely pagan ideal to flat allegorical figures or hackneyed conventions of romance. A banal piece of literature will no doubt feature banal dragons; the dragons portrayed in the four works examined here each represent an unanticipated challenge to the audience horizon of expectations concerning dragons and dragon slayers that is better explained in terms of the medieval tendency toward continuous variation on a underlying pattern than in terms of the modern idea of evolution. In Jauss's words:

> ... the metaphorics of the courses of development, function, and decay can be replaced by the nonteleological concept of the playing out of a limited number of possibilities. In this concept a masterwork is definable in terms of an alteration of the horizon of the genre that is as unexpected as it is enriching.[1]

Clearly, according to this definition of the word, *Beowulf, Vǫlsunga saga, Das Nibelungenlied*, and even *Þiðreks saga af Bern* are 'masterworks;' each alters the horizon of expectations concerning dragons and dragon slayings in a distinctive way. At the same time, each of the four works is related to the others in terms of genre and potential intertexts, since the number of possibilities for dragon stories is limited by chronotopic (that is, generic) restraints on the types of narrative that may admit dragons at all.

Most dragon stories take place within a variant of what, following Bakhtin, I have called 'adventure time,' because this chronotope allows for the sudden incursion of alien elements—be they supernatural or simply foreign—into the familiar world of everyday life, which may itself be conceptualized as mythic, historic, or marvelous in its own right. Change in either the temporal or the spatial aspect of the basic chronotope mandates a corresponding change in the nature and roles of both dragon and hero. The dragon may be presented, as it is in *Beowulf* and *Das Nibelungenlied*, as an inhabitant of a world "other" than the human world in time or space, from which it invades this world in the form either of a hostile intruder or a (monstrous) guest. In such cases the hero is a person who can understand and deal with such otherworldly intrusions successfully, while the felt proximity between worlds determines whether the otherworldly incursion is perceived as terrifying or comic. Alternatively, the dragon may be conceptualized as it is in *Vǫlsunga saga*, as an extraordinary denizen of a mythic past that is also the world of gods and human beings; in this case the sudden change in circumstance or incursion of an alien element that characterizes the 'adventure time' chronotope beomes internal rather than external and manifests itself as a physical or psychological metamorphosis, be it the transformation of a man into a dragon or of a child into an adult. Or, as is the case in *Þiðreks saga af Bern*, the entire world may be conceived of as marvelous, along with all of its inhabitants, so that dragons become simply one opportunity for adventure among others, the dragon slaying yet another means of glorification for the best and strongest of heroes.

Other intertexts for dragons exist, of course, including many that are chronotopically distinct from heroic literature. Biblical and hagiographic texts, for example, would have made significant contributions to audience expectations about dragons in the Middle Ages, as would the studies of natural, political, and military historical dragons surveyed in Chapter I. Nonetheless, as we have seen throughout this investigation, the dragons of Germanic heroic literature are more closely related to the serpentine monsters fought by the gods of Indo-European myth than to any specifically Christian conception of the *serpens antiquus* as a type of Satan or to purely secular ideas about exotic animals or military insignia. The Indo-European myths concerning dragon slayings represent the sacred violence which is associated with the creation of cosmic order as it is told in monologic discourse; heroic dragon slayings, although they function as representations of the human violence associated with the establishment of societal order, are necessarily retold dialogically, and thus sublate (i.e., simultaneously conceal and reveal) rather than transform, reciprocal human violence into the unilateral violence of the dragon slaying. For this reason hero and monster are often recognizably akin, twin antagonists having greater affinities with each other than with the rest of humanity: heroes in these narratives may exhibit 'dragonish' behavior, or acquire 'dragonish' characteristics such as horn-hard skin or esoteric knowledge, as a result of an encounter with the monster.

On another, more human level, the dragon slaying in many narratives establishes a new or renewed ontological order as well. Heroes who kill dragons are often portrayed as doing so in a confrontation that establishes the hero's humanity in contradistinction to the monstrosity of the dragon, or that initiates the hero into adulthood and a central place in human society after the liminality of childhood and adolescence, or, even more fundamentally, that validates the hero's existence, his Being, in opposition to the dragon as a representative of non-Being, of a present absence whose monstrous (non)existence is an eternal reminder of the void. In these cases the dragon's hoard becomes a signifier of Being itself, and as such may spark a renewed cycle of reciprocal violence rooted in mimetic desire, or even a new dragon slaying as a sublation of that violence.

The past few decades have seen a renewed popular fascination with dragons and dragon slayers, manifested primarily in the endlessly repeated plots of sword and sorcery romances and in the mass-produced artwork that illustrates their fantastic characters and themes. Speculation as to the reasons behind the popularity of any fashionable trend is perilous at best, yet it may not be farfetched to suggest that the current appeal of the dragon is in fact related to the monster's function in traditional heroic literature. For a world in which the possibility of nuclear obliteration competes with the potential for ecological disaster as the most likely means of human destruction, the dragon may once again serve as a potent reminder of the ultimate danger involved in unending, reciprocal human violence, the threat of human annihilation. By telling and retelling the stories of dragon-slaying heroes, our age like past ages may be seeking to assert the existence and power of its goodness, its *humanitas*, in the face of what must often seem the inevitable, inescapable, and ever nearer triumph of our own dragons.

Notes

Notes to Chapter 1

[1] J.R.R. Tolkien, "*Beowulf:* The Monsters and the Critics," *Proceedings of the British Academy* 22 (1936), pp. 245–295, reprinted in *An Anthology of Beowulf Criticism*, ed. L.E. Nicholson (Notre Dame: University of Notre Dame Press, 1963), pp. 51–103. For a discussion of the relationship between medieval scholarship and the popular idea of the Middle Ages, see Paul Zumthor, *Speaking of the Middle Ages* (Lincoln, NE: University of Nebraska Press, 1986), pp. 8–13.

[2] Gwyn Jones, *Kings, Beasts and Heroes* (London: Oxford University Press, 1972), p. 16.

[3] Mikhail M. Bakhtin, *Problems of Dostoevsky's Poetics*, ed. and trans. Caryl Emerson (Minneapolis: University of Minnesota Press, 1984), p. 202.

[4] Mikhail M. Bakhtin, *The Dialogic Imagination*, ed. Michael Holquist, trans. Caryl Emerson and Michael Holquist (Austin: University of Texas Press, 1981), pp. 279–80.

[5] Cp. Bakhtin: "I call meaning the *answers* to the questions. That which does not answer any question is devoid of meaning for us. . . . The answering character of meaning. Meaning always answers some questions." Cited by Tzvetan Todorov from a previously untranslated Russian text, *Estetika slovesnogo tvorchestva* [The aesthetics of verbal creation, Moscow: S.G. Bocharov, 1979], in *Mikhail Bakhtin: The Dialogic Principle* (Minneapolis: University of Minnesota Press, 1984), p. 54. Cp. also Hans Robert Jauss, *Question and Answer: Forms of Dialogic Understanding*, ed. and trans. Michael Hays (Minneapolis: University of Minnesota Press, 1989).

[6] For a good example of the critique of objectivist historicism, see Hans Robert Jauss, *Toward an Aesthetic of Reception*, trans. Timothy Bahti (Minneapolis: University of Minnesota Press, 1982), pp. 20–1.

[7] "The Alterity and Modernity of Medieval Literature," trans. Timothy Bahti, *New Literary History* 10 (1979): pp. 187ff.

[8] Thomas Hahn, "The Premodern Text and the Postmodern Reader," *Exemplaria* 2 (1990): p. 11.

[9] Jauss, "Alterity and Modernity," p. 182. Cp. Bakhtin: "The first task is to understand the work as the author understood it, without leaving the limits of his understanding. . . . The second task is to use one's temporal and cultural exotopy. Inclusion in our context (alien to the author)." (Cited in Todorov, *Mikhail Bakhtin*, p. 109)

[10] Jauss, *Toward an Aesthetic of Reception*, p. 28.

[11] Ibid., p. 24.

[12] Jauss, *Question and Answer*, p. 207.

[13] Bakhtin, *Dialogic Imagination*, p. 417.

[14]Jauss, *Toward an Aesthetic of Reception*, p. 19.

[15]Jauss, "Alterity and Modernity," p. 189.

[16]Ibid., p. 190.

[17]G. Elliott Smith, *The Evolution of the Dragon* (Manchester: At the University Press, 1919), p. 77.

[18] Calvert Watkins, "How to Kill a Dragon in Indo-European," *Studies in Memory of Warren Cowgill (1929–1985)*, Papers from the Fourth East Coast Indo-European Conference, Cornell University, June 6–9, 1985, ed. Calvert Watkins (Berlin and New York: Walter de Gruyter, 1987), p. 271. Hereafter cited in text as *HK*. Unfortunately, Watkins' book, also entitled *How to Kill a Dragon in Indo-European* (New York: Oxford University Press, 1995), appeared too late for me to make use of it in this text. See also Joseph Fontenrose, *Python: A Study of Delphic Myth and Its Origins* (Berkeley: University of California Press, 1959) for further examples of what Fontenrose calls the "combat myth".

[19]Bakhtin, *Dialogic Imagination*, p. 15.

[20]Jauss, *Question and Answer*, p. 57.

[21]Ibid.

[22]I use the term 'formula' here in its linguistic sense; I do not intend it to have the specific, technical meaning it has been given by scholars studying oral-formulaic literature. See Albert B. Lord, *The Singer of Tales* (Cambridge: Harvard University Press, 1960).

[23]Jauss, *Question and Answer*, p. 56. Cp. Bakhtin: "In the past, everything is good: all the really good things (i.e., the 'first' things) occur *only* in this past. The epic absolute past is the single source and beginning of everything good for all later times as well" (*Dialogic Imagination*, p. 15).

[24]Littleton, "The 'Kingship in Heaven' Theme," in *Myth and Law Among the Indo-Europeans*, ed. Jaan Puhvel (Berkeley: University of California Press, 1970), p. 84. Littleton explains that "[i]n each instance a single pattern of events is present: an existing generation of gods was preceded by two (and in some cases three) earlier generations of supernatural beings, each succeeding generation being presided over by a 'king in heaven' who has usurped (or at least assumed) the power of his predecessor. Moreover, there is generally a fourth figure, a monster of some sort, who, acting on behalf of the deposed 'king' (in the Iranian and Babylonian versions . . . the monster became identified with the deposed 'king' himself), presents a challenge to the final heavenly ruler and must be overcome" (p. 84). For an explication of this myth in its Judeo-Christian form, see John Day, *God's Conflict with the Dragon and the Sea* (Cambridge: Cambridge University Press, 1985).

[25]Littleton, p. 92.

[26]David K. Danow, *The Thought of Mikhail Bakhtin: From Word to Culture*, (New York: St. Martin's Press, 1991), p. 64.

[27]René Girard, *Violence and the Sacred*, trans. Patrick Gregory (Baltimore and London: Johns Hopkins University Press, 1977); hereafter cited in the text as *VS*. See also Girard's later book, *The Scapegoat*, trans. Yvonne Freccero (Baltimore: Johns Hopkins, 1986).

[28]Cp. Watkins, who points out that the hero "can be a sort of monster . . . unpredictable violence is always latent" (*HK*, p. 294).

[29]"The thing signified . . . is the destruction of all signification" because language is "made up of differences" (*VS*, 64).

[30]Kenneth Burke, *Language as Symbolic Action: Essays on Life, Literature, and Method* (Berkeley: University of California Press, 1966), pp. 419–79.

[31]Eric Gould, *Mythical Intentions in Modern Literature* (Princeton: Princeton University Press, 1981), p. 109.

[32]Ibid., p. 43.

[33]Ibid., p. 67.

[34]Burke, p. 430. Burke further points out, following Bergson, that "we can't really *think* of nothing. The nearest we can come to it is to think of annihilating something, a feat which on closer inspection will be found to force upon us the thought of the annihilator or of a substituted image such as a black spot, etc." (p. 437). In the dragon myth, these alternatives are combined, for the dragon, the 'substituted image,' is, in its role as monstrous double, at the same time the obverse of the 'annihilator.'

[35]Gould, p. 66.

[36]Some scholars have theorized that the concluding stanzas of *Vǫluspá* are not in fact original, but instead constitute a late (c. 1000) addition to the poem and are therefore attributable to Christian influence. Yet this in no way negates the significance of the dragon Niðhǫggr within the context of the myth itself. As Paul C. Bauschatz has argued, "It is clear that there is nothing in the final stanzas of *Vǫluspá* that runs seriously counter to the mythic elements that the whole of the poem presents" (*The Well and the Tree: World and Time in Early Germanic Culture* [Amherst: University of Massachusetts Press, 1982], p. 204n).

[37]Snorri Sturluson, *The Prose Edda: Tales from Norse Mythology*, trans. Jean I. Young (Berkeley: University of California Press, 1954), p. 43.

[38]Hilda R. Ellis Davidson, *Gods and Myths of Northern Europe* (Baltimore: Penguin, 1964), p. 160.

[39]"Maxims II," 26a-27b. In *The Anglo-Saxon Minor Poems*, ASPR VI, ed. Elliott Van Kirk Dobbie (New York: Columbia University Press, 1942).

[40]David Williams, *Cain and Beowulf: A Study in Secular Allegory* (Toronto: University of Toronto Press, 1982), p. 64.

[41]On the level of folktale, the similarity between dragon and dragon slayer often manifests itself humorously in the form of fantastic and monstrous homemade 'armor' which, in Jacqueline Simpson's words, turns the hero into "a ludicrous-looking monster, a sort of parody-dragon" [*British Dragons* (London: B.T. Batsford, 1980, p. 122).

[42]Isidore of Seville, *Etymologiarum Sive Originum* (Book XII), ed. W.M. Lindsay (Oxford: Clarendon, 1911).

[43]*Differentiae* I, 9; cited by Jacques LeGoff, "Ecclesiastical Culture and Folklore in the Middle Ages: Saint Marcellus of Paris and the Dragon," trans. Arthur Goldhammer,

in *Time, Work, and Culture in the Middle Ages (Pour un autre Moyen Age: temps, travail et culture en Occident)* (Chicago and London: University of Chicago Press, 1980), p. 167; 333n.

⁴⁴Cited in M.J. Swanton, *Crisis and Development in Germanic Society 700–800: Beowulf and the Burden of Kingship* (Göppingen: Kümmerle, 1982), p. 137.

⁴⁵Stanley Rypins, ed. *Three Old English Prose Texts in MS. Cotton Vitellius A xv.* EETS o.s. 161 (London: Oxford University Press, 1924), p. 59.

⁴⁶Claude Lecouteux, "Der Drache," *Zeitschrift für deutsches Altertum und deutsche Literature* 108 (1979): pp. 15-21.

⁴⁷Nora K. Chadwick, "Norse Ghosts: A Study in the *Draugr* and the *Haugbúi*," *Folk-Lore* 57 (1948): p. 110n.

⁴⁸Alan K. Brown, "The Firedrake in *Beowulf*," *Neophilologus* 64 (1980): pp. 439–43.

⁴⁹C. Plummer, ed. *The Anglo-Saxon Chronicle* (Oxford: Oxford University Press, 1893).

⁵⁰Brown suggests a meteor (p. 450); cp. also W. G. Cooke, "'Firy Drakes and Blazing-Bearded Light'" *English Studies* 61 (1980): pp. 97–103. Hilda R. Ellis Davidson, in *Gods and Myths of Northern Europe* suggests the *aurora* (p. 160).

⁵¹Cp. Friedrich Wild, *Drachen im Beowulf und andere Drachen: Mit einem Anhand Drachenfeldzeichen, Drachenwappen und St. Georg* (Wien: Hermann Bohlaus, 1962), p. 11.

⁵²LeGoff, "Ecclesiastical Culture," p. 176.

⁵³Ibid., p. 175.

⁵⁴Mircea Eliade, *The Myth of the Eternal Return* (New York: 1954), p. 43.

⁵⁵Otto Höfler, *Siegfried, Arminius und die Symbolik* (Heidelberg: Carl Winter, 1961), p. 17. For a specific response to Höfler, see Heinrich Beck, "Zu Otto Höflers Siegfried-Arminius Untersuchung," *Beitrage zur Geschichte der Deutschen Sprache und Literatur* 107 (1985): pp. 91–107.

⁵⁶Annelise Talbot, "Sigemund the Dragon-Slayer," *Folklore* 94 (1983): p. 158.

⁵⁷Zumthor, *Speaking of the Middle Ages*, p. 47. Zumthor asserts the necessity of distinguishing intertextuality "very clearly . . . from the biologizing idea of 'sources'" (p. 77).

⁵⁸Cited in LeGoff, "Ecclesiastical Culture," p. 166.

Notes to Chapter 2

¹A complete bibliography of publications on the *Beowulf* dragon is of course impossible to include here. The interested reader would probably want to start with Tolkien's essay, and then go on to the discussions (cited in full in the Bibliography) by Adrien Bonjour, "Monsters Crouching and Critics Rampant: Or the *Beowulf* Dragon Debated"; Alan K. Brown, "The Firedrake in *Beowulf*"; Daniel G. Calder, "Setting and Ethos: The

Pattern of Measure and Limit in *Beowulf*"; Signe M. Carlson, "The Monsters of *Beowulf*: Creations of Literary Scholars"; Nora K. Chadwick, "The Monsters and *Beowulf*"; Michael D. Cherniss, "The Progress of the Hoard in *Beowulf*"; Arthur E. DuBois, "The Unity of *Beowulf*" and "The Dragon in *Beowulf*"; T.M. Gang, "Approaches to *Beowulf*"; G.N. Garmonsway and Jacqueline Simpson, tr., *Beowulf and its Analogues*; Andreas Haarder, *Beowulf: The Appeal of a Poem*; Edward R. Irving, Jr. *A Reading of Beowulf* and *Rereading Beowulf*; Christopher Knipp, "*Beowulf* 2210-2323: Repetition in the Description of the Dragon's Hoard"; Bruce Mitchell, "'Until the Dragon Comes . . .' Some Thoughts on *Beowulf*"; Jerome Oetgen, "Order and Chaos in the World of *Beowulf*"; H.L. Rogers, "Beowulf's Three Great Fights"; Kenneth Sisam, "Beowulf's Fight with the Dragon"; and Raymond P. Tripp, Jr., *More About the Fight With the Dragon: Beowulf 2208b-3182, Commentary, Edition, and Translation*.

[2]A detailed description of the MS is available in Kevin S. Kiernan, *Beowulf and the Beowulf Manuscript* (New Brunswick, NJ: Rutgers University Press, 1981); see also Kemp Malone, ed., *The Nowell Codex (British Museum Cotton Vitellius A. XV, Second MS)*, Early English Manuscripts in Facsimile, 12 (Copenhagen: Rosenkilde & Bagger, 1963).

[3]The three prose texts have been edited by Stanley Rypins, *Three Old English Prose Texts in MS. Cotton Vitellius A. xv.*, EETS o.s. 161 (London: Oxford University Press, 1924).

[4]Kenneth Sisam, *Studies in the History of Old English Literature* (Oxford: Clarendon Press, 1953), p. 96. Saint Christopher's connection with monsters is explained by the fact that "[a]ccording to the *Old English Martyrology*, he had a dog's head, and his locks were extraordinarily long, and his eyes gleamed as bright as the morning star, and his teeth were as sharp as a boar's tusks" (Sisam, p. 66; cited by Kiernan, p. 140n). For more recent discussions of the relationship between *Beowulf* and the Alexandrian marvels, see Andrew Orchard, *Pride and Prodigies: Studies in the Monsters of the Beowulf Manuscript* (Cambridge: D.S. Brewer, 1995) and William E. Brynteson, "*Beowulf*, Monsters, and Manuscripts: Classical Associations," *Res Publica Literarum* 5 (1982): pp. 41–57.

[5]For example, Kevin Kiernan states that "[t]he real objection to the thesis that *Beowulf* was the fourth item in a decidedly eccentric *Liber Monstrorum* is the implication that the 11th century Anglo-Saxons had no sophisticated appreciation for an original epic in their own tongue. . . . even the dullest anthologist would realize that Grendel outmonstered anything *The Wonders of the East* had to offer, much less *Alexander's Letter* or St. Christopher's curious pedigree" (ibid., 140).

[6]See, in addition to Kiernan's book noted above, Colin Chase, ed., *The Dating of "Beowulf"* (Toronto: University of Toronto Press, 1981), and Patricia Prousa, "The Date of *Beowulf* Reconsidered: The Tenth Century?" *Neuphilologische Mitteilungen* 82 (1981): pp. 276–88.

[7]Rypins, p. 59.

[8]Ibid., p. 19.

[9]Ibid., pp. 20–1.

[10]Franco Porsia, ed., *Liber Monstrorum* (Bari: Dedalo Libri, 1976), p. 138. For discussions of the relationship of the *Liber Monstrorum* to *Beowulf,* see Dorothy Whitelock, *The Audience of Beowulf* (Oxford: Clarendon Press, 1951), pp. 46–53, and L.G. Whitbread, "The *Liber Monstrorum* and *Beowulf,*" *Mediaeval Studies* 36 (1974): pp. 434–71. For an argument against the idea that the *Liber* was compiled in England, see Ann Knock, "The *Liber Monstrorum*: An Unpublished Manuscript and Some Reconsiderations," *Scriptorium* 32 (1978): pp. 19–28.

[11]Ibid., p. 276.

[12]Whitelock, p. 69. A translation of Saxo's account of the dragon fight can be found in Garmonsway and Simpson, *Beowulf and Its Analogues* (New York: E.P. Dutton, 1971), p. 337.

[13]Whitelock, pp. 69–70.

[14]Alan K. Brown, "The Firedrake in *Beowulf,*" *Neophilologus* 64 (1980), p. 444.

[15]James Carney, *Studies in Irish Literature and History* (Dublin, 1955), pp. 123–4.

[16]Brown, p. 444.

[17]Nora K. Chadwick, "The Monsters and *Beowulf,*" in *The Anglo-Saxons: Studies in Some Aspects of Their History and Culture Presented to Bruce Dickens,* ed. Peter Clemoes (London: Bowes and Bowes, 1959), p. 178. On the triplicity of the monsters, see also Peter Buchholz, *Vorzeitkunde: Mündliches Erzählen und Überliefern im mittelalterlichen Skandinavien nach dem Zeugnis von Fornaldarsaga und eddischer Dichtung* (Neumünster: Karl Wachholtz, 1980), p. 56, and Axel Olrik's "law of three," discussed in his 1909 essay "Epic Laws of Folk Narrative," in *The Study of Folklore,* ed. Alan Dundes (Englewood Cliffs, NJ: Prentice Hall, 1965), p. 134.

[18]Ibid., p. 186.

[19]George Clark, *Beowulf* (Boston: Twayne Publishers, 1990), p. 30. Cp. Chadwick, p. 186.

[20]Chadwick, "Monsters and *Beowulf,*" p. 186. In addition, in 1971 George Clark noted that the exploits of a character in *Njáls Saga,* Þorkell hákr, also fit into Chadwick's pattern, and suitably enough, since Þorkell can trace his ancestry back to Ketill Hængr. See George Clark, "*Beowulf* and *Njáls-saga,*" in *Proceedings of the First International Saga Conference, University of Edinburgh, 1971,* ed. Peter Foote, Hermann Pálsson, and Desmond Slay (London: Viking Society for Northern Research, 1973): pp. 66–87.

[21] *Hálfdanar Saga Eysteinssonar,* ed. Guðni Jónsson and Bjarni Vilhjalmsson, *Fornaldarsǫgur Norðurlanda* (Reykjavik: Bókaútgáfan Forni, 1943), p. 311.

[22] Hermann Pálsson and Paul Edwards, trans., *Seven Viking Romances* (London: Penguin Books, 1985), p. 192.

[23]Ibid., p. 318.

[24]Chadwick, "Monsters and Beowulf," p. 186.

[25]The first discussion of *Beowulf* as an orally composed poem is Francis P. Magoun, Jr, "The Oral-Formulaic Character of Anglo-Saxon Narrative Poetry," *Speculum* 28 (1953): pp. 446–67; rpt. in *An Anthology of Beowulf Criticism,* ed. Lewis E. Nicholson (Notre Dame: University of Notre Dame Press, 1963), pp. 189–221. A more recent

discussion may be found in John Miles Foley, *Traditional Oral Epic: The Odyssey, Beowulf, and the Serbo-Croatian Return Song* (Berkeley: University of California Press, 1990).

[26]See Larry D. Benson, "The Literary Character of Anglo-Saxon Formulaic Poetry," *PMLA* 81 (1966): 334–41.

[27]See John D. Niles, *Beowulf: The Poem and Its Tradition* (Cambridge, MA & London: Harvard University Press, 1983), who states that: "he is presented as a living creature of the same general sort as any lion, bear, or other wild beast, only more fearsome" (p. 25); cp. George Clark, *Beowulf*, pp. 127–30. Bernard F. Huppé, in *The Hero in the Earthly City: A Reading of Beowulf* (Binghamton: State University of New York Press, 1984), calls the dragon "the greatest of nature's monstrosities" (p. 55). For an earlier view of the dragon-as-wild-animal see T.M. Gang, "Approaches to *Beowulf*," *Review of English Studies* 3 (1952): pp. 1–12.

[28] Margaret Goldsmith, *The Mode and Meaning of Beowulf* (London: Athlone Press, 1970), is still the best critic to take this approach.

[29]G.V. Smithers [*The Making of Beowulf*, Inaugural Lecture of the Professor of English Language Delivered in the Appleby Lecture Theatre on 18 May 1961 (Durham, England: University of Durham Press, 1961)] notes that *Beowulf* provides the only known exception to the story-pattern of a Last Survivor transforming himself into a dragon (p. 12), and suggests that the poet erred through ignorance in separating the two (p. 17). More recently, Raymond P. Tripp, Jr [*More About the Fight With the Dragon: Beowulf 2208b–3182, Commentary, Edition, and Translation* (Washington, D.C.: University Press of America, 1983)] argues that the damaged condition of the MS has led scholars to misread the text which, once restored, reveals a saga-like 'human' dragon. For support for Tripp's view, see Peter C. Braeger, "Connotations of (*Earm*)*Sceapen*: *Beowulf* ll. 2228–9 and the Shape-Shifting Dragon," *Essays in Literature* 13 (1986): pp. 327–30.

[30]Tolkien, "*Beowulf*: The Monsters and the Critics," pp. 58ff. Ker's assertion is in *The Dark Ages*, p. 253.

[31]W.P. Ker, *Epic and Romance* (London: MacMillan, 1931), p. 168.

[32]M.M. Bakhtin, *The Dialogic Imagination*, p. 12; 61–3.

[33]In ll. 2212b, 2290b, 2402b, 2549b, and 3131b. All quotations from *Beowulf* are from Fr. Klaeber, *Beowulf and the Fight at Finnsburg*, 3rd. ed. (Boston: D.C. Heath, 1950). Unless otherwise noted, translations are from E. Talbot Donaldson's *Beowulf: A New Prose Translation* (New York: W. W. Norton, 1966).

[34]In ll. 2287a, 2307a, 2316a, 2343b, 2348a, 2400a, 2519a, 2567b, 2629b, 2669b, 2705b, 2745b, 2759b, 2771b, 2827a, 2902b, 3039a, 3132a.

[35]Earlier in the poem there are two other compounds, *wyrmcynnes* "of the race of serpents," (1425b), in reference to the *sædracan* "sea-dragons" of the Grendelmere, and *wyrmfah* "with serpentine ornamentation" (1698a), describing the sword Beowulf finds in the Grendels' underwater hall.

[36]See Paul Beekman Taylor, "Some Uses of Etymology in the Reading of Medieval Germanic Texts," in *Hermeneutics and Medieval Culture*, ed. Patrick J. Gallacher and Helen Damico (Albany: State University of New York Press, 1989), pp. 109–20.

[37]Bakhtin, *Dialogic Imagination*, p. 61; emphasis in the original.

[38]Donaldson's translation is "shining with surging flames," which does not retain the sense that the dragon's body is itself *fah*, "marked" by the fire.

[39]Kenneth Sisam, "Beowulf's Fight With the Dragon," *Review of English Studies* 9 (1958), p. 134.

[40]Tripp, p. 93.

[41]For a discussion of the word, see Claude M. Lotspeich, "Old English Etymologies," *Journal of English and Germanic Philology* 40 (1941): pp. 1–4; Marion Lois Huffines, "Old English *Aglæca*: Magic and Moral Decline of Monsters and Men," *Semasia* 1 (1974): pp. 71–81; Doreen M.E. Gillam, "The Use of the Term 'Æglæca' in *Beowulf* at Lines 893 and 2592," *Studia Germanica Gandensia* 3 (1961): pp. 145–69; and Sherman Kuhn, "Old English *Aglæca*—Middle Irish *Oclach*" in *Linguistic Method: Essays in Honor of Herbert Penzl*, ed. Irmengard Rauch and Gerald F. Carr (The Hague: Mouton, 1979), pp. 213–30.

[42]Emile Benveniste, *La Vocabulaire des institutions indo-européennes*, 2 vols. (Paris, 1969), 2:78-79. Cited by Girard, *VS*, pp. 263-4.

[43]Critics who deal with the similarities between monsters and men in *Beowulf* include S. L. Dragland, "Monster-Man in *Beowulf*," *Neophilologus* 61 (1977): pp. 606–18; Harry Berger and H. Marshall Leicester, Jr., "The Limits of Heroism in *Beowulf*," in *Old English Studies in Honour of John C. Pope*, ed. Robert B. Burlin and Edward B. Irving, Jr. (Toronto: University of Toronto Press, 1974), pp. 37–80; Peter F. Fisher, "The Trials of the Epic Hero in *Beowulf*," *PMLA* 73 (1958): pp. 171–83; Stanley B. Greenfield, "'Gifstol' and Goldhoard in *Beowulf*," in *Pope Studies*, pp. 107–18; and Edward B. Irving, Jr, *A Reading of Beowulf* (New Haven: Yale University Press, 1968).

[44]Berger and Leicester, pp. 66.

[45]Irving, *A Reading of Beowulf*, p. 201.

[46]Kathryn Hume, "The Concept of the Hall in Old English Poetry," *Anglo-Saxon England* 3 (1974), p. 68.

[47]Irving, *A Reading of Beowulf*, p. 209.

[48]Berger and Leicester, p. 66.

[49]F.H. Whitman, "Corrosive Blood in *Beowulf*," *Neophilologus* 61 (1977): p. 276.

[50]I am indebted for the use of the term 'sublation' to John P. Hermann, *Allegories of War: Language and Violence in Old English Poetry* (Ann Arbor: University of Michigan Press, 1989), pp. 3, 55.

[51]Thomas D. Hill, "Scyld Scefing and the '*Stirps Regia*': Pagan Myth and Christian Kingship in *Beowulf*," in *Magister Regis: Studies in Honor of Robert Earl Kaske*, ed. Arthur Gross, *et al.* (New York: Fordham University Press, 1986), p. 41.

[52]Cp. W.T.H. Jackson, who reads *Beowulf* in terms of "hero-intruders" who can be either heroic or monstrous in *The Hero and the King: an Epic Theme* (New York: Columbia University Press, 1982), and Charles Dahlberg, who discusses *Beowulf* in light of Jackson's theory in *The Literature of Unlikeness* (Hanover, NH: University Press of New England, 1988), p. 48.

[53]See Stanley B. Greenfield, "A Touch of the Monstrous in the Hero, or Beowulf Re-Marvellized," in *Pope Studies*, pp. 119–37; and S.L. Dragland, pp. 606–18.

[54]Irving, *A Reading of Beowulf*, pp. 110–11.

[55] Klaeber emends MS *sendeþ*, "sends" to *snedeþ*, "feasts." He notes, however, that *sendan* "has been suspected of being a relic of old heathen sacrificial terminology" (152n), and cites *Hávamál* 145.3 ff. as an example of an analogous Old Norse usage in a specifically sacrificial context. The most likely meaning of the O.E. word in the context of *Beowulf* is "send to death," perhaps, as Klaeber suggests, with "a vague idea of 'sacrifice'" (p. 152n). For a discussion of the interrelated themes of sleeping, feasting, and killing in *Beowulf*, see Joanne De Lavan Foley, "Feasts and Anti-Feasts in *Beowulf* and the *Odyssey*," in John Miles Foley, ed. *Oral Traditional Literature: A Festschrift for Albert Bates Lord* (Columbia, MO: Slavica Publishers, 1980), pp. 235–61.

[56]Klaeber glosses *wælgæst* in this line as "murderous sprite" instead of "guest," assuming that *gæst* here is a variant of *gāst*, "ghost, spirit, sprite, demon," instead of *gist*, "guest, stranger, foe." Bosworth and Toller [Joseph Bosworth, *An Anglo-Saxon Dictionary*, ed. and enlarged by T. Northcote Toller (London: Oxford University Press, 1898; rpt. 1976)] assume the opposite, and I have followed their lead here.

[57]Clark, *Beowulf*, p. 50.

[58]See also Kathryn Hume, "The Theme and Structure of *Beowulf*," *Studies in Philology* 72 (1975): p. 5, who states that "the controlling theme of the poem . . . is *threats to social order*" (emphasis in original).

[59]Cp. Jackson, who points out that "the orientation of epics is strongly social" (p. 135).

[60]Hermann, p. 125.

[61]See, for example, Tomoaki Mizuno, "Beowulf as a Terrible Stranger," *Journal of Indo-European Studies* 17 (1989): pp. 1–46, and Fidel Fajardo-Acosta, *The Condemnation of Heroism in the Tragedy of Beowulf* (Lewiston, NY: Edwin Mellen Press, 1989). Fajardo-Acosta's creative identification of Grendel's mother with Healfdane's daughter and of Grendel as the product of an incestuous union with Hroðgar has interesting Girardian implications, since incest is common in scapegoat myths as a further eradication of social differences.

[62]Clark, *Beowulf*, p. 92.

[63]For a good survey of the critical debate concerning the Christianity of *Beowulf*, as well as a sensitive reading of the various explicitly Christian elements in the poem, see Mary A. Parker, *Beowulf and Christianity* (New York: Peter Lang Publishing, 1987).

[64]Tolkien, "*Beowulf*: The Monsters and the Critics," p. 73.

[65]*Dialogic Imagination*, p. 84.

[66]Ibid., p. 85.

[67]See Clark, *Beowulf*, p. ix; John D. Niles, *Beowulf*, p. 3; Edward B. Irving, Jr, *Rereading Beowulf*, p. 7; Stanley B. Greenfield, "*Beowulf* and Epic Tragedy," in *Hero and Exile*, p. 17; and W. F. Bolton, *Alcuin and Beowulf: An Eighth Century View* (New Brunswick, N.J.: Rutgers University Press, 1978), p. 170.

[68]David Williams, *Cain and Beowulf: A Study in Secular Allegory* (Toronto: University of Toronto Press, 1982), p. 5.

[69]*"Beowulf:* The Monsters and the Critics," p. 74.

[70]*Dialogic Imagination*, p. 252.

[71]Fred C. Robinson, *Beowulf and the Appositive Style* (Knoxville: University of Tennessee Press, 1985), p. 89n. Hereafter cited in the text as *BA*.

[72]Niles, p. 181. See also Roberta Frank, "The *Beowulf* Poet's Sense of History," in *The Wisdom of Poetry: Essays in Early English Literature in Honor of Morton W. Bloomfield*, ed. Larry D. Benson and Siegfried Wenzel (Kalamazoo, MI: Medieval Institute Publications, 1982), pp. 53–65.

[73]Ibid.

[74]Bakhtin, *Dialogic Imagination*, p. 252; emphasis in original.

[75]Ibid., emphasis in original.

[76]Ibid.

[77]*"Beowulf:* The Monsters and the Critics," pp. 72–3.

[78]Niles points out that "wherever Beowulf stands geographically [at the Grendelmere] . . . he is approaching an entry to the otherworld" (p. 17).

[79]Irving, *Rereading Beowulf*, p. 100.

[80]*Dialogic Imagination*, pp. 94–5.

[81]Bakhtin, *Problems of Dostoevsky's Poetics*, p. 185; emphasis in original.

[82]Paul Beekman Taylor, "Heorot, Earth, and Asgard: Christian Poetry and Pagan Myth," *Tennessee Studies in Literature* 11 (1966): pp. 119–30.

[83]Cp. Bakhtin's discussion of the relationship between tropes and double voicing (*Dialogic Imagination*, pp. 237, 327–8).

[84]Cp. Gillian R. Overing, who emphasizes "the temporary nature of metaphoric resolution and . . . the continual metonymic reassertion of the ambiguity of double vision" [*Language, Sign, and Gender in Beowulf* (Carbondale & Edwardsville, IL: Southern Illinois University Press, 1990)], p. 9.

[85]*"Beowulf:* The Monsters and the Critics," p. 92.

[86]J.R.R. Tolkien, "The Homecoming of Beorhtnoth, Beorhthelm's Son," *Essays and Studies*, n.s. 6 (1953), p. 16. For recent discussions of *lofgeornost*, see Robinson, pp. 80–2, Niles, pp. 237–42, and Clark, pp. 136–42.

[87]Bakhtin, *Problems of Dostoevsky's Poetics*, p. 75.

NOTES TO CHAPTER 3

[1]The saga's intertexts include two other works to be discussed in this study, *Das Nibelungenlied* and *Þiðreks saga af Bern*. In the Scandinavian tradition one may also cite the *Prose Edda of Snorri Sturluson* (c. 1225), the fourteenth-century *Norna-Gests*

Þáttr, the fifteenth-century *Vǫlsungsrímur*, and a scattering of ballads in Norwegian, Swedish, Danish and Faroese. The German tradition also includes Albrecht von Scharfenberg's *Seifrid de Ardemont* (c. 1280, a text which links Siegfried with the Arthurian material), the 15th century *Anhang zum Heldenbuch* and *Das Lied vom Hürnen Seyfrid*, and a 16th century drama by Hans Sachs, *Der Hürnen Seufrid*. In addition, there must have been a flourishing oral tradition, lost to us, of stories and poems concerning Sigurðr/Siegfried and Fáfnir.

[2]For a complete discussion of the saga author's use of his sources, see R.G. Finch, "The Treatment of Poetic Sources by the Compiler of *Vǫlsunga Saga*," *Saga-Book of the Viking Society* 16 (1962): pp. 315–53.

[3]Ibid., p. 353.

[4]Rory McTurk points out that fifteen was in fact the age of majority in medieval Norway, [*Studies in Ragnars saga Loðbrókar and Its Major Scandinavian Analogues*, Medium Ævum Monographs New Series XV (Oxford: Society for the Study of Mediæval Languages and Literature, 1991), p. 52].

[5]Nora K. Chadwick, "The Monsters and *Beowulf*," pp. 186–7.

[6]H.R. Ellis Davidson, "Gods and Heroes in Stone," in *The Early Cultures of North-West Europe*, H. M. Chadwick Memorial Studies, ed. Sir Cyril Fox and Bruce Dickins (Cambridge: University Press, 1950), pp. 123–39.

[7]Jesse L. Byock, "Sigurðr Fáfnisbani: An Eddic Hero Carved on Norwegian Stave Churches," in *Poetry in the Scandinavian Middle Ages: Proceedings of the Seventh International Saga Conference*, ed. Teresa Pàroli (Spoleto: Presso la Sede del Centro Studi, 1990), pp. 619–28.

[8]Byock, p. 620.

[9]At least some implicit Christian influence must be assumed, given the dates of the composition and MSS of each text.

[10]Ibid., p. 628.

[11]Stephen A. Mitchell, *Heroic Sagas and Ballads* (Ithaca & London: Cornell University Press, 1991), p. 29.

[12]Ibid, p. 28.

[13]Hermann Pálsson and Paul Edwards, *Legendary Fiction in Medieval Iceland* (Reykjavik: Bókaútgáfa Minningarsjóðs, 1971), p. 97.

[14]Ibid., p. 98.

[15]These examples are also cited by Mitchell, p. 84. Unless otherwise noted, all citations and translations from *Vǫlsunga saga* are from R.G. Finch, ed. and trans., *The Saga of the Vǫlsungs* (London: Thomas Nelson & Sons, 1968).

[16]Pálsson and Edwards, p. 16.

[17]Mitchell, p. 28.

[18]Cp. Pálsson and Edwards, "In the hands of the authors of these tales the mythic and actual are often allowed to flow into one another" (p. 34).

[19]Kathryn Hume, "From Saga to Romance: The Use of Monsters in Old Norse Literature," *Studies in Philology* 77 (1980): p. 15.

[20]I owe this comparison to William C. Johnson, Jr, "*Beowulf* and the *Vǫlsungasaga*," *In Geardagum II: Essays on Old and Middle English Language and Literature*, ed. Loren C. Gruber and Dean Loganbill (Denver: Society for New Language Study, 1979): pp. 42–53.

[21]Johnson, p. 44.

[22]Ibid., p. 45.

[23]Ibid.

[24]Other *fornaldarsǫgur* in which Óðinn plays a significant part include *Hrólfs saga kraka*, *Ketils saga hœngs*, *Ǫrvar-Odds saga*, *Gautreks saga*, *Sǫrla þáttr*, *Heiðreks saga*, and *Hálfs saga ok Hálfsrekka*. See Mitchell, p. 62.

[25]Gabriel Turville-Petre, "The Cult of Óðinn in Iceland," in *Nine Norse Studies* (London: Viking Society for Northern Research, 1972), p. 2. Cp. Mitchell, who calls Óðinn a "suspicious character" (p. 62).

[26]E.O.G. Turville-Petre, *Myth and Religion of the North: The Religion of Ancient Scandinavia* (London: Weidenfeld and Nicolson, 1964), p. 63.

[27]John L. Greenway, *The Golden Horns: Mythic Imagination and the Nordic Past* (Athens, GA: University of Georgia Press, 1977), p. 33.

[28]See Finch, "Treatment," as well as P. Wieselgren, "Quellenstudien zur Völsungasaga" *Acta et Commentationes Universitatis Tartuensis* (1935–6): pp. 34–8. The Eddic poems themselves are apparently also late compositions; see Lee M. Hollander, "Were the Mythological Poems of the Edda Composed in the Pre-Christian Era?" *JEGP* 26 (1927): pp. 96–105.

[29]Bakhtin, *The Dialogic Imagination*, p. 111.

[30]Ibid., pp. 111–12.

[31]Ibid., p. 113.

[32]For a recent discussion of this phenomenon, see Hilda R. Ellis Davidson, "Shape-Changing in the Old Norse Sagas," in J.R. Porter and W.M.S. Russell, eds., *Animals in Folklore* (Cambridge and Totowa, N.J.: Published by D.S. Brewer and Rowman & Littlefield for the Folklore Society, 1978): pp. 126–42.

[33]Bakhtin, *Dialogic Imagination*, p. 115.

[34]For a discussion of this setting from an oral-comparative point of view, see Donald K. Fry, "The Cliff of Death in Old English Poetry," in *Comparative Research on Oral Traditions: A Memorial for Milman Parry*, ed. John Miles Foley (Columbus, OH: Slavica Publishers, 1985), pp. 213-233.

[35]Hilda R. Ellis, "The Hoard of the Nibelungs," *Modern Language Review* 37 (1942), p. 476. The best general discussion of the *draugar* is still Nora K. Chadwick, "Norse Ghosts: A Study in the *Draugr* and the *Haugbúi*," *Folk-Lore* 57 (1948): pp. 50–65, 106–27.

[36]Ellis, p. 476.

[37]Nora Chadwick, "Norse Ghosts," p. 51.

[38]Jan de Vries, *Heroic Song and Heroic Legend*, trans. B.J. Timmer (London: Oxford University Press, 1963), pp. 220–1. Cp. Mircea Eliade, who states that the purpose of initiation is "to produce a decisive alteration in the religious and social status of the person to be initiated . . . initiation is equivalent to a basic change in existential condition" [*Rites and Symbols of Initiation: The Mysteries of Birth and Rebirth*, trans. Willard R. Trask (N.Y.: Harper Torchbooks, 1958), p. x].

[39]Victor Turner, *The Ritual Process: Structure and Anti-Structure* (Ithaca: Cornell University Press, 1969), pp. 94–5, 166. Turner cites Arnold van Gennep as the original source of this terminology [*The Rites of Passage*, trans. Monika B. Vizedom & Gabrielle L. Caffee (London: Routledge & Kegan Paul, 1909)].

[40]Turner, p. 95.

[41]I have adopted this term from Kaaren Grimstad's article "The Revenge of Vǫlundr," in *Edda: A Collection of Essays*, ed. R.J. Glendinning & Haraldur Bessason (Manitoba: University of Manitoba Press, 1983), pp. 187–209.

[42]For specific discussions of these initiation motifs and their manifestations in other sagas, see A. Margaret Arent, "The Heroic Pattern: Old Germanic Helmets, *Beowulf*, and *Grettis Saga*," in *Old Norse Literature and Mythology: A Symposium*, ed. Edgar C. Polomé (Austin: University of Texas Press, 1969), pp. 130–99; and Mary Danielli, "Initiation Ceremonial from Norse Literature," *Folk-Lore* 56 (1945): pp. 229–45.

[43]For an early discussion of initiation in the saga, see de Vries, pp. 217–26; cp. also Rory McTurk, pp. 35ff.

[44]Cp. Bakhtin: "The idea of testing . . . does not know development, becoming, a man's *gradual* formation. Testing begins with an already formed person and subjects him to a trial in the light of an ideal also already formed" (*Dialogic Imagination*, p. 392).

[45]Arent, p. 137. Cp. Anne Holtsmark, "On the Werewolf Motif in *Egil's saga Skallagrímssonar*," *Scientia Islandica* 1 (1968): pp. 7–9.

[46]Mary R. Gerstein, "Germanic *Warg*: The Outlaw as Werwolf," in *Myth in Indo-European Antiquity*, ed. Gerald James Larson (Berkeley: University of California Press, 1974), pp. 133–4. See also Winfred P. Lehmann, "On Reflections of Germanic Legal Terminology and Situations in the Edda," in Edgar C. Palomé, ed., *Old Norse Literature and Mythology: A Symposium* (Austin: University of Texas Press, 1969): pp. 227–43.

[47]R.G. Finch speculates that the very name 'Sinfjǫtli,' translated as 'he of the ash-(cinder) gold fetter,' could be construed as a kenning for wolf (*Saga*, p. 10n).

[48]Cited in Mitchell, p. 56.

[49]Grimstad, pp. 202–3.

[50]Grimstad cites Edith Marold's comments on the suitability of the smith's role in cultic rituals such as initiations: "Er is durch seine Arbeit dämonischen Wesen verbunden, ist selbst Zauberer. Die Gegnerschaft zum Teufel und Drachen stellt ihn in kosmologische

Zusammenhänge hinein. Als Verkünder der Weisheit, als Übermittler der Kultur bei der Initiation steht er an einer zentralen Stelle des Kultes" ["He is connected through his work with demonic beings, is himself a magician. His opposition to the devil and the dragon puts him into a cosmological context. As a messenger of wisdom, a transmitter of culture, he stands in a central position in the cult in regard to initiation."] ["Der Schmied im germanischen Altertum," unpublished Diss. Wien, 1967, 538]. Cp. Eliade, who remarks that "access to sacrality is manifested, among other things, by a prodigious increase in heat ... a relation shown by the close connection between smiths, shamans, and warriors" (*Rites and Symbols*, p. 86).

[51]Geoffrey R. Russom, "A Germanic Concept of Nobility in *The Gifts of Men* and *Beowulf*," *Speculum* 53 (1978): p. 5.

[52]Eliade, *Rites and Symbols*, pp. 35-7.

[53]Ibid., pp. 50-1.

[54]The description, which does not occur in the Eddic poetry, is borrowed directly from *Þiðreks saga af Bern*.

[55]Ruth Righter-Gould, "The *Fornaldar Sögur Norðurlanda*: A Structural Analysis," *Scandinavian Studies* 52 (1980), p. 427. There are, however, other examples of exceptions to the rule: the narrator of *Helgisaga Ólafs konungs Haraldssonar* waits until chap. 30 to describe his hero, "just as Snorri Sturluson postpones his unforgettable description of Egil Skalla-Grimsson until the viking-poet becomes the dominant figure of his saga," Paul Schach, *Icelandic Sagas* (Boston: Twayne, 1984), p. 54.

[56]Johnson calls it "a Germanic 'cosmology quiz,'" p. 51; George K. Anderson terms it a "rather ridiculous paratheological dialogue" [*The Saga of the Volsungs: Together With Excerpts from the Nornageststhattr and Three Chapters from the Prose Edda* (Newark: University of Delaware Press, 1982)], p. 23. More serious discussions of the dialogue occur in Alv Kragerud, "De mytologiske spørsmål i Fåvnesmål," *Arkiv för nordisk filologi* 96 (1981): pp. 9-48; and Kathryn Hume, "From Saga to Romance," p. 9.

[57]James David Mason, "Monsters With Human Voices: The Anthropomorphic Adversary of the Hero in Old English and Old Norse Literature," unpublished Diss. Tennessee, 1976.

[58]Stefan Einarsson, *A History of Icelandic Literature* (New York: Johns Hopkins Press for the American Scandinavian Foundation, 1957), p. 37.

[59]The most recent and comprehensive study of the genre is Karen Swenson, *Performing Definitions: Two Genres of Insult in Old Norse Literature* (Columbia, SC: Camden House, 1991). But although Swenson devotes an entire chapter to flytings between human beings and monsters, she does not mention the conversation between Sigurðr and Fáfnir.

[60]For a discussion of some of the exceptions, see Joaquín Martínez-Pizarro, "Woman-to-Man *Senna*," in *Poetry in the Scandinavian Middle Ages: Proceedings of the Seventh International Saga Conference*, ed. Teresa Pàroli (Spoleto: Presso la Sede del Centro Studi, 1990), pp. 339-50.

[61]R.W. Chambers, *Beowulf: An Introduction*, p. 96.

[62]Ward Parks, *Verbal Dueling in Heroic Narrative: The Homeric and Old English Traditions* (Princeton: Princeton University Press, 1990), pp. 13, 26; see also John H. McDowell, "Verbal Dueling," in *A Handbook of Discourse Analysis*, vol. 3, ed. Teun A. Van Dijk (London: Academic Press, 1985), p. 208; and Walter J. Ong, *Fighting for Life: Contest, Sexuality, and Consciousness* (Ithaca: Cornell University Press, 1981), pp. 64–76.

[63]Swenson, p. 37.

[64]Cp. the *draugr* appearing in two versions of the *Saga of Óláfr Tryggvason* and in *Tóka Þattr Tókason*, discussed by Nora Chadwick in "Norse Ghosts," p. 120. See also Eliade: ". . . this sojourn among the dead is not without its rewards. The novices will receive revelations of secret lore. For the dead know more than the living" (*Rites and Symbols*, p. 37).

[65]Most recently Kari Ellen Gade, "*Sigurðr—Gofuct dýr*: A Note on *Fáfnismál* St. 2," *Arkiv för nordisk filologi* 105 (1990): pp. 57–68.

[66]Cp. *Helgakviða Hundingsbana II*, 38 and *Guðrúnarkviða II*, 2. Lee M. Hollander takes this interpretation for granted, rendering *Gofugt dýr* in *Fáfnismál* 12 as 'Stag' in his translation of *The Poetic Edda* (Austin: University of Texas Press, 1962), p. 199. For further discussion of the hart motif in the story of Sigurðr/Siegfried, see Otto Höfler, *Siegfried, Arminius und die Symbolik* (Heidelberg: Carl Winter Universitatsverlag, 1961), pp. 48–69.

[67]R.C. Boer, 1922; cited in Finch, p. 31n.

[68]The implication that the norns offer obstetrical aid to mothers is strange since the norns' appearance at a childbed is usually to determine or announce the child's fate; the words *kjósa frá* are glossed "to assist in the delivery of a child" only in reference to this passage and its source in *Fáfnismál* 12; otherwise, they are translated "to take away from, to separate from." Chester Nathan Gould's early suggestion that the reference is not "to obstetrical aid, but to stealing babies" may be correct. Cp. Gould, "'Which Are the Norns Who Take Children From Mothers?'" *Modern Language Notes* 42 (1927), pp. 221.

[69]Cp. *Sigrdrífumál* 18, and *Hávamál* 143 and 160. Alv Kragerud discusses these passages, pp. 12–14.

[70]Kragerud, p. 15. Thus it may be also be an ominous sign that Sigurðr's initiation master in the saga is a dwarf.

[71]Kragerud, p. 16; Patricia Terry, trans., *Poems of the Elder Edda*, rev. ed. (Philadelphia: University of Pennsylvania Press, 1990), p. 154.

[72]Finch, p. 32n; Jesse Byock, trans. *The Saga of the Volsungs: The Norse Epic of Sigurd the Dragon Slayer* (Berkeley: University of California Press, 1990), p. 64.

[73]Amory, Frederic, "Kenning," in Phillip Pulsiano, ed., *Medieval Scandinavia: An Encyclopedia* (New York: Garland, 1989). The term is also used by Margaret Clunies Ross in her discussion of "Voice and Voices in Eddic Poetry," in Teresa Pàroli, ed., *Poetry in the Scandinavian Middle Ages: Proceedings of the Seventh International Saga Conference* (Spoleto: Presso la Sede del Centro Studi, 1990), pp. 219–30.

[74]Kragerud, pp. 18–19. The reference is to *Fáfnismál* 15.

[75]Heusler and Ranisch, *Eddica Minora: Dichtungen eddischer Art aus den Fornaldarsögur und anderen Prosawerken* (Dortmund, 1903; rpt. Darmstadt, 1974), p. xli; Harris, "Beowulf's Last Words," *Speculum* 67 (1992): pp. 1–32.

[76]Cp. de Vries, "The creature is a symbol of chaos; he who is going to be initiated must pass through this creature to be born a new man" (p. 222). See also Eliade, *Rites and Symbols*, pp. xii; 36.

[77]Precisely what the *ægishjálmr* is remains an open question. The word does appear in other contexts; D.J. Beard reports that, in *Sǫrla þáttr*, Ivar is advised to attack Hogne "from behind, as no-one can kill him face-to-face because he has the '*oegishjálmr*' in his eyes . . . . The phrase, '*hafa ægishjálm í augum*' is still used in Iceland to denote a magical overawing power of the eye" ["*Á þá bitu engi járn*: A Brief Note on the Concept of Invulnerability in the Old Norse Sagas," in *Studies in English Language and Early Literature in Honour of Paul Christophersen*, ed. P.M. Tilling (New University of Ulster, Occasional Papers in Linguistics and Language Learning, no. 8, 1981)], p. 26.

[78]Andrew J. McKenna, *Violence and Difference: Girard, Derrida, and Deconstruction* (Urbana & Chicago: University of Illinois Press, 1992), p. 72.

NOTES TO CHAPTER 4

[1]All references to *Das Nibelungenlied* are to Helmut de Boor's 21st edition (Wiesbaden: F. A. Brockhaus, 1979).

[2]For a recent summary of source-studies, see Theodore M. Andersson, *A Preface to the Nibelungenlied* (Stanford, CA: Stanford University Press, 1987), pp. 105–17. The argument for an oral background to the poem is presented by Edward R. Haymes, *The Nibelungenlied: History and Interpretation* (Urbana and Chicago: University of Illinois Press, 1986), pp. 21–33.

[3]In addition to Andersson and Haymes, for a recent interpretive study see Otfrid Ehrismann, *Nibelungenlied: Epoche—Werk—Wirkung* (Munich: C.H. Beck, 1987).

[4]Andreas Heusler, *Nibelungensage und Nibelungenlied: Die Stoffgeschichte des deutschen Heldenepos* (Dortmund: Ruhfus, 1920).

[5]Andersson, *Preface*, p. 117. The most detailed study of the hypothetical sources of Part I is Theodore M. Andersson, *The Legend of Brynhild* (Ithaca and London: Cornell University Press, 1980). Not all scholars agree with Andersson's assumptions as to the poem's sources. For a contrary view, see Franz Bauml's review of *The Legend of Brynhild* in *Speculum* 57 (1982): 346–9.

[6]Translations of *Das Nibelungenlied*, unless otherwise noted, are from A. T. Hatto, *The Nibelungenlied* (Harmondsworth: Penguin, 1969).

[7]Andersson, *Preface*, p. 84ff.

[8]Obviously, the wooing of Kriemhilt is also a significant 'romance' element in the poem; Alain Renoir has shown the episode to "conform on all points to nearly every rule set forth in the *De Amore* of Andreas Capellanus." See his "Levels of Meaning in

the *Nibelungenlied*: Sîfrit's Courtship," *Neuphilologische Mitteilungen* 61 (1960), p. 353.

⁹"He has a twofold existence." Walter Johannes Schröder, *Das Nibelungenlied: Versuch einer Deutung* (Halle: Max Niemeyer, 1954), p. 24.

¹⁰"Siegfried has a double character." Friedrich Neumann, *Das Nibelungenlied in seiner Zeit* (Göttingen: Vandenhoeck and Ruprecht, 1967), p. 11.

¹¹Mowatt, D.G., "Studies Toward an Interpretation of the 'Nibelungenlied'," *German Life and Letters* 14 (1961), p. 265.

¹²Hatto, p. 315.

¹³"The characters of the *Nibelungenlied* maintain their old ways to the extent that these are required by the basic story. They take on the behavior of courtly knights and ladies whenever the older conduct is not dictated by the plot." Neumann, pp. 16–17.

¹⁴Andersson, *Legend of Brynhild*, p. 164.

¹⁵"When the older poetry has spoken, one's invention is no longer free," Neumann, p. 12. Additionally, Walter Johannes Schröder characterizes the freedom of the poet as "kaum etwas anderes als die Freiheit der Wahl: er wählt aus dem Vorhandenen eines der darin vorgegebenen Motive aus und macht es zum beherrschenden . . . . Andere Motive . . . treten dadurch in funktionale Stellung zurück und werden notwendigerweise in ihrer Reichweite verkürzt" (. . . scarcely other than the freedom of choice: he chooses from the available material one of the given motifs and makes it predominant . . . . The other motifs become functionally unimportant and are of necessity abridged" [p. 16].

¹⁶Haymes, *Nibelungenlied*, p. 42.

¹⁷Edward R. Haymes, "Once again: 'Schichten der Ethik im Nibelungenlied'," in William C. McDonald and Winder McConnell, eds., *Fide et Amore: A Festschrift for Hugo Bekker* (Göppingen: Kümmerle, 1990), pp. 149–56.

¹⁸Haymes, *Nibelungenlied*, p. 49.

¹⁹Ibid., p. 56.

²⁰Ibid., p. 66.

²¹Ibid., pp. 73–90.

²²M.M. Bakhtin, *Dialogic Imagination*, p. 91.

²³These epithets are used to describe Gîselher some two dozen times, from (1, 4) to (30, 2371).

²⁴Bakhtin, *Dialogic Imagination*, p. 91.

²⁵Ibid., p. 99.

²⁶In addition to the examples cited in the text, see D.G. Mowatt and Hugh Sacker, *The Nibelungenlied: An Interpretive Commentary* (Toronto: University of Toronto Press, 1967); Jan de Vries multiplies the differences and sees "three worlds . . . which are continually overlapping": the world "of Worms and Etzel's stronghold in the sphere of the Migration period," the more modern world "of about the year 1200," and the world of Isenstein, "a mythical realm that seems to belong to the remotest past" [*Heroic Song*

and Heroic Legend, p. 64]. In a more striking divergence from other critics, Walter Falk [*Das Nibelungenlied in seiner Epoche: Revision eines romantischen Mythos* (Heidelberg: Winter, 1974), p. 121] sees Sîfrit as inhabiting both an outer world of physical reality and "eine traumhafte, psychische Innenwelt" ["a dreamlike, psychic inner world"]. Falk regards all the events partaking of the supernatural as psychological, not physical, occurrences.

[27]"Nibelungenland and Isenstein lie in the far north; temporally they belong to a remote antiquity. Here Siegfried won the hoard and *tarnkappe*, here and then he slew the dragon and bathed in its blood . . . . The North of myth and folktale stands in opposition to the historical South." Schröder, p. 22.

[28]Winder McConnell, *The Nibelungenlied* (Boston: Twayne Publishers, 1984), pp. 28–30; 42–5.

[29]Bakhtin, *Dialogic Imagination*, pp. 151–2.

[30]Ibid, p. 152.

[31]Ibid., p. 23.

[32]Ibid., p. 23.

[33]Hilda Ellis comments on the identity between the *tarnkappe* and the *ægishjálmr* in "The Hoard of the Nibelungs," *Modern Language Review* 37 (1947), pp. 476–7.

[34]Cp. W.T.H. Jackson's discussion of the hero-intruder motif in *Das Nibelungenlied*, pp. 36–54.

[35]Bakhtin, *Dialogic Imagination*, p. 248, emphasis in the original. Cp. also *Problems of Dostoevsky's Poetics*, pp. 169–70.

[36]Hatto, p. 328.

[37]Ward Parks has explored the relationship between agonistic modes of behavior and guest-host bonding in some detail; he concludes that "contests in the battlefield pattern can modulate fairly easily and naturally into the guest-host mold, if the contestants discover grounds to justify this movement." p. 79.

[38]Carl S. Singer, "The Hunting Contest: An Interpretation of the Sixteenth *Aventiure* of *Das Nibelungenlied*," *Germanic Review* 42 (1967), p. 172.

[39]Campbell, Joseph, *The Hero With a Thousand Faces* (Princeton: Princeton University Press, 1949; rpt. 1968).

[40]Mathias Lexer defines MHG *gast* as both Modern German *fremder* "foreigner, stranger" and *gast* "visitor, guest." Cp. *Mittelhochdeutsches Taschenwörterbuch*, 35 Auflage (Stuttgart: S. Hirzel Verlag, 1979).

[41]Haymes, *Nibelungenlied*, pp. 73–90, discusses Hagen as a 'dark' hero. Cp. also Edward R. Haymes and Stephanie Cain Van D'Elden, eds., *The Dark Figure in Medieval German and Germanic Literature* (Göppingen: Kümmerle, 1986). I am also indebted throughout this entire section to long conversations with my friend and colleague Lynn Thelen, whose ideas on doubles and doubling within *Das Nibelungenlied* have become inextricably intertwined with my own.

[42]Mowatt & Sacker, p. 92.

[43]Andersson, *Preface*, p. 139.

[44]Haymes, *Nibelungenlied*, p. 63.

[45]Otfrid Ehrismann attributes Sîfrit's murder to his *übermuot*, "pride, arrogance"; Hugo Bekker has argued that his death is one result of his failure to marry Prünhilt himself [*The Nibelungenlied: A Literary Analysis* (Toronto: University of Toronto Press, 1971), pp. 84–100].

[46]Réne Girard, *Things Hidden Since the Foundation of the World*, trans. Stephen Bann (Books II and III) and Michael Metteer (Book I) (Stanford: Stanford University Press, 1987), p. 78; emphasis in the original.

[47]Cp. Winder McConnell, who asks, "Is Siegfried's murder not just as deplorable thirteen years after the fact as it was on the day it was committed? The answer offered implicitly by the poet seems to be a categorical 'No!' . . . Even Siegmund, Siegfried's father, never pursues the matter once he returns to Xanten" (p. 36).

[48]Cp. Haymes, *Nibelungenlied*, p. 78.

[49]Cp. Haymes, pp. 73–90; Winder McConnell goes so far as to say that "Compared with Siegfried, Hagen is the greater hero" (p. 36).

[50]Haymes points out that Sîfrit's murder is here seen as "a badge of honor, a heroic deed that actually adds to Hagen's stature" (*Nibelungenlied*, p. 74). He also discusses the scene in terms of Icelandic saga analogues (pp. 79–80).

[51]Jackson, p. 47.

[52]". . . permeated with the darkness and wildness of supernatural power." Gottfried Weber, *Das Nibelungenlied: Problem und Idee* (Stuttgart: J.B. Metzlersche, 1963), p. 136.

[53]They are, of course, actually Burgundians, but are called 'Nibelungs' throughout Part II of the poem. The confusion in nomenclature probably owes its existence to a change in source, although it serves to underscore the comparison between the two episodes.

[54]Hatto, p. 399. Cp. Haymes, who calls the crossing a "symbolic entry into the realm of death," p. 77; and Stephen L. Waites, who states that "in the fall of the Burgundians we are dealing with the Journey to the Other World" ("The *Nibelungenlied* as Heroic Epic," in Felix J. Oinas, *Heroic Epic and Saga* (Bloomington and London: Indiana University Press, 1978), p. 138.

[55]Haymes, *Nibelungenlied*, p. 77.

[56]The hoard does contain one treasure that is more than gold: a *rüetelin* "tiny rod," which, *der daz het erkunnet, der möhte meister sîn / wol in aller werlde über ietslîchen man* "if any had found its secret, he could have been lord of all mankind!" (19, 1124). This treasure of treasures remains undiscovered and unused by Sîfrit and by the Burgundians, although some critics have used it to support an interpretation of the hoard as a symbol of power. Helmut De Boor rightly comments that "Die sonst bewußte zurückgedrängte Freude an Märchenhaftem bricht hier ganz unmotiviert durch. Diese Wünschelrute spielt sachlich gar keine Rolle" ("The pleasure in folktale elements that is elsewhere deliberately repressed breaks in here in a totally unmotivated way. The wishing-rod itself has no role to play") (p. 184n).

NOTES TO CHAPTER 5

[1]There are, of course, other versions of the tale. Norse retellings include *Skaldskaparmál*, c. 1225; *Nornagests þáttr*, fourteenth-century; *Vǫlsungsrimur*, c. 1400; and various Norwegian and Faroese ballads, c. 1300–1400. In German there are *Seifrid de Ardemont* (in which Seifrid becomes a knight of Arthur's Round Table), c. 1280; *Das Leid vom Hürnen Seyfrid*, fifteenth-century; and a drama, *Der Hürnen Seufrid*, by Hans Sachs, 1557. For manuscript history and description, see Henrik Bertelsen, ed., *Þiðriks saga af Bern* (Copenhagen: S.L. Mollers, 1905–11).

[2]Some scholars have argued for an earlier date of composition. Theodore M. Andersson posits an original composition in Soest as early as 1200 ["An Interpretation of Thidreks saga," in *Structure and Meaning in Old Norse Literature: New Approaches to Textual Analysis and Literary Criticism of Edda And Saga Narrative*, ed. John Lindow, Lars Lönnroth, and Gerd Wolfgang Weber (Odense: Odense University Press, 1986), pp. 356–59]. Alternatively, Marina Mundt places the composition in Norway at 1230–40. See her "Observations on the Influence of Þiðreks Saga on Icelandic Saga Writing," in *Proceedings of the First International Saga Conference, University of Edinburgh, 1971*, ed. Peter Foote, Hermann Pálsson, and Desmond Slay (London: Viking Society for Northern Research, 1973), p. 354.

[3]The origin of this idea lies with Andreas Heusler. See Edward R. Haymes, trans., *The Saga of Thidrek of Bern* (New York and London: Garland Publishing, 1988), p. xx.

[4]The specific saga genre of *Þiðreks saga* has often been debated, with some scholars assigning it to the *fornaldarsǫgur*, others to the *riddarasǫgur*, and others, such as Marianne E. Kalinke, finally assigning it 'a class by itself' [*King Arthur North-by-Northwest: The Matiére de Bretagne in Old Norse-Icelandic Romances*, Bibliotheca Arnamagnæana 37 (Copenhagen: C.A. Reitzels Boghandel, 1981), p. 2. For discussions of the saga's genre, see Andersson, "An Interpretation of *Þiðreks saga*," pp. 352–6; Peter Hallberg, "Some Aspects of the Fornaldarsǫgur as a Corpus," *Arkiv for nordisk filologi* 97 (1982), pp. 1–35; and Haymes, tr. *The Saga of Thidrek of Bern*, p. xxi.

[5]Cited in Tolkien, "*Beowulf*: The Monsters and the Critics," p. 69.

[6]Hilda R. Ellis, "The Hoard of the Nibelungs," *Modern Language Review* 37 (1942), p. 473.

[7]R.G. Finch, *The Saga of the Völsungs*, p. viii. Cp. also William J. Paff, who speaks of the saga's "characteristic naiveté and vulgarity" [*The Geographical and Ethnic Names in the Þidriks Saga* (Cambridge: Harvard University Press, 1959), p. 3], and George K. Anderson, who drily remarks that the saga is "an overambitious work" [*The Saga of the Volsungs: Together with Excerpts from the Nornageststháttr and Three Chapters from the Prose Edda* (Newark: University of Delaware Press, 1982), p. 221]. Roswitha Wisniewski, taking a more moderate approach, calls the author neither a "verballhornenden Stümper" [bowdlerizing bungler] nor a "großen Dichter" [great poet], [*Die Darstellung des Niflungenunterganges in der Thidrekssaga: Eine Quellenkritische Untersuchung* (Tübingen: Max Niemeyer, 1961), p. 21].

[8]Bakhtin, *Dialogic Imagination*, p. 154, emphasis in original.

[9]Ibid., p. 152.

[10]Ibid., p. 154.

[11]Ibid., p. 153.

[12]Kathryn Hume, "From Saga to Romance," p. 3.

[13]All quotations from *Þiðrekssaga af Bern* are taken from Guðni Jónsson's edition (Reykjavik: 1962). Translations are from Edward R. Haymes, *The Saga of Thidrek of Bern* (New York & London: Garland Publishing, 1988).

[14]Michael Curschmann, "The Prologue of *Þiðreks Saga*: Thirteenth Century Reflections on Oral Traditional Literature," *Scandinavian Studies* 56 (1984), pp. 141–2.

[15]Haymes comments on the essentially conservative nature of stories offered primarily for entertainment (*Nibelungenlied*, p. 25), a characteristic which ought to be kept in mind when considering the thematic structures of *Þiðreks saga*.

[16]The same could be said of most of the Norse sagas dealing with fabulous elements. Peter Hallberg asserts that the saga's *Formáli* could, "*mutatis mutandi*, have been accepted by most writers of such texts as an apology for the genre as a whole" ("Some Aspects," p. 8).

[17]Kathryn Hume, "From Saga to Romance," p. 24.

[18]The prologue author is almost certainly a cleric, and the saga author, if he is not identical with the author of the prologue, at least "seems to have known clerical traditions as well as oral heroic songs and stories about his hero" (Haymes, *Saga of Thidrek*, p. xxvii).

[19]Curschmann, p. 142. See Ernst Walter, "Zur Entstehung der Thidrikssaga" in *Jahrbuch des Vereins für niederdeutsche Sprachforschung*, 83 (1960), pp. 23–8 for a summary of the possible relationships between the prologue author and the sagaman.

[20]Jauss, *Question and Answer*, p. 8.

[21]Cp. Geir T. Zoëga, *A Concise Dictionary of Old Icelandic* (Oxford: Clarendon, 1910; rpt. 1975), which does not list 'dragon' as a possible meaning.

[22]Marianne E. Kalinke calls the situation "ludicrous"and adds that "[t]he potentially parodistic character of the scene is unmistakable, regardless how the author of *Þiðreks saga* intended an audience to react" (*King Arthur North-by-Northwest*, p. 195).

[23]Cp. Kalinke, who states "Authorial focus in *Þiðriks saga* is on the beast—through extensive description—and on the victim—through extended dialogue, or to be more exact, monologue, since Þiðrikr and Fasold do not reply with words . . ." (*King Arthur North-by-Northwest*, p. 194).

[24]Haymes translates *andskoti* as "demon."

[25]This episode is not original with the saga, nor with the character of Þiðrekr himself; it has been imported into *Þiðreks saga* from German romances dealing with Ortnit and Wolfdietrich. For an English version of the tales, see J. W. Thomas, tr. *Ortnit and Wolfdietrich: Two Medieval Romances* (Columbia, SC: Camden House, 1986).

[26]According to Marianne E. Kalinke, in addition to *Ivens saga*, the lion-knight motif appears in *Hrolfs saga*, *Ectors saga*, the fragmentary *Grega saga*, *Kára saga Kárasonar*,

Konraðs saga keisarasonar, Vilhjálms saga sjóðs, and *Sigurðar saga Þǫgla* [Marianne E. Kalinke, *Bridal-Quest Romance in Medieval Iceland,* Islandica XLVI (Ithaca and London: Cornell University Press, 1990), p. 58]. For another discussion of this motif, see Richard L. Harris, "The Lion-Knight Legend in Iceland and the Valþjófsstaðir Door," *Viator* 1 (1970): 125–45.

[27]Bakhtin sees the "stretching and compression" of time evident in Sigurðr sveinn's abnormally rapid physical development as characteristic of the romance chronotope; see *Dialogic Imagination,* p. 155.

[28]Jackson, however, does not explicitly discuss *Þiðreks saga* in his book. The parallels between chap. 168 of the saga and *Aventiure* 8 of *Das Nibelungenlied* were first noted by Helmut de Boor, "Kapitel 168 der *Thidrekssaga,*" in *Edda, Skalden, Saga,* ed. Hermann Schneider (Heidelberg: Carl Winter, 1952), pp. 157–72.

[29]Andersson points out that the episode "echoes the anecdote of Alexander and Bucephalus in the *Alexanderlied*" and is another reason to look to an early composition in Germany ("An Interpretation," p. 363).

[30]Peter Hallberg also discusses this episode, noting that it is "as if Þiðrekr were changed into a fire-spitting dragon" ("Some Aspects," p. 32).

[31]Cp. *hans nafn mun aldrigi t nast i þyðverskri tungu ok slikt sama með Norðmönnum* (chap. 348), "his name will never die in the German language, and the same among the Northmen."

NOTES TO CHAPTER 6

[1]Jauss, *Toward an Aesthetic of Reception,* p. 94.

Bibliography

Amory, Frederic. "Kenning." In *Medieval Scandinavia: An Encyclopedia*, edited by Phillip Pulsiano. New York: Garland Publishing, 1989.

Anderson, George K., trans. *The Saga of the Volsungs: Together with Excerpts from the Nornageststhattr and Three Chapters from the Prose Edda*. Newark: University of Delaware Press, 1982.

Andersson, Theodore M. *The Legend of Brynhild*. Islandica XLIII. Ithaca: Cornell University Press, 1980.

———. The Thief in *Beowulf.*" *Speculum* 59 (1984): 493-508.

———. "An Interpretation of *Þiðreks Saga*." In *Structure and Meaning in Old Norse Literature: New Approaches to Textual Analysis and Literary Criticism*, edited by John Lindow, Lars Lönnroth and Gerd Wolfgang Weber, 347–77. Odense: Odense University Press, 1986.

———. *A Preface to the Nibelungenlied*. Stanford: Stanford University Press, 1987.

Arent, A. Margaret. "The Heroic Pattern: Old Germanic Helmets, Beowulf, and Grettis Saga." In *Old Norse Literature and Mythology: A Symposium*, edited by Edgar C. Polomé, 130–99. Austin: University of Texas Press, 1969.

Bakhtin, Mikhail M. *The Dialogic Imagination*. Edited by Michael Holquist. Translated by Caryl Emerson and Michael Holquist. Austin: University of Texas Press, 1981.

———. *Problems of Dostoevsky's Poetics*. Edited and translated by Caryl Emerson. Minneapolis: University of Minnesota Press, 1984.

Bauschatz, Paul C. *The Well and the Tree: World and Time in Early Germanic Culture*. Amherst: University of Massachusetts Press, 1982.

Beard, D.J. "*Á þá bitu engi járn*: a Brief Note on the Concept of Invulnerability in the Old Norse Sagas." In *Studies in English Language and Early Literature in Honour of Paul Christophersen*, edited by P.M. Tilling, 13–31. Belfast: New University of Ulster, 1981.

Beck, Heinrich. "Zu Otto Höflers Siegfried-Armninius Untersuchung." *Beitrage zur Geschichte der Deutschen Sprache und Literatur* 107 (1985): 91–107.

Bekker, Hugo. *The Nibelungenlied: A Literary Analysis*. Toronto: University of Toronto Press, 1971.

Benson, Larry D. "The Literary Character of Anglo-Saxon Formulaic Poetry." *PMLA* 81 (1966): 334–41.

Berger, Harry, and H. Marshall Leicester. "The Limits of Heroism in *Beowulf*." In *Old English Studies in Honour of John C. Pope*, edited by Robert B. Burlin and Edward B. Irving, 37–80. Toronto: University of Toronto Press, 1974.

Bertelsen, Henrik, ed. *Þiðriks Saga Af Bern*. Copenhagen: S. L. Mollers, 1905–11.

Bocharov, S.G. *Estetika slovesnogo tvorchestva* [The Aesthetics of Verbal Creation]. Moscow, 1979.

Bolton, W.F. *Alcuin and Beowulf: An Eighth Century View.* New Brunswick, NJ: Rutgers University Press, 1978.

Bonjour, Adrian. "Monsters Crouching and Critics Rampant: Or the *Beowulf* Dragon Debated." In *Twelve Beowulf Papers 1940–1960*, 97–114. Neuchatel: Faculté des Lettres, 1962.

de Boor, Helmut. "Kapitel 168 der *Thidrekssaga*." In *Edda, Skalden, Saga*, edited by Hermann Schneider, 157–72. Heidelberg: Carl Winter, 1952.

———, ed. *Das Nibelungenlied.* 21st ed. Deutsche Klassiker des Mittelalters. Wiesbaden: F.A. Brockhaus, 1979.

Braeger, Peter C. "Connotations of (*Earm*) *Sceapen: Beowulf* ll. 2228–2229 and the Shape-Shifting Dragon." *Essays in Literature* 13 (1986): 327–330.

Brown, Alan K. "The Firedrake in *Beowulf.*" *Neophilologus* 64 (1980): 439–60.

Brynteson, William E. "*Beowulf*, Monsters, and Manuscripts: Classical Associations." *Res Publica Literarum* 5 (1982): 41–57.

Buchholz, Peter. *Vorzeitkunde: Mündliches Erzählen und Überliefern im mittelalterlichen Skandinavien nach dem Zeugnis von Fornaldarsaga und eddischer Dichtung.* Neumünster: Karl Wachholz, 1980.

Burke, Kenneth. *Language as Symbolic Action: Essays on Life, Literature, and Method.* Berkeley: University of California Press, 1966.

Byock, Jesse L. "Sigurðr Fáfnisbani: an Eddic Hero Carved on Norwegian Stave Churches." In *Poetry in the Scandinavian Middle Ages*, edited by Teresa Pàroli, 619–28. Proceedings of the Seventh International Saga Conference. Spoleto: Presso la Sede del Centro Studi, 1990.

———, trans. *The Saga of the Volsungs: the Norse Epic of Sigurd the Dragon Slayer.* Berkeley: University of California Press, 1990.

Calder, Daniel G. "Setting and Ethos: The Pattern of Measure and Limit in *Beowulf.*" *Studies in Philology* 69 (1972): 21–37.

Campbell, Joseph. *The Hero with a Thousand Faces.* Princeton: Princeton University Press, 1949; rpt. 1968.

Carlson, Signe M. "The Monsters of *Beowulf*: Creations of Literary Scholars." *Journal of American Folklore* 80 (1967): 357–64.

Carney, James. *Studies in Irish Literature and History.* Dublin, 1955.

Chadwick, H. Munro. *The Heroic Age.* Cambridge: Cambridge University Press, 1912. Rpt. 1967.

Chadwick, Nora K. "Norse Ghosts: A Study in the *Draugr* and the *Haugbúi.*" *Folk-Lore* 57 (1948): 50–65, 106–27.

———. "The Monsters and *Beowulf.*" In *The Anglo-Saxons: Studies in Some Aspects of Their History and Culture Presented to Bruce Dickens*, edited by Peter Clemoes, 171–203. London: Bowes and Bowes, 1959.

Chambers, R.W. *Beowulf: An Introduction*. 3rd ed., suppl. by C.L. Wrenn. Cambridge: Cambridge University Press, 1963.

Chase, Colin, ed. *The Dating of "Beowulf"*. Toronto: University of Toronto Press, 1981.

Cherniss, Michael D. "The Progress of the Hoard in *Beowulf*." *Philological Quarterly* 47 (1968): 473–86.

Chickering, Howell D. Jr., ed. & trans. *Beowulf: A Dual-Language Edition*. New York: Anchor Books, 1977.

Clark, George. "*Beowulf* and *Njálssaga*." In *Proceedings of the First International Saga Conference, University of Edinburgh, 1971*, edited by Peter Foote, Hermann Pálsson and Desmond Slay, 66–87. London: Viking Society for Northern Research, 1973.

————. *Beowulf*. Twayne's English Authors Series. Boston: Twayne Publishers, 1990.

Clover, Carol J. "Scene in Saga Composition." *Arkiv för nordisk filologi* 89 (1974): 57–83.

————. "The Germanic Context of the Unferþ Episode." *Speculum* 55 (1980): 444–68.

Cooke, W.G. "'Firy Drakes and Blazing-Bearded Light'." *English Studies* 61 (1980): 97–103.

Crawford, S.J., ed. *Byrhtferth's Manual*. EETS o.s. 177. London: Oxford University Press, 1929.

Curschmann, Michael. "The Prologue of *Þiðreks Saga*: Thirteenth Century Reflections on Oral Traditional Literature." *Scandinavian Studies* 56 (1984): 140–51.

Dahlberg, Charles. *The Literature of Unlikeness*. Hanover, NH: University Press of New England, 1988.

Danielli, Mary. "Initiation Ceremonial from Norse Literature." *Folk-Lore* 56 (1945): 229–45.

Danow, David K. *The Thought of Mikhail Bakhtin: From Word to Culture*. New York: St. Martin's Press, 1991.

Day, John. *God's Conflict with the Dragon and the Sea*. Cambridge: Cambridge University Press, 1985.

Dobbie, Elliott Van Kirk, ed. *The Anglo-Saxon Minor Poems*. ASPR VI. New York: Columbia University Press, 1942.

Dragland, S.L. "Monster-Man in *Beowulf*." *Neophilologus* 61 (1977): 606–18.

Dronke, Ursula. "Beowulf and Ragnarök." *Saga-Book of the Viking Society* 17 (1968): 302–25.

DuBois, Arthur E. "The Unity of *Beowulf*." *PMLA* 49 (1934): 374–405.

————. "The Dragon in *Beowulf*." *PMLA* 72 (1957): 819–22.

Duncan, Ian. "Epitaphs for Æglæcan: Narrative Strife in *Beowulf*." In *Beowulf*, edited by Harold Bloom, 111–30. New York: Chelsea House Publishers, 1987.

Ehrismann, Otfrid. *Nibelungenlied: Epoche-Werk-Wirkung*. München: C. H. Beck, 1987.

Einarsson, Stefan. *A History of Icelandic Literature*. New York: Johns Hopkins Press for the American Scandinavian Foundation, 1957.

Eliade, Mircea. *The Myth of the Eternal Return*. New York, 1954.

―――. *Rites and Symbols of Initiation: the Mysteries of Birth and Rebirth*. Translated by Willard R. Trask. New York: Harper & Row, 1958.

―――. *The Sacred and the Profane*. Translated by Willard R. Trask. New York: Harcourt, 1959.

Ellis, Hilda R. "The Hoard of the Nibelungs." *Modern Language Review* 37 (1942): 466–79.

Ellis-Davidson, H.R. "Gods and Heroes in Stone." In *The Early Cultures of North-West Europe*, edited by Sir Cyril Fox and Bruce Dickens, 123–39. H.M. Chadwick Memorial Studies. Cambridge: Cambridge University Press, 1950.

―――. *Gods and Myths of Northern Europe*. Baltimore: Penguin, 1964.

―――. "Shape Changing in the Old Norse Sagas." In *Animals in Folklore*, edited by J. R. Porter and W. M. S. Russell, 126–42. Cambridge and Totowa, NJ: D.S. Brewer and Rowman and Littlefield, 1978.

―――. "Insults and Riddles in the *Edda* Poems." In *Edda: A Collection of Essays*, edited by R.J. Glendinning and Haraldur Bessason, 25–46. Manitoba: University of Manitoba Press, 1983.

Fajardo-Acosta, Fidel. *The Condemnation of Heroism in the Tragedy of Beowulf*. Lewiston, NY: Edwin Mellen Press, 1989.

Falk, Walter. *Das Nibelungenlied in seiner Epoche: Revision eines romantischen Mythos*. Heidelberg: Winter, 1974.

Finch, R. G. "The Treatment of Poetic Sources by the Compiler of *Vǫlsunga Saga*." *Saga-Book of the Viking Society* 16 (1962): 315–53.

―――, ed. and trans. *The Saga of the Völsungs*. London: Thomas Nelson & Sons, 1968.

Fisher, Peter F. "The Trials of the Epic Hero in *Beowulf*." *PMLA* 73 (1958): 171–83.

Foley, Joanne De Lavan. "Feasts and Anti-Feasts in *Beowulf* and the *Odyssey*." In *Oral Traditional Literature: A Festschrift for Albert Bates Lord*, edited by John Miles Foley, 235–61. Columbus, MO: Slavica Publishers, 1981.

Foley, John Miles. *Traditional Oral Epic: The Odyssey, Beowulf, and the Serbo-Croatian Return Song*. Berkeley: University of California Press, 1990.

Fontenrose, Joseph. *Python: A Study of Delphic Myth and Its Origins*. Berkeley: University of California Press, 1959.

Frank, Roberta. "The *Beowulf* Poet's Sense of History." In *The Wisdom of Poetry: Essays in Early English Literature in Honor of Morton W. Bloomfield*, edited by Larry D. Benson and Siegfried Wenzel, 53–65. Kalamazoo, MI: Medieval Institute Publications, 1982.

Fry, Donald K. "The Cliff of Death in Old English Poetry." In *Comparative Research on Oral Traditions: a Memorial for Milman Parry*, edited by John Miles Foley, 213–233. Columbus, OH: Slavica Publishers, 1985.

Gade, Kari Ellen. "*Sigurðr—Gǫfuct Dýr*: a Note on *Fáfnismál* St. 2." *Arkiv för nordisk filologi* 105 (1990): 57–68.

Gang, T. M. "Approaches to *Beowulf.*" *Review of English Studies* 3 (1952): 1–12.

Gardner, John. "Guilt and the World's Complexity: the Murder of Ongentheow and the Slaying of the Dragon." In *Anglo-Saxon Poetry: Essays in Appreciation for John C. McGalliard*, edited by Lewis E. Nicholson and Dolores Warwick Frese, 14–22. Notre Dame: University of Notre Dame Press, 1975.

Garmonsway, G.N. "Anglo-Saxon Heroic Attitudes." In *Franciplegius: Medieval and Linguistic Studies in Honor of Francis Peabody Magoun, Jr.*, edited by Jess B. Bessinger and Robert P. Creed, 139–46. New York: New York University Press, 1965.

———, and Jacqueline Simpson, tr. *Beowulf and Its Analogues*. New York: E. P. Dutton, 1968.

van Gennep, Arnold. *The Rites of Passage*. Translated by Monika B. Vizedom and Gabrielle L. Caffee. London: Routledge and Kegan Paul, 1909.

Gerstein, Mary R. "Germanic *Warg*: The Outlaw as Werwolf." In *Myth in Indo-European Antiquity*, edited by Gerald James Larson, 131–56. Berkeley: University of California Press, 1974.

Gillam, Doreen M.E. "The Use of the Term 'Æglæca' in *Beowulf* at Lines 893 and 2592." *Studia Germanica Gandensia* 3 (1961): 145–69.

Girard, René. *Violence and the Sacred*. Translated by Patrick Gregory. Baltimore: The Johns Hopkins University Press, 1977.

———. *The Scapegoat*. Translated by Yvonne Freccero. Baltimore: The Johns Hopkins University Press, 1986.

———. *Things Hidden Since the Foundation of the World*. Translated by Stephan Bann and Michael Metteer. Stanford: Stanford University Press, 1987.

Goldsmith, Margaret. "The Christian Perspective in *Beowulf.*" In *Studies in Old English Literature in Honor of Arthur G. Brodeur*, edited by Stanley B. Greenfield, 71–90. Oregon: University of Oregon Books, 1963.

———. *The Mode and Meaning of Beowulf*. London: Athlone Press, 1970.

Gould, Chester Nathan. "'Which Are the Norns Who Take Children from Mothers?'." *Modern Language Notes* 42 (1927): 218–21.

Gould, Eric. *Mythical Intentions in Modern Literature*. Princeton: Princeton University Press, 1981.

Greenfield, Stanley B. "'Gifstol' and Goldhoard in *Beowulf.*" In *Old English Studies in Honour of John C. Pope*, edited by Robert B. Durlin and Edward B. Irving, 37–80. Toronto: University of Toronto Press, 1974.

————. "A Touch of the Monstrous in the Hero, or *Beowulf* Re-Marvellized." In *Old English Studies in Honour of John C. Pope*, edited by Robert B. Burlin and Edward B. Irving Jr, 119–37. Toronto: University of Toronto Press, 1974.

Greenway, John L. *The Golden Horns: Mythic Imagination and the Nordic Past*. Athens, GA: University of Georgia Press, 1977.

Grimstad, Kaaren. "The Revenge of Völundr." In *Edda: A Collection of Essays*, edited by R. J. Glendinning and Haraldur Bessason, 187–209. Manitoba: University of Manitoba Press, 1983.

Haarder, Andreas. *Beowulf: The Appeal of a Poem*. Viborg: Akademisk Forlag, 1975.

Haber, Tom Burns. *A Comparative Study of the Beowulf and the Aeneid*. New York: Phaeton Press, 1931. Rpt. 1968.

Hahn, Thomas. "The Premodern Text and the Postmodern Reader." *Exemplaria* 2 (1990): 1–21.

Hallberg, Peter. "The Syncretic Saga Mind: A Discussion of a New Approach to the Icelandic Sagas." *Mediaeval Scandinavia* 7 (1973): 102–17.

————. "Some Aspects of the *Fornaldarsögur* as a Corpus." *Arkiv för nordisk filologi* 97 (1982): 1–35.

Harris, Joseph. "Reflections on Genre and Intertextuality in Eddic Poetry." In *Poetry in the Scandinavian Middle Ages*, edited by Teresa Pàroli, 231–43. Proceedings of the Seventh International Saga Conference. Spoleto: Presso la Sede del Centro Studi, 1990.

————. "Beowulf's Last Words." *Speculum* 67 (1992): 1–32.

Harris, Richard. "The Lion-Knight Legend in Iceland and the Valþjófsstaðir Door." *Viator* 1 (1971): 125–47.

Hatto, A. T., trans. *The Nibelungenlied*. Harmondsworth: Penguin, 1965. Rpt. 1969.

Haymes, Edward R. *The Nibelungenlied: History and Interpretation*. Illinois Medieval Monographs II. Urbana: University of Illinois Press, 1986.

————, trans. *The Saga of Thidrek of Bern*. New York & London: Garland Publishing, 1988.

————. "Once Again 'Schichten Der Ethik' in the *Nibelungenlied*." In *Fide Et Amore: a Festschrift for Hugo Bekker on His Sixty-Fifth Birthday*, edited by William C. McDonald and Winder McConnell, 149–56. Göppingen: Kümmerle, 1990.

———— and Stephanie Cain Van D'Elden, eds. *The Dark Figure in Medieval German and Germanic Literature*. Göppingen: Kümmerle Verlag, 1986.

Heinrichs, Anne. "*Annat Er Várt Eðli*: The Type of the Prepatriarchal Woman in Old Norse Literature." In *Structure and Meaning in Old Norse Literature: New Approaches to Textual Analysis and Literary Criticism*, edited by John Lindow, Lars Lönnroth and Gerd Wolfgang Weber, 110–40. Odense: Odense University Press, 1986.

Helterman, Jeffrey. "Beowulf: the Archetype Enters History." *English Literary History* 35 (1968): 1–20.

Hermann, John P. *Allegories of War: Language and Violence in Old English Poetry*. Ann Arbor: University of Michigan Press, 1989.

Heusler, Andreas. *Nibelungensage und Nibelungenlied: Die Stoffgeschichte des deutschen Heldenepos*. Dortmund: Ruhfus, 1920.

────── and Wilhelm Ranisch. *Eddica Minora: Dichtungen eddischen Art aus den Fornaldarsögur und anderen Prosawerken*. Dortmund, 1903. Rpt. 1974.

Hill, Thomas D. "Two Notes on Patristic Allusion in *Andreas*." *Anglia* 84 (1966): 156–62.

──────. "Scyld Scefing and the '*Stirps Regia*': Pagan Myth and Christian Kingship in *Beowulf*." In *Magister Regis: Studies in Honor of Robert Earl Kaske*, edited by Arthur Gross and et al., 37–47. New York: Fordham University Press, 1986.

Hoffman, Werner. *Das Siegfriedbild in der Forschung*. Darmstadt: Wissenschaftliche Buchgesellschaft, 1979.

Höfler, Otto. *Siegfried, Arminius und die Symbolik*. Heidelberg: Carl Winter, 1961.

──────. *Siegfried, Arminius und der Nibelungenhort*. Wien: Verlag der Österreichischen Akademie der Wissenschaften, 1978.

Hollander, Lee M. "Were the Mythological Poems of the Edda Composed in the Pre-Christian Era?" *JEGP* 26 (1927): 96–105.

──────, trans. *The Poetic Edda*. Austin: University of Texas Press, 1962.

Holtsmark, Anne. "On the Werewolf Motif in *Egil's Saga Skallagrímssonar*." *Scientia Islandica* 1 (1968): 7–9.

Huffines, Marion Lois. "Old English *Aglæca*: Magic and Moral Decline of Monsters and Men." *Semasia* 1 (1974): 71–81.

Hume, Kathryn. "The Concept of the Hall in Old English Poetry." *Anglo-Saxon England* 3 (1974): 63–74.

──────. "The Theme and Structure of *Beowulf*." *Studies in Philology* 72 (1975): 1–27.

──────. "From Saga to Romance: The Use of Monsters in Old Norse Literature." *Studies in Philology* 77 (1980): 1–25.

Huppé, Bernard F. *The Hero in the Earthly City: A Reading of Beowulf*. Binghamton: State University of New York Press, 1984.

Irving, Edward B., Jr. *A Reading of Beowulf*. New Haven: Yale University Press, 1968.

──────. *Rereading Beowulf*. Philadelphia: University of Pennsylvania Press, 1989.

Isidore of Seville. *Etymologiarum Sive Originum*. Edited by W. M. Lindsay. Oxford: Clarendon, 1911.

Jackson, W. T. H. *The Hero and the King: An Epic Theme*. New York: Columbia University Press, 1982.

Jacobus de Voragine. *The Golden Legend*. Translated by Granger Ryan and Helmut Ripperger. New York: Longmans, 1941. Rpt. Arno Press, 1969.

Jauss, Hans Robert. "The Alterity and Modernity of Medieval Literature." Translated by Timothy Bahti. *New Literary History* 10 (1979): 181–227.

————. *Toward an Aesthetic of Reception*. Translated by Timothy Bahti. Minneapolis: University of Minnesota Press, 1982.

————. *Question and Answer: Forms of Dialogic Understanding*. Edited and translated by Michael Hays. Minneapolis: University of Minnesota Press, 1989.

Johnson, William C., Jr. "*Beowulf* and the *Völsungasaga*." In *In Geardagum II: Essays on Old and Middle English Language and Literature*, edited by Loren C. Gruber and Dean Loganbill, 42–53. Denver: Society for New Language Study, 1979.

Jones, Gwyn. *Kings, Beasts, and Heroes*. London: Oxford University Press, 1972.

Jónsson, Guðni, ed. *Þiðrekssaga af Bern*. 2 vol. Reykjavik: Litbra, 1962.

————, and Bjarni Vilhjalmsson, eds. *Fornaldarsögur Norðurlanda*. 3 vol. Reykjavik: Bokautgafan Forni, 1943.

Kalinke, Marianne E. *King Arthur North-by-Northwest: The Matiére De Bretagne in Old Norse-Icelandic Romances*. Bibliotheca Arnamagnæana 37. Copenhagen: C.A. Reitzels Boghandel, 1981.

————. *Bridal-Quest Romance in Medieval Iceland*. Islandica 46. Ithaca & London: Cornell University Press, 1990.

Ker, W.P. *The Dark Ages*. London, 1904.

————. *Epic and Romance*. 2nd edition 1908. London: MacMillan, 1931.

Kiernan, Kevin S. "The Eleventh-Century Origin of *Beowulf* and the *Beowulf* Manuscript." In *The Dating of Beowulf*, edited by Colin Chase, 9–22. Toronto: University of Toronto Press, 1981.

————. *Beowulf and the Beowulf Manuscript*. New Brunswick, NJ: Rutgers University Press, 1981.

Klaeber, Frederick, ed. *Beowulf and the Fight at Finnsburg*. 3rd ed. Boston: D.C. Heath, 1950.

Knipp, Christopher. "*Beowulf* 2210–2323: Repetition in the Description of the Dragon's Hoard." *Neuphilologische Mitteilungen* 73 (1972): 775–85.

Knock, Ann. "The *Liber Monstrorum*: An Unpublished Manuscript and Some Reconsiderations." *Scriptorium* 32 (1978): 19–28.

Kragerud, Alv. "De Mytologiske Spørsmål i Fåvnesmål." *Arkiv för nordisk filologi* 96 (1981): 9–48.

Krapp, George Philip, and Elliott Van Kirk Dobbie, eds. *The Exeter Book*. ASPR III. New York: Columbia University Press, 1936.

Kristjánsson, Jónas. *Eddas and Sagas*. Reykjavík: Hið íslenska bókmenntafélag, 1992.

Kroll, Norma. "Beowulf: The Hero as Keeper of Human Polity." *Modern Philology* 84 (1986): 117–129.

Kuhn, Sherman M. "Old English *Aglæca*—Middle Irish *Oclach*." In *Linguistic Method: Essays in Honor of Herbert Penzl*, edited by Irmengard Rauch and Gerald F. Carr, 213–30. The Hague: Mouton, 1979.

Lapidge, Michael. "*Beowulf*, Aldhelm, the *Liber Monstrorum*, and Wessex." *Studi Medievali* 23 (1982): 151–192.

Lecouteux, Claude. "Der Drache." *Zeitschrift für deutsches Altertum und deutche Literature* 108 (1979): 13–31.

LeGoff, Jacques. "Ecclesiastical Culture and Folklore in the Middle Ages: Saint Marcellus of Paris and the Dragon." Translated by Arthur Goldhammer. In *Time, Work, and Culture in the Middle Ages (Pour Un Autre Moyen Age: temps, Travail Et Culture En Occident)*, 159–88. Chicago and London: University of Chicago Press, 1980.

Lehmann, Winfred P. "On Reflections of Germanic Legal Terminology and Situations in the Edda." In *Old Norse Literature and Mythology: A Symposium*, edited by Edgar C. Palomé, 227–43. Austin: University of Texas Press, 1969.

Lexer, Mathias. *Mittelhochdeutsches Taschenwörterbuch*. Stuttgart: S. Hirzel, 1979.

Leyerle, John. "Beowulf the Hero and King." *Medium Aevum* 34 (1965): 89–102.

Lionarons, Joyce Tally. "The Sign of a Hero: Dragon-Slaying in *Þiðreks saga af Bern*. *Proceedings of the Medieval Association of the Midwest* 2 (1993), 47–57.

———. *Beowulf*: Myth and Monsters. *English Studies* 77 (1996), 1–14.

Littleton, C. Scott. "The 'Kingship in Heaven' Theme." In *Myth and Law Among the Indo-Europeans*, edited by Jaan Puhvel, 83–122. Berkeley: University of California Press, 1970.

Loganbill, Dean. "Time and Monsters in *Beowulf*." In *In Geardagum: Essays in Old English Language and Literature*, edited by Loren C. Gruber and Dean Loganbill, 26–35. Denver: Society for New Language Study, 1979.

Lönnroth, Lars. "The Noble Heathen: a Theme in the Sagas." *Scandinavian Studies* 41 (1969): 1–29.

———. "The Double Scene of Arrow Odd's Drinking Contest." In *Medieval Narrative: a Symposium*, edited by Hans Bekker-Nielson, Peter Foote, Andreas Haarder and Preben Meulengracht Sørensen, 94–119. Odense: Odense University Press, 1979.

Lord, Albert B. *The Singer of Tales*. Cambridge: Cambridge University Press, 1960.

Lotspeich, Claude M. "Old English Etymologies." *Journal of English and Germanic Philology* 40 (1941): 1–4.

Magoun, Francis P. "The Oral-Formulaic Character of Anglo-Saxon Narrative Poetry." In *An Anthology of Beowulf Criticism*. Reprinted from *Speculum* 28 (1953): 446–67, edited by Lewis E. Nicholson, 189–221. Notre Dame: University of Notre Dame Press, 1963.

Malone, Kemp, ed. *The Nowell Codex (British Museum Cotton Vitellius A. XV, Second MS)*. Early English Manuscripts in Facsimile, 12. Copenhagen: Rosenkilde & Bagger, 1963.

Martínez-Pizarro, Joaquín. "Woman-to-Man *Senna*." In *Poetry in the Scandinavian Middle Ages*, edited by Teresa Pàroli, 339–50. Proceedings of the Seventh International Saga Conference. Spoleto: Presso la Sede del Centro Studi, 1990.

Mason, James David. "Monsters with Human Voices; The Anthropomorphic Adversary of the Hero in Old English and Old Norse Literature." diss. *DAI* 37 (1976): 2834A.

McConnell, Winder. *The Nibelungenlied*. Boston: Twayne Publishers, 1984.

McDowell, John H. "Verbal Dueling." In *A Handbook of Discourse Analysis*, edited by Teun A. Van Dijk. London: Academic Press, 1985.

McKenna, Andrew J. *Violence and Difference: Girard, Derrida, and Deconstruction*. Urbana & Chicago: University of Illinois Press, 1992.

McTurk, Rory. *Studies in Ragnars Saga Loðbrókar and Its Major Scandinavian Analogues*. Oxford: Society for the Study of Mediæval Languages and Literature, 1991.

Mitchell, Bruce. "'Until the Dragon Comes...' Some Thoughts on *Beowulf*." *Neophilologus* 47 (1963): 126–38.

Mitchell, Stephen A. *Heroic Sagas and Ballads*. Ithaca & London: Cornell University Press, 1991.

Mizuno, Tomoaki. "Beowulf as a Terrible Stranger." *Journal of Indo-European Studies* 17 (1989): 1–46.

Mowatt, D. G. "Studies Toward an Interpretation of the 'Nibelungenlied'." *German Life and Letters* 14 (1961): 257–70.

———— and Hugh Sacker. *The Nibelungenlied: A Interpretive Commentary*. Toronto: University of Toronto Press, 1967.

Mueller, Werner A. *The Nibelungenlied Today: Its Substance, Essence, and Significance*. Chapel Hill: University of North Carolina Press, 1962.

Mundt, Marina. "Observations on the Influence of *Þiðreks Saga* on Icelandic Saga Writing." In *Proceedings of the First International Saga Conference, University of Edinburgh, 1971*, edited by Peter Foote, Hermann Pálsson and Desmond Slay, 335–59. London: Viking Society for Northern Research, 1973.

Nagel, Bert. *Das Nibelungenlied: Stoff—Form—Ethos*. Frankfurt: Hirschgraben, 1965.

Nagler, Michael N. "*Beowulf* in the Context of Myth." In *Old English Literature in Context*, edited by John D. Niles, 143–56. Cambridge and Totowa, NJ: D.S. Brewer; Rowman and Littlefield, 1980.

Neumann, Friedrich. *Das Nibelungenlied in Seiner Zeit*. Gottingen: Vandenhoeck & Ruprecht, 1967.

Niles, John D. *Beowulf: The Poem and Its Tradition*. Cambridge, MA & London: Harvard University Press, 1983.

Oetgen, Jerome. "Order and Chaos in the World of *Beowulf*." *American Benedictine Review* 29 (1978): 134–52.

Olrik, Axel. "Epic Laws of Folk Narrative." In *The Study of Folklore*, edited by Alan Dundee. Englewood Cliffs, NJ: Prentice Hall, 1965.

Ong, Walter J. *Fighting for Life: Contest, Sexuality, and Consciousness*. Ithaca: Cornell University Press, 1981.

Overing, Gillian. *Language, Sign, and Gender in Beowulf*. Carbondale and Edwardsville, IL: Southern Illinois University Press, 1990.

Ovid. *Metamorphosis*. Translated by Mary M. Innes. Baltimore: Penguin, 1955.

Ovidius Naso, Publius. *Ovid in Six Volumes.* 3rd ed. Edited by G. P. Gould. Cambridge: Harvard University Press, 1977.

Paff, William J. *The Geographical and Ethnic Names in the Þiðriks Saga.* Cambridge, MA: Harvard University Press, 1959.

Pálsson, Hermann, and Paul Edwards. *Legendary Fiction in Medieval Iceland.* Reykjavik: Studia Islandica 30, 1971.

————, trans. *Seven Viking Romances.* London: Penguin Books, 1985.

Parker, Mary A. *Beowulf and Christianity.* New York: Peter Lang Publishing, 1987.

Parks, Ward. *Verbal Dueling in Heroic Narrative: The Homeric and Old English Traditions.* Princeton: Princeton University Press, 1990.

Petroff, Elizabeth Alvilda. "Transforming the World: The Serpent Dragon and the Virgin Saint." In *Body and Soul: Essays on Medieval Women and Mysticism*, 97–109. Oxford: Oxford University Press, 1994.

Ploss, Emil. *Siegfried-Sigurd, der Drachenkämpfer: Untersuchungen zur germanischdeutschen Heldensage* . Köln: Bölau Verlag, 1966.

Plummer, C., ed. *The Anglo-Saxon Chronicle.* Oxford: Oxford University Press, 1893.

Porsia, Franco, ed. *Liber Monstrorum.* Bari: Dedalo Libri, 1976.

Prousa, Patricia. "The Date of *Beowulf* Reconsidered: the Tenth Century?" *Neuphilologische Mitteilungen* 82 (1981): 276–88.

Renoir, Alain. "Levels of Meaning in the *Nibelungenlied*: Sifrit's Courtship." *Neuphilologische Mitteilungen* 61 (1960): 353–61.

Righter-Gould, Ruth. "The *Fornaldar Sögur Norðurlanda*: A Structural Analysis." *Scandinavian Studies* 52 (1980): 423–41.

Robinson, Fred C. *Beowulf and the Appositive Style.* Knoxville: University of Tennessee Press, 1985.

Rogers, H. L. "Beowulf's Three Great Fights." *Review of English Studies* 6 (1955): 339–55.

Ross, Margaret Clunies. "Voice and Voices in Eddic Poetry." In *Poetry in the Scandinavian Middle Ages*, edited by Teresa Pàroli, 219–30. Proceedings of the Seventh International Saga Conference. Spoleto: Presso la Sede del Centro Studi, 1990.

Russom, Geoffrey R. "A Germanic Concept of Nobility in *The Gifts of Men* and *Beowulf.*" *Speculum* 53 (1978): 1–15.

Rypins, Stanley, ed. *Three Old English Prose Texts in MS. Cotton Vitellius A XV.* EETS o.s. 161. London: Oxford University Press, 1924.

Schach, Paul. *Icelandic Sagas.* Boston: Twayne, 1984.

Schichler, Robert Lawrence. "Heorot and Dragon-Slaying in *Beowulf.*" *Proceedings of the PMR Conference* 11 (1986): 159–175.

Schröder, Walter Johannes. *Das Nibelungenlied: Versuch Einer Deutung.* Halle (Salle)ı Max Niemeyer, 1954.

Serres, Michel. *The Parasite*. Translated by Lawrence R. Schehr. Baltimore & London: Johns Hopkins University Press, 1982.

Simpson, Jacqueline. *British Dragons*. London: Batsford, 1980.

Singer, Carl S. "The Hunting Contest: An Interpretation of the Sixteenth *Aventiure* of the *Nibelungenlied*." *Germanic Review* 42 (1967): 166–74.

Sisam, Kenneth. *Studies in the History of Old English Literature*. Oxford: Clarendon Press, 1953.

———. "Beowulf's Fight with the Dragon." *Review of English Studies* 9 (1958): 129–40.

Smith, G. Elliot. *The Evolution of the Dragon*. Manchester: At the University Press, 1919.

Smithers, G. V. *The Making of Beowulf*. Inaugural Lecture of the Professor of English Language Delivered in the Appleby Lecture Theatre on 18 May 1961. Durham, England: University of Durham Press, 1961.

Stanley, E. G. "The Narrative Art of *Beowulf*." In *Medieval Narrative: A Symposium*, edited by Hans Bekker-Nielson, Peter Foote, Andreas Haarder and Preben Meulengracht Sørensen, 58–81. Odense: Odense University Press, 1979.

Steblin-Kamenskij, M. I. "Valkyries and Heroes." *Arkiv för nordisk filologi* 97 (1982): 81–93.

Sturluson, Snorri. *The Prose Edda: Tales from Norse Mythology*. Translated by Jean I. Young. Berkeley: University of California Press, 1954.

Swanton, M.J. *Crisis and Development in Germanic Society 700–800: Beowulf and the Burden of Kingship*. Göppingen: Kümmerle Verlag, 1982.

Swenson, Karen. *Performing Definitions: Two Genres of Insult in Old Norse Literature*. Columbia, SC: Camden House, 1991.

Taylor, Paul Beekman. "Heorot, Earth, and Asgard: Christian Poetry and Pagan Myth." *Tennessee Studies in Literature* 11 (1966): 119–130.

———. "The Traditional Language of Treasure in *Beowulf*." *Journal of English and Germanic Philology* 85 (1986): 191–205.

———. "Some Uses of Etymology in the Reading of Medieval Germanic Texts." In *Hermeneutics and Medieval Culture*, edited by Patrick J. Gallacher and Helen Damico, 109–120. Albany: State University of New York Press, 1989.

Terry, Patricia, trans. *Poems of the Elder Edda*. Philadelphia: University of Pennsylvania Press, 1990.

Thompson, Claiborne W. "Moral Values in the Icelandic Sagas: Recent Re-evaluations." In *The Epic in Medieval Society: Aesthetic and Moral Values*, edited by Harald Scholler, 347–60. Tübingen: Max Niemeyer Verlag, 1977.

Todorov, Tzvetan. *Mikhail Bakhtin: The Dialogic Principle*. Translated by Wlad Godzich. Minneapolis: University of Minnesota Press, 1984.

Tolkien, J.R.R. "*Beowulf:* The Monsters and the Critics." In *An Anthology of Beowulf Criticism.* Reprinted from *Proceedings of the British Academy* 22 (1936) 245–295, edited by L.E. Nicholson, 51–103. Notre Dame: University of Notre Dame Press, 1963.

Tripp, Raymond P., Jr. *More About the Fight with the Dragon: Beowulf 2208b–3182, Commentary, Edition, and Translation.* Washington, D.C.: University Press of America, 1983.

Turner, Victor. *The Ritual Process: Structure and Anti-Structure.* Ithaca: Cornell University Press, 1969.

Turville-Petre, E.O.G. *Myth and Religion of the North: The Religion of Ancient Scandinavia.* London: Weidenfeld and Nicolson, 1964.

Turville-Petre, Gabriel. *Origins of Icelandic Literature.* Oxford: Clarendon, 1953.

―――. *Nine Norse Studies.* London: Viking Society for Northern Research, 1972.

de Vries, Jan. *Heroic Song and Heroic Legend.* Translated by B.J. Timmer. London: Oxford University Press, 1963.

Waddell, Helen. *Beasts and Saints.* London: Constable, 1934.

Wahlgren, Erik. *The Maiden King in Iceland.* Chicago: University of Chicago Libraries, 1938.

Waites, Stephen. "The *Nibelungenlied* as Heroic Epic." In *Heroic Epic and Saga*, edited by Felix J. Oinas. Bloomington and London: Indiana University Press, 1978.

Walter, Ernst. "Zur Enstehung Der Thidrikssaga." *Jahrbuch des Vereins für niederdeutsche Sprachforschung* 83 (1960): 23–28.

Watkins, Calvert. "How to Kill a Dragon in Indo-European." In *Studies in Memory of Warren Cowgill (1929–1985).* Papers from the Fourth East Coast Indo-European Conference, edited by Calvert Watkins, 270–99. New York: Walter de Gruyter, 1987.

―――. *How To Kill A Dragon in Indo-European.* New York: Oxford University Press, 1995.

Weber, Gerd Wolfgang. "The Decadence of Feudal Myth—Towards a Theory of *Riddarasaga* and Romance." In *Structure and Meaning in Old Norse Literature: New Approaches to Textual Analysis and Literary Criticism*, edited by John Lindow, Lars Lönnroth and Gerd Wolfgang Weber, 415–54. Odense: Odense University Press, 1986.

Weber, Gottfried. *Das Nibelungenlied: Problem Und Idee.* Stuttgart: J.B. Metzlersche, 1963.

Whitbread, L.G. "The *Liber Monstrorum* and *Beowulf.*" *Mediaeval Studies* 36 (1974): 434–471.

White, T. H. *The Book of Beasts: Being a Translation from a Latin Bestiary of the 12th Century.* London: Jonathan Cape, 1954.

Whitelock, Dorothy. *The Audience of Beowulf.* Oxford: Clarendon Press, 1951.

Whitman, F.H. "Corrosive Blood in *Beowulf.*" *Neophilologus* 61 (1977): 276.

Wild, Friedrich. *Drachen im Beowulf und andere Drachen: Mit einem Anhang Drachenfeldzeichen, Drachenwappen und St. Georg.* Wien: Hermann Bohlaus Nachf., 1962.

Williams, David. *Cain and Beowulf: A Study in Secular Allegory.* Toronto: University of Toronto Press, 1982.

Wisniewski, Roswitha. *Die Darstellung des Niflungenunterganges in der Thidrekssaga: Eine Quellenkritische Untersuchung.* Tübingen: Max Niemeyer, 1961.

Wyss, Ulrich. "Struktur Der Thidrekssaga." *Acta Germanica* 13 (1980): 69–86.

Zoëga, Geir T. *A Concise Dictionary of Old Icelandic.* Oxford: Clarendon, 1910; rpt. 1975.

Zumthor, Paul. *Speaking of the Middle Ages.* Translated by Sarah White. Lincoln, NE: University of Nebraska Press, 1986.

Index

DATE DUE

FEB 2 8 2002	